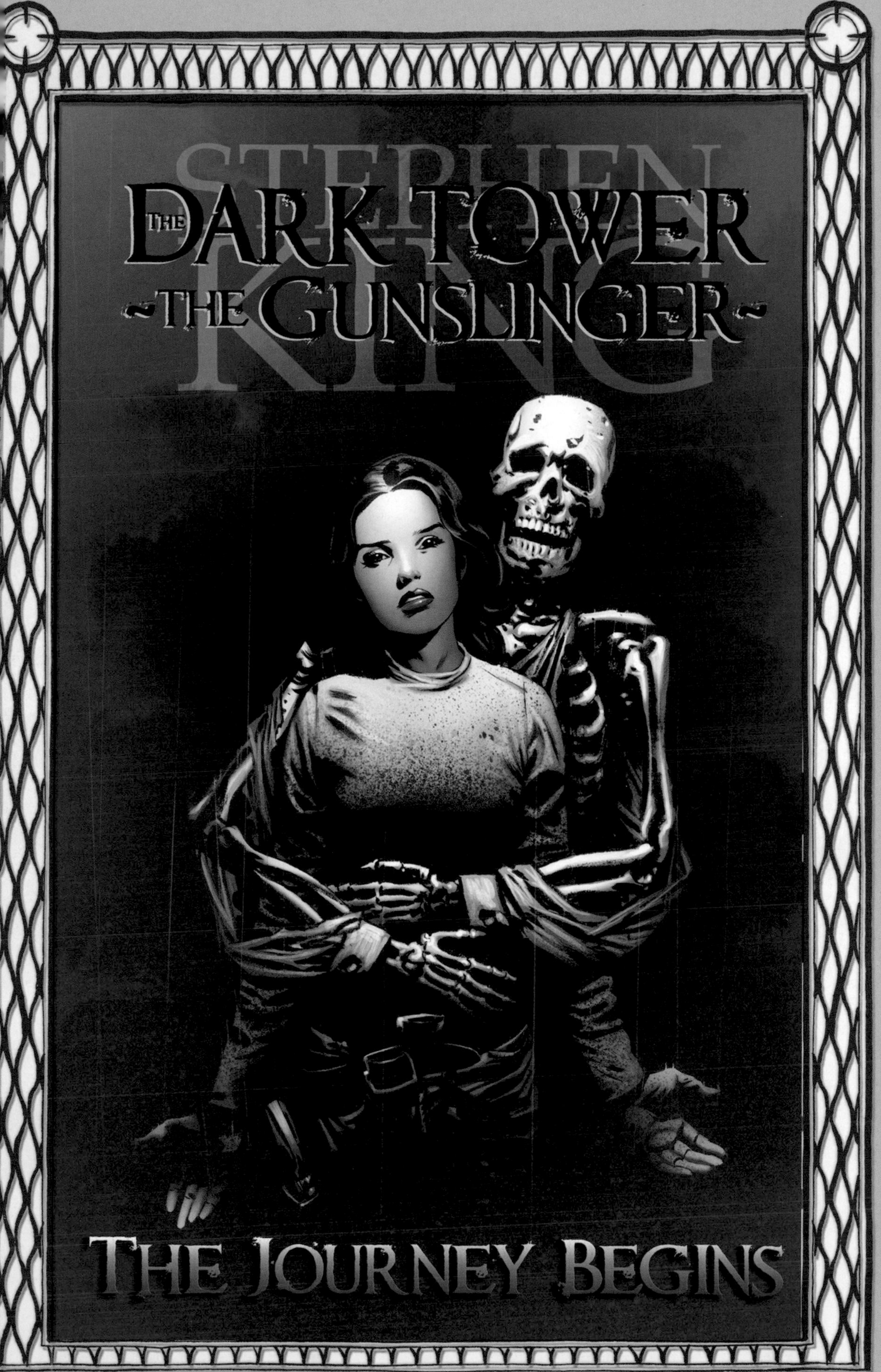
STEPHEN KING
THE DARK TOWER
THE GUNSLINGER
THE JOURNEY BEGINS

THE DARK TOWER
~THE GUNSLINGER~

THE JOURNEY BEGINS

CREATIVE DIRECTOR AND EXECUTIVE DIRECTOR
STEPHEN KING

PLOTTTING AND CONSULTATION
ROBIN FURTH

SCRIPT
PETER DAVID

ART
SEAN PHILLIPS & RICHARD ISANOVE

LETTERING
VC'S RUS WOOTON

PRODUCTION
ANTHONY DIAL, IRENE Y. LEE,
JEFF POWELL & TAYLOR ESPOSITO

ASSISTANT EDITORS
MICHAEL HORWITZ & CHARLIE BECKERMAN

SENIOR EDITOR
RALPH MACCHIO

COVER ART
SEAN PHILLIPS & RICHARD ISANOVE

DARK TOWER: THE GUNSLINGER — THE JOURNEY BEGINS. Contains material originally published in magazine form as DARK TOWER: THE GUNSLINGER — THE JOURNEY BEGINS #1-5. First printing 2011. ISBN# 978-0-7851-4709-1. Published by MARVEL WORLDWIDE, INC., a subsidiary of MARVEL ENTERTAINMENT, LLC. OFFICE OF PUBLICATION: 135 W. 50th Street, New York, NY 10020. Copyright © 2010 and 2011 Stephen King. All rights reserved. $24.99 per copy in the U.S. and $27.99 in Canada (GST #R127032852); Canadian Agreement #40668537. All characters featured in this publication and the distinctive names and likenesses thereof, and all related indicia are trademarks of Stephen King. No similarity between any of the names, characters, persons, and/or institutions in this magazine with those of any living or dead person or institution is intended, and any such similarity which may exist is purely coincidental. Marvel and its logos are TM & © Marvel Characters, Inc. **Printed in the U.S.A.** ALAN FINE, EVP - Office of the President, Marvel Worldwide, Inc. and EVP & CMO Marvel Characters B.V.; DAN BUCKLEY, Chief Executive Officer and Publisher - Print, Animation & Digital Media; JIM SOKOLOWSKI, Chief Operating Officer; DAVID GABRIEL, SVP of Publishing Sales & Circulation; DAVID BOGART, SVP of Business Affairs & Talent Management; MICHAEL PASCIULLO, VP Merchandising & Communications; JIM O'KEEFE, VP of Operations & Logistics; DAN CARR, Executive Director of Publishing Technology; JUSTIN F. GABRIE, Director of Publishing & Editorial Operations; SUSAN CRESPI, Editorial Operations Manager; ALEX MORALES, Publishing Operations Manager; STAN LEE, Chairman Emeritus. For information regarding advertising in Marvel Comics or on Marvel.com, please contact Ron Stern, VP of Business Development, at rstern@marvel.com. For Marvel subscription inquiries, please call 800-217-9158. **Manufactured between 11/22/10 and 12/29/10 by R.R. DONNELLEY, INC., SALEM, VA, USA.**

10 9 8 7 6 5 4 3 2 1

COLLECTION EDITOR
MARK D. BEAZLEY

EDITORIAL ASSISTANTS
JOE HOCHSTEIN & JAMES EMMETT

ASSISTANT EDITORS
NELSON RIBEIRO & ALEX STARBUCK

EDITOR, SPECIAL PROJECTS
JENNIFER GRÜNWALD

SENIOR EDITOR, SPECIAL PROJECTS
JEFF YOUNGQUIST

SENIOR VICE PRESIDENT OF SALES
DAVID GABRIEL

SENIOR VICE PRESIDENT OF STRATEGIC DEVELOPMENT
RUWAN JAYATILLEKE

BOOK DESIGN
SPRING HOTELING & PATRICK MCGRATH

EDITOR IN CHIEF
JOE QUESADA

PUBLISHER
DAN BUCKLEY

SPECIAL THANKS TO
CHUCK VERRILL, MARSHA DEFILIPPO, RALPH VICINANZA,
BARBARA ANN MCINTYRE, BRIAN STARK, JIM NAUSEDAS,
JIM MCCANN, ARUNE SINGH, JEFF SUTER, JOHN BARBER,
LAUREN SANKOVITCH & CHRIS ELIOPOULOS

FOR MORE INFORMATION ON DARK TOWER COMICS, VISIT MARVEL.COM/DARKTOWER.
TO FIND MARVEL COMICS AT A LOCAL COMIC SHOP, CALL 1-888-COMICBOOK.

INTRODUCTION

Dear Fellow Constant Readers:

Welcome to the first issue of our new Dark Tower saga. Gilead has fallen, the Affiliation's finest have been massacred at the Battle of Jericho Hill, yet our protagonist, Roland Deschain, has miraculously survived. And perhaps the word *miraculous* is an even more apt description than we may suspect. For how many men are mistaken for corpses and thrown onto funeral pyres, only to rise again like avenging furies? Like many heroes before him, Roland has become very skilled at outwitting death. Although almost all of his boyhood companions are now ash and smoke, Roland refuses to follow them to the clearing while his quest remains unfinished. He is determined to reach that field of red roses where the Dark Tower stands, and when he enters that imposing edifice he will climb to the top and demand justice from whatever god or demon resides there. And when that justice is done, Gilead will live again, and Roland's departed companions will rise from the dead and he will embrace them once more . . . or so he hopes.

If you are like me, you have awaited this moment with a mixture of excitement and trepidation. For years I have known that the last of Roland's youth would burn on a funeral pyre atop Jericho Hill, but I also knew that the man who escaped those corpse flames was destined to become something very different from the angry but idealistic boy we first met in *The Gunslinger Born*. If I ever got the chance to plot another thirty-issue story arc (which I fervently hoped would happen), I would have to show how a boy so completely devoted to his ka-tet could become the bitter, lonely, and dangerous drifter we meet in the first of the Dark Tower novels. How in the world could I even begin to undertake such a gargantuan task? Well, what you hold in your hands is my attempt to do just that.

Moving from the end of *The Battle of Jericho Hill* to the beginning of *The Gunslinger: The Journey Begins* was a dizzying task. While plotting the first Dark Tower series I felt that I had many signposts to guide me. I knew that after Roland and his friends escaped Hambry they would have to trek through forests and across the Xay River before they reached Gilead. I knew that Roland's mind would be lost inside Maerlyn's Grapefruit, and that our tet's homecoming would not be easy. Roland was destined to kill his treacherous mother, Cort would be poisoned, and Roland's father would be killed by a traitor's knife. Gilead had to fall, and the shadow of Jericho Hill loomed large. But of the twelve years following the Battle of Jericho Hill, I knew very little. Of course I was familiar with the names of some of the adversaries Roland would encounter while casting about for the trail of the Man in Black, and I knew in great detail his dangerous liaison with a certain otherworldly lady in Eluria (which I will not discuss now!) but otherwise, I was in the dark. And to tell you the truth, despite so many years of traveling unknown roads with Roland, such darkness makes me profoundly uneasy.

How could I bridge those undocumented years? How could I segue from Roland, the dinh of a powerful ka-tet, to Roland, the drifter? How could I smoothly transport our tale from the fertile Mid-World of Roland's youth to the ruined landscape of the Mohaine Desert? And scariest of all, how could I open the story told in *The Gunslinger* when we had already used the famous first line of that novel as an opening for *The Gunslinger Born*? (*The man in black fled across the desert, and the gunslinger followed...*) I approached these daunting tasks the way writers have always had to approach formidable obstacles—one word at a time.

Luckily for me, these Dark Tower comics have two fabulous editors—Ralph Macchio and Mike Horwitz. To my fear that we might repeat ourselves by opening *The Journey Begins* in the same way that we opened *The Gunslinger Born*, they had the perfect answer. Let's use that repetition in an interesting fashion. Let's *purposefully* echo the beginning of *The Gunslinger Born*, but let's try to add some extra layers of meaning. Their words got me thinking. In fact, by the time I returned to my word processor, my brain was spinning so fast that smoke was probably coming out of my ears. In the opening of *The Gunslinger Born*, we had emphasized Roland's *pursuit* of the Man in Black. But in *The Journey Begins*, I wanted to stress that while Roland is chasing his enemy, the Man in Black is quite purposefully *leading Roland on*. The difference is subtle, but also profound. Here is an excerpt from that part of my original outline:

As Ralph and Mike suggested, let's begin this new arc by playing off the opening pages of *The Gunslinger Born*...only we'll add a new twist! The Man in Black (aka Marten/ Walter) is a sorcerer, and he's playing his own game with Roland, so let's make use of this information. (As Peter mentioned in the earlier opening, the Man in Black is a sly old fox. In fact, we're going to see him demonstrate his slyness over and over in this 30 issue story.)

And as for how to segue from Jericho Hill to the Mohaine Desert, the answer all of a sudden seemed obvious. The first section of the original *Gunslinger* novel is told in flashback—Roland is recounting his adventures to a desert dweller named Brown. Hence, all we had to do was flashback further—not to the horrors that Roland experienced in a town called Tull, *but all the way back* to the horrors of Jericho Hill. And to segue from Roland, the dinh of a tet to Roland, the loner, let's *witness* his bereavement. As Mike Horwitz suggested, let's see him bid goodbye to all of his dead friends lying atop that pyre, *especially* Aileen. But each time I started visualizing that scene, my favorite bit of *Carrie* flashed before my eyes. What if one of Roland's companions isn't *quite* dead? What if a hand reaches out of that *pyre* and grabs him...?

Anyway, my fellow Constant Readers, I hope you have enjoyed this tale. And thanks, as always, for staying with us. Roland appreciates your company, and so do we.

Long days and pleasant nights—
Robin Furth

IN A WORLD THAT HAS MOVED ON...

Roland Deschain is the last descendant of the line of Arthur Eld. His late father, Steven, was the king of the barony of Gilead. Seeking to emulate his father, Roland was the youngest man to ever become a gunslinger. Great forces have swirled around him since that day.

When Gilead was under attack by the armies of evil led by Walter O'Dim and the Good Man, John Farson, Steven Deschain was killed. His forces of the White known as The Affiliation faltered in their defense of the city. Roland and his ka-tet became Gilead's final barrier, and they, too, failed.

And for nigh unto ten years, Roland, the lone survivor of that last, losing battle, has pursued his destiny. His quest is to reach the mysterious Dark Tower wherein he can set this out-of-synch world right. And the key to his goal lies with the Man in Black, who Roland now doggedly tracks.

STEPHEN KING

THE DARK TOWER
~THE GUNSLINGER~

THE JOURNEY BEGINS
CHAPTER ONE

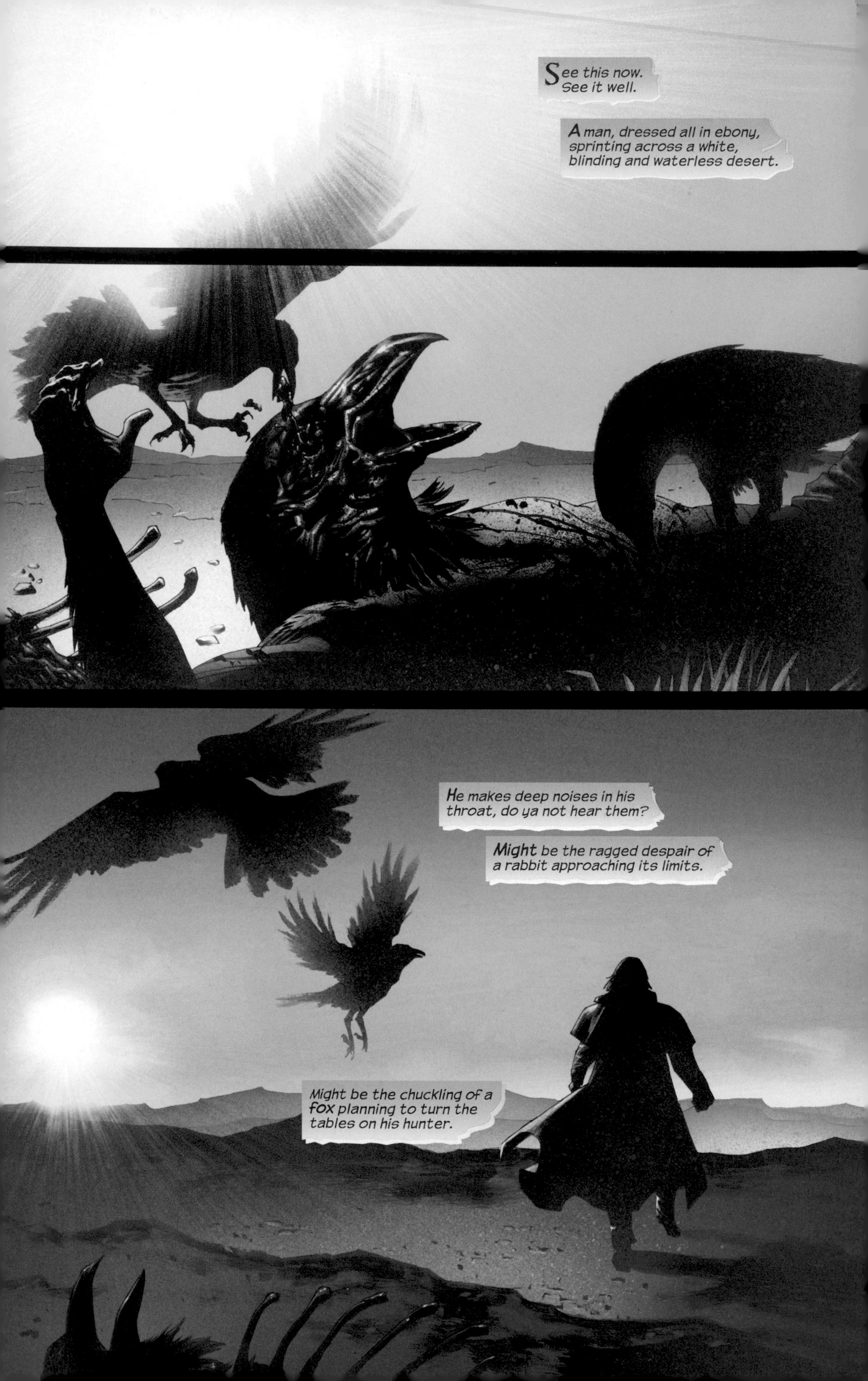

See this now. See it well.
A man, dressed all in ebony, sprinting across a white, blinding and waterless desert.
He makes deep noises in his throat, do ya not hear them?
Might be the ragged despair of a rabbit approaching its limits.
Might be the chuckling of a fox planning to turn the tables on his hunter.

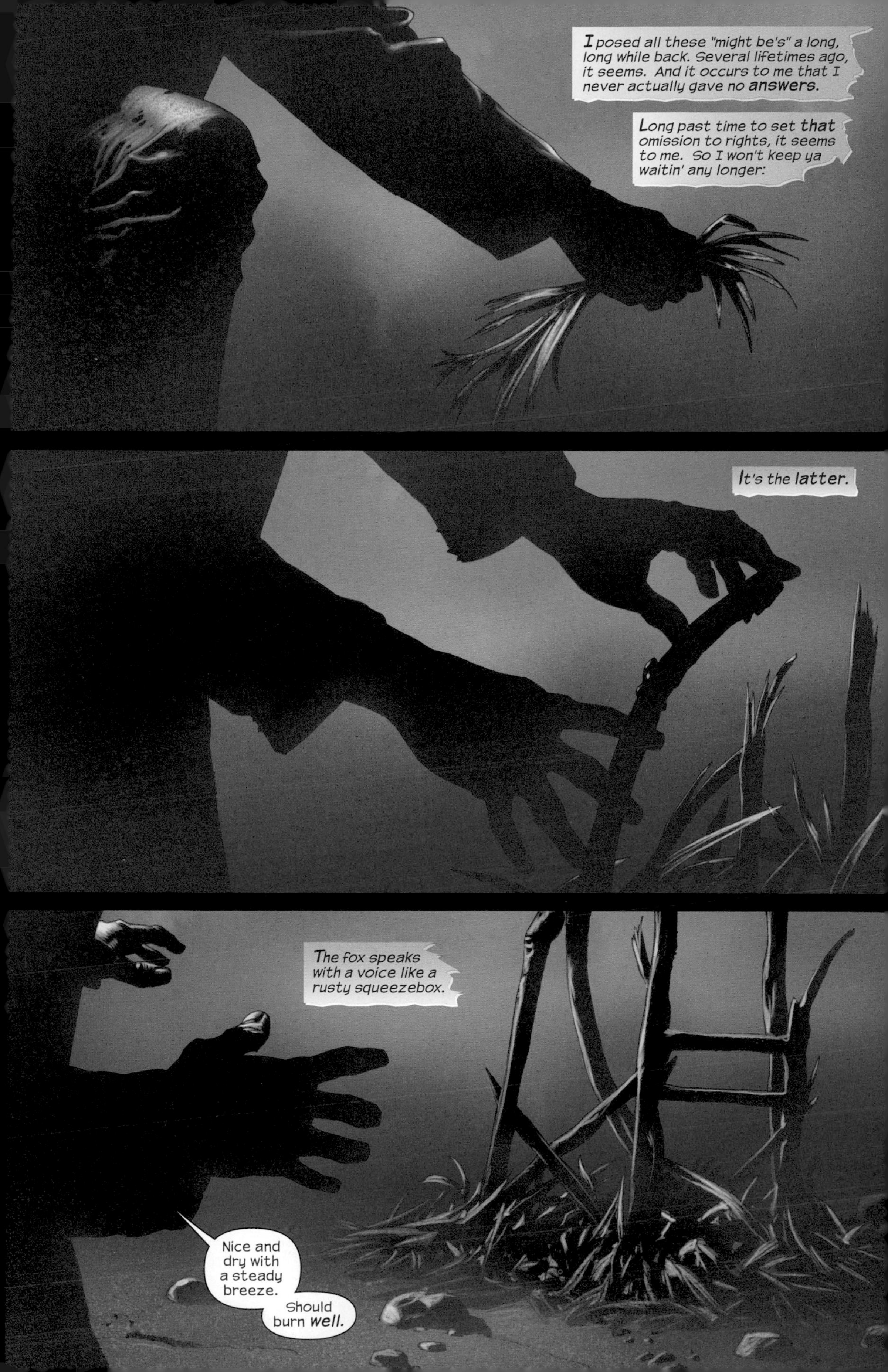
I posed all these "might be's" a long, long while back. Several lifetimes ago, it seems. And it occurs to me that I never actually gave no answers.
Long past time to set that omission to rights, it seems to me. So I won't keep ya waitin' any longer:
It's the latter.
The fox speaks with a voice like a rusty squeezebox.
Nice and dry with a steady breeze.
Should burn well.

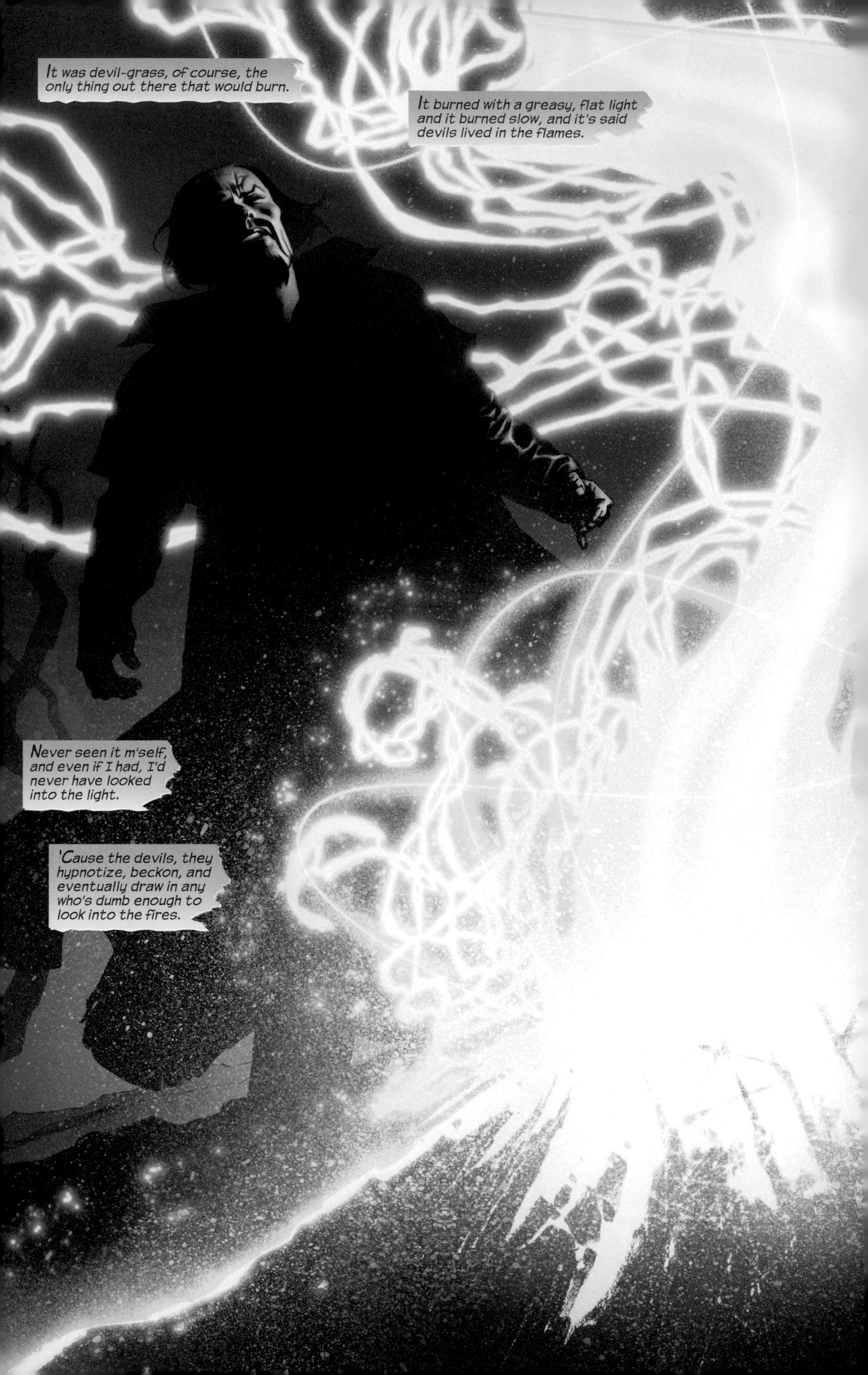
It was devil-grass, of course, the only thing out there that would burn.
It burned with a greasy, flat light and it burned slow, and it's said devils lived in the flames.
Never seen it m'self, and even if I had, I'd never have looked into the light.
'Cause the devils, they hypnotize, beckon, and eventually draw in any who's dumb enough to look into the fires.

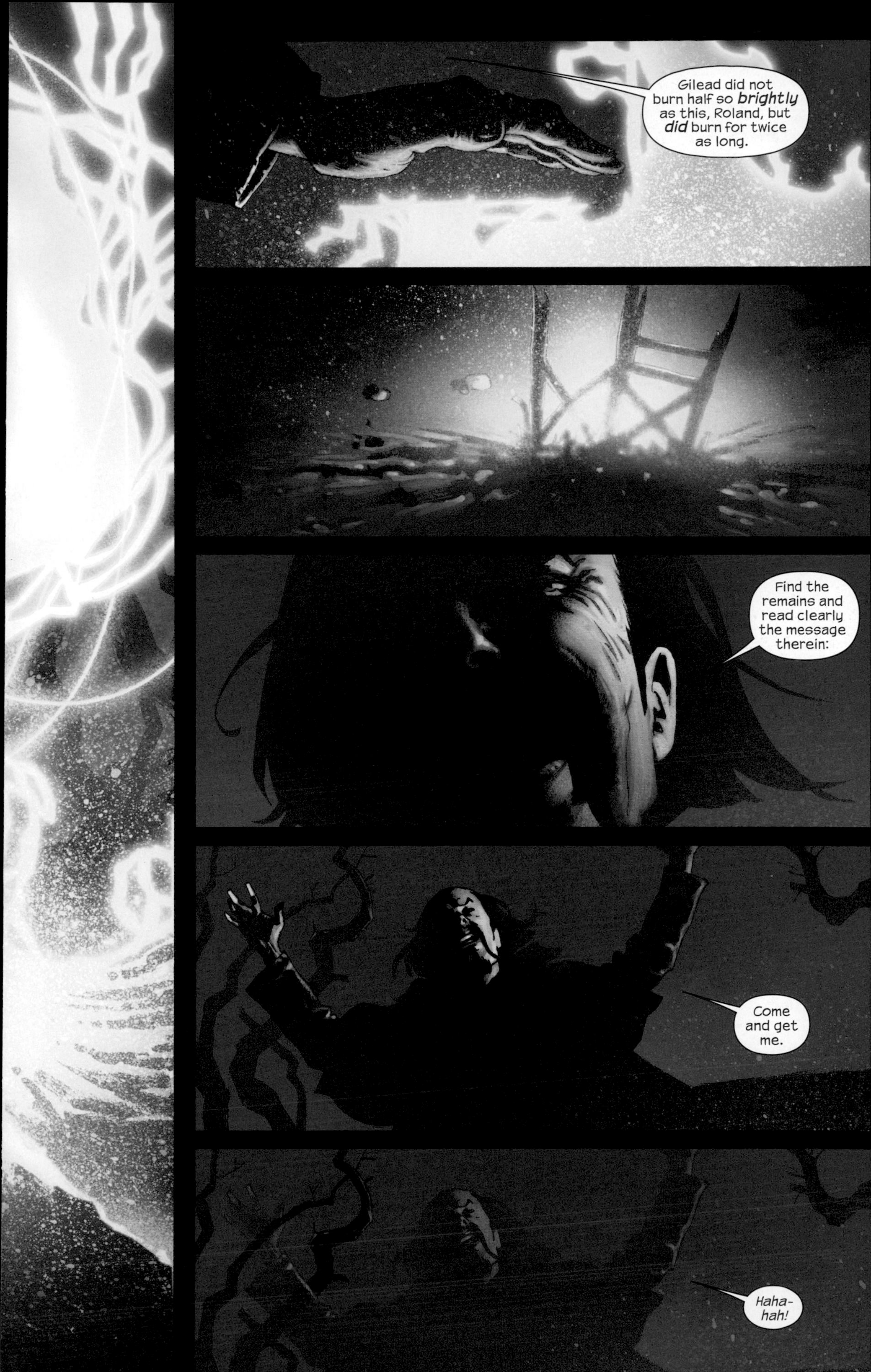
Gilead did not burn half so brightly as this, Roland, but did burn for twice as long.
Find the remains and read clearly the message therein:
Come and get me.
Haha-hah!

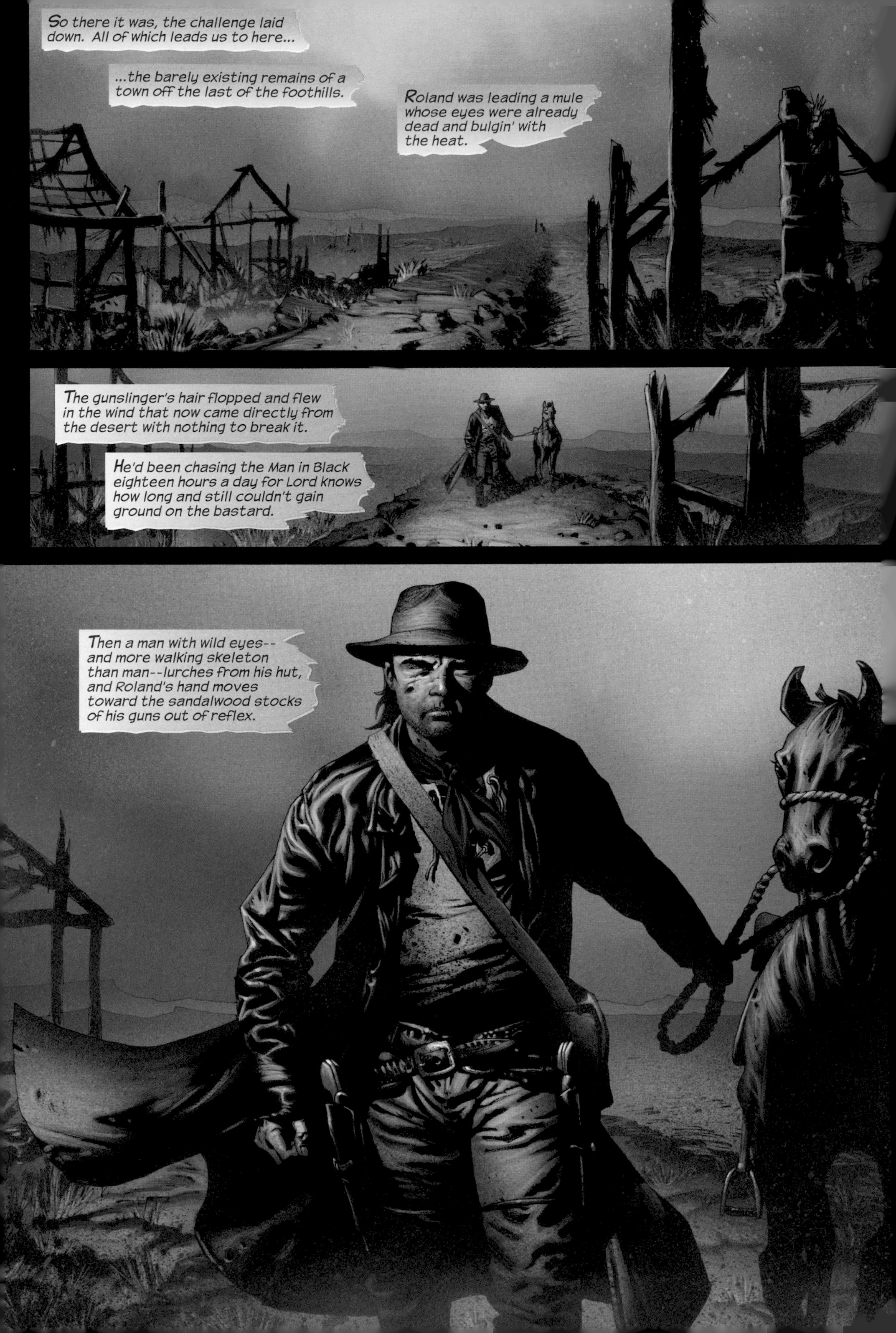
So there it was, the challenge laid down. All of which leads us to here...
...the barely existing remains of a town off the last of the foothills.
Roland was leading a mule whose eyes were already dead and bulgin' with the heat.
The gunslinger's hair flopped and flew in the wind that now came directly from the desert with nothing to break it.
He'd been chasing the Man in Black eighteen hours a day for Lord knows how long and still couldn't gain ground on the bastard.
Then a man with wild eyes--and more walking skeleton than man--lurches from his hut, and Roland's hand moves toward the sandalwood stocks of his guns out of reflex.

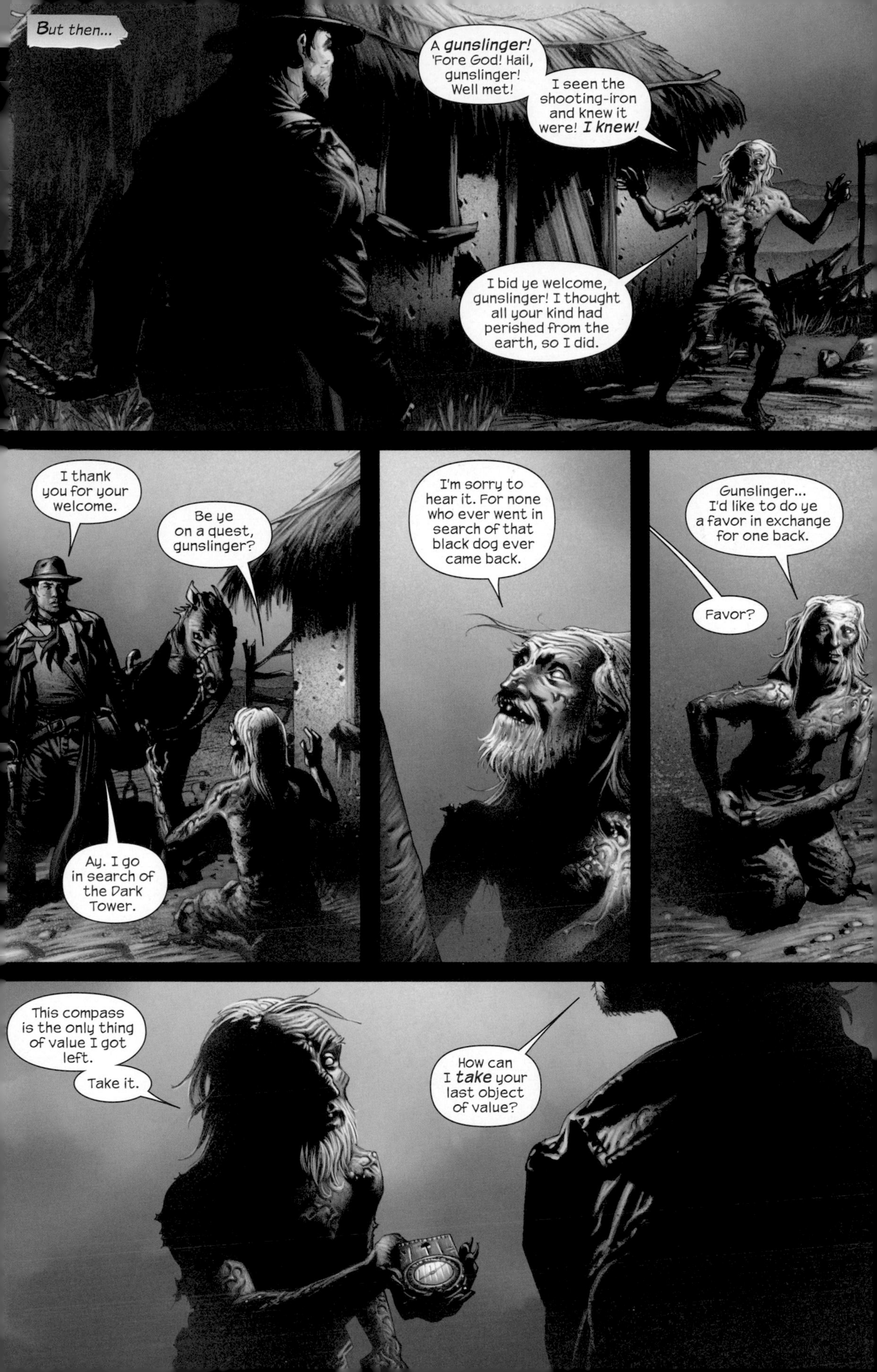
But then...
A gunslinger! 'Fore God! Hail, gunslinger! Well met!
I seen the shooting-iron and knew it were! I knew!
I bid ye welcome, gunslinger! I thought all your kind had perished from the earth, so I did.
I thank you for your welcome.
Be ye on a quest, gunslinger?
Ay. I go in search of the Dark Tower.
I'm sorry to hear it. For none who ever went in search of that black dog ever came back.
Gunslinger... I'd like to do ye a favor in exchange for one back.
Favor?
This compass is the only thing of value I got left.
Take it.
How can I take your last object of value?

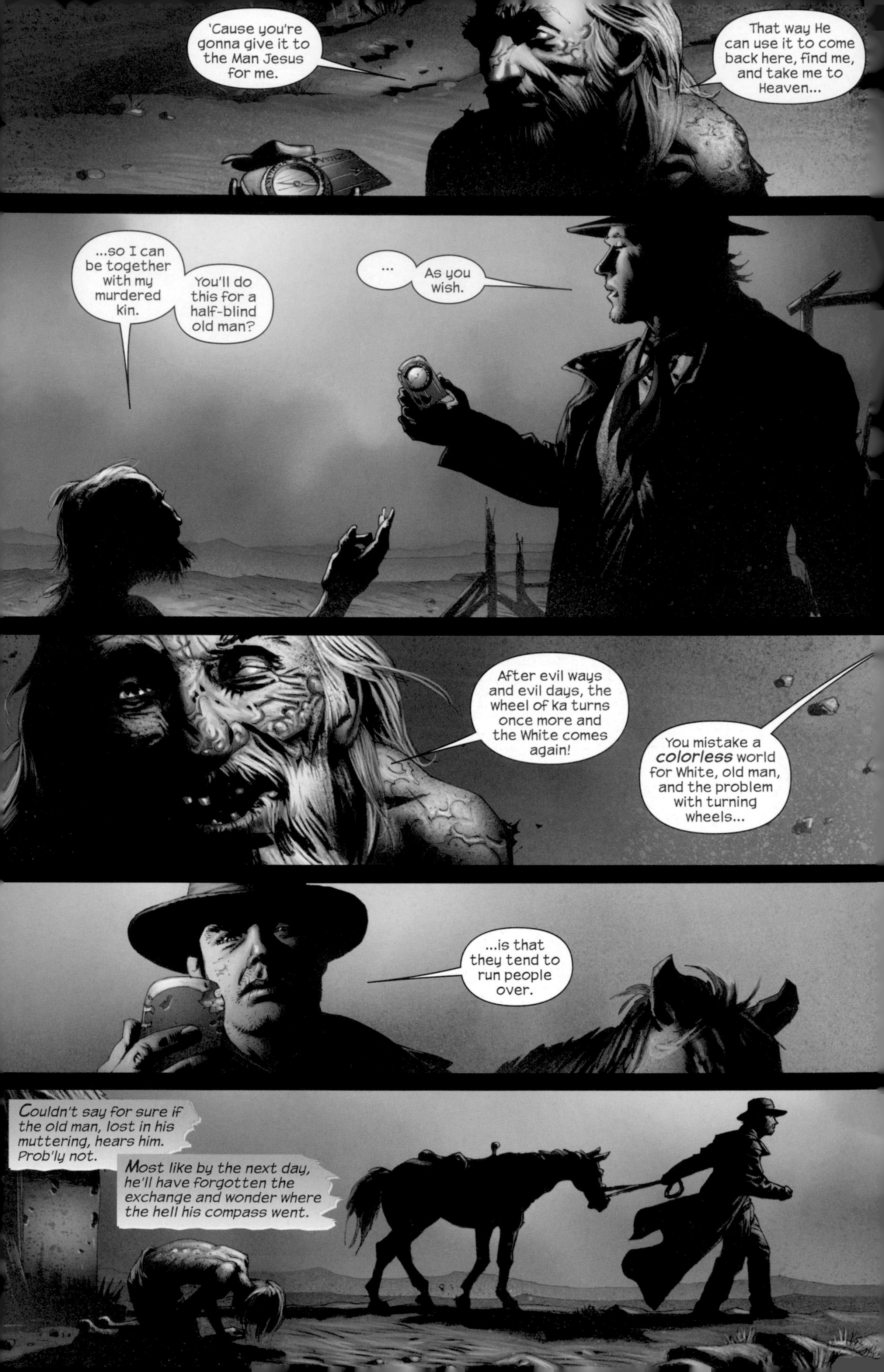
'Cause you're gonna give it to the Man Jesus for me.
That way He can use it to come back here, find me, and take me to Heaven...
...so I can be together with my murdered kin.
You'll do this for a half-blind old man?
...
As you wish.
After evil ways and evil days, the wheel of ka turns once more and the White comes again!
You mistake a *colorless* world for White, old man, and the problem with turning wheels...
...is that they tend to run people over.
Couldn't say for sure if the old man, lost in his muttering, hears him. Prob'ly not.
Most like by the next day, he'll have forgotten the exchange and wonder where the hell his compass went.

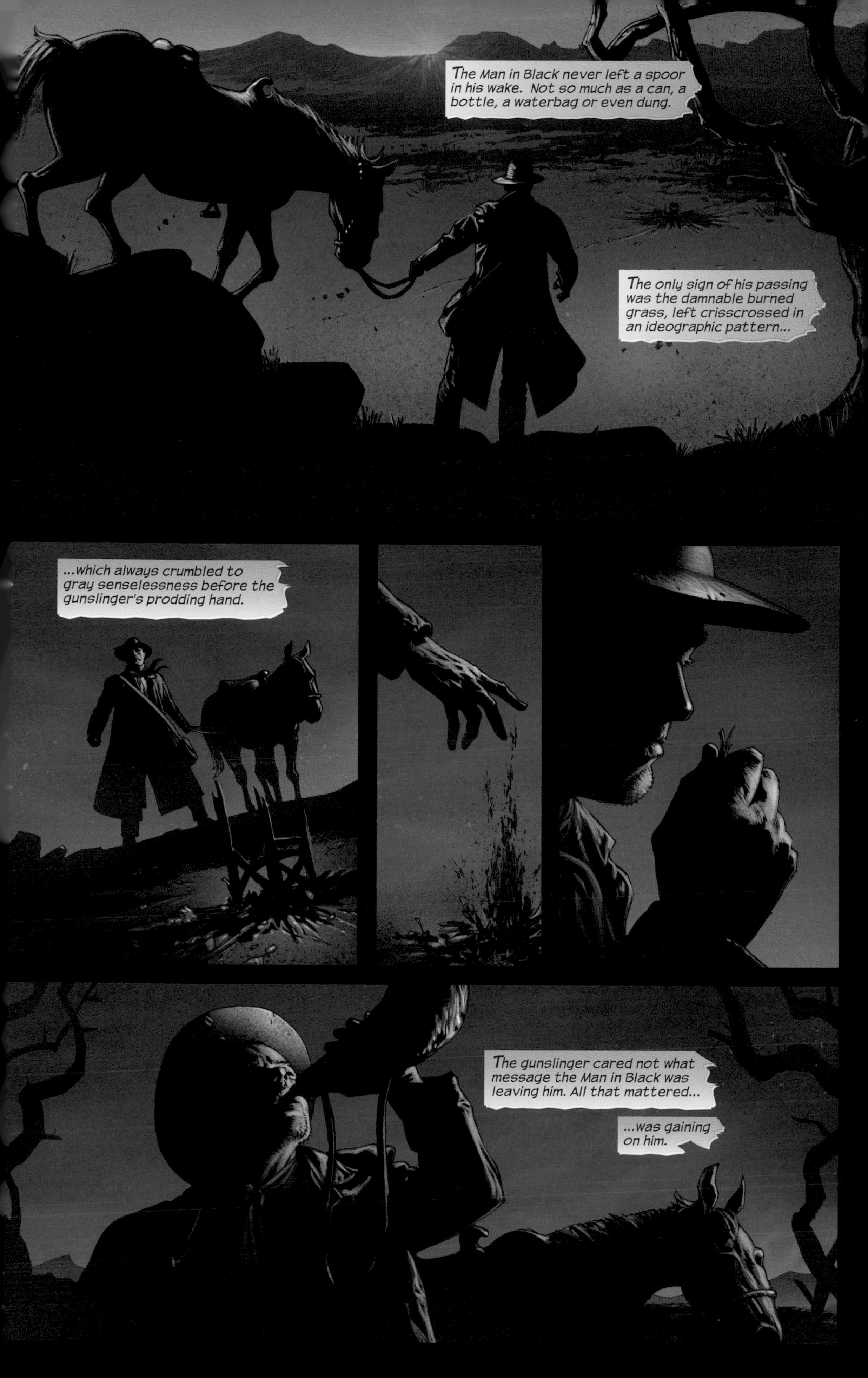
The Man in Black never left a spoor in his wake. Not so much as a can, a bottle, a waterbag or even dung.
The only sign of his passing was the damnable burned grass, left crisscrossed in an ideographic pattern...
...which always crumbled to gray senselessness before the gunslinger's prodding hand.
The gunslinger cared not what message the Man in Black was leaving him. All that mattered...
...was gaining on him.

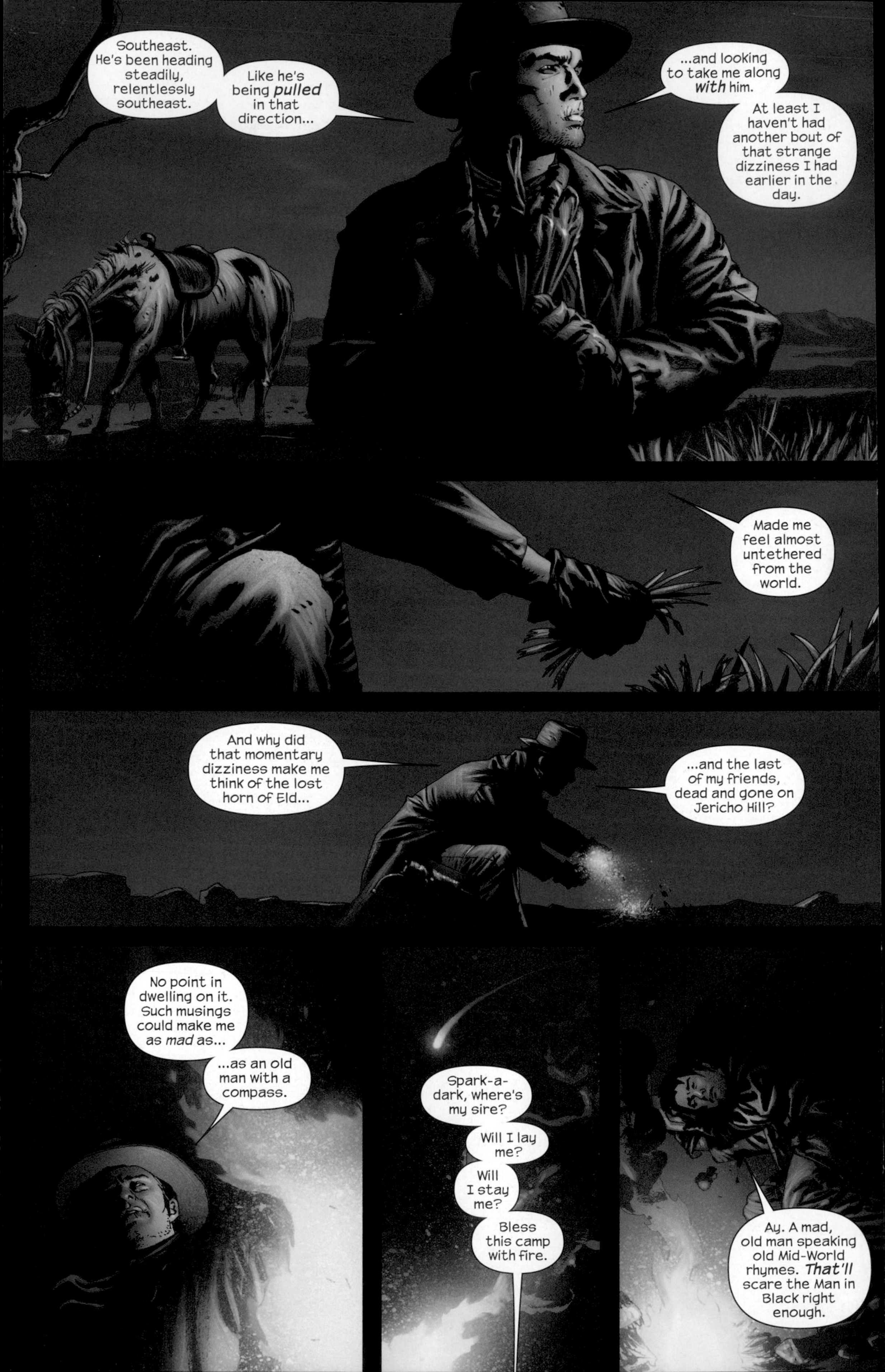
Southeast. He's been heading steadily, relentlessly southeast.
Like he's being pulled in that direction...
...and looking to take me along with him.
At least I haven't had another bout of that strange dizziness I had earlier in the day.
Made me feel almost untethered from the world.
And why did that momentary dizziness make me think of the lost horn of Eld...
...and the last of my friends, dead and gone on Jericho Hill?
No point in dwelling on it. Such musings could make me as mad as...
...as an old man with a compass.
Spark-a-dark, where's my sire?
Will I lay me?
Will I stay me?
Bless this camp with fire.
Ay. A mad, old man speaking old Mid-World rhymes. That'll scare the Man in Black right enough.

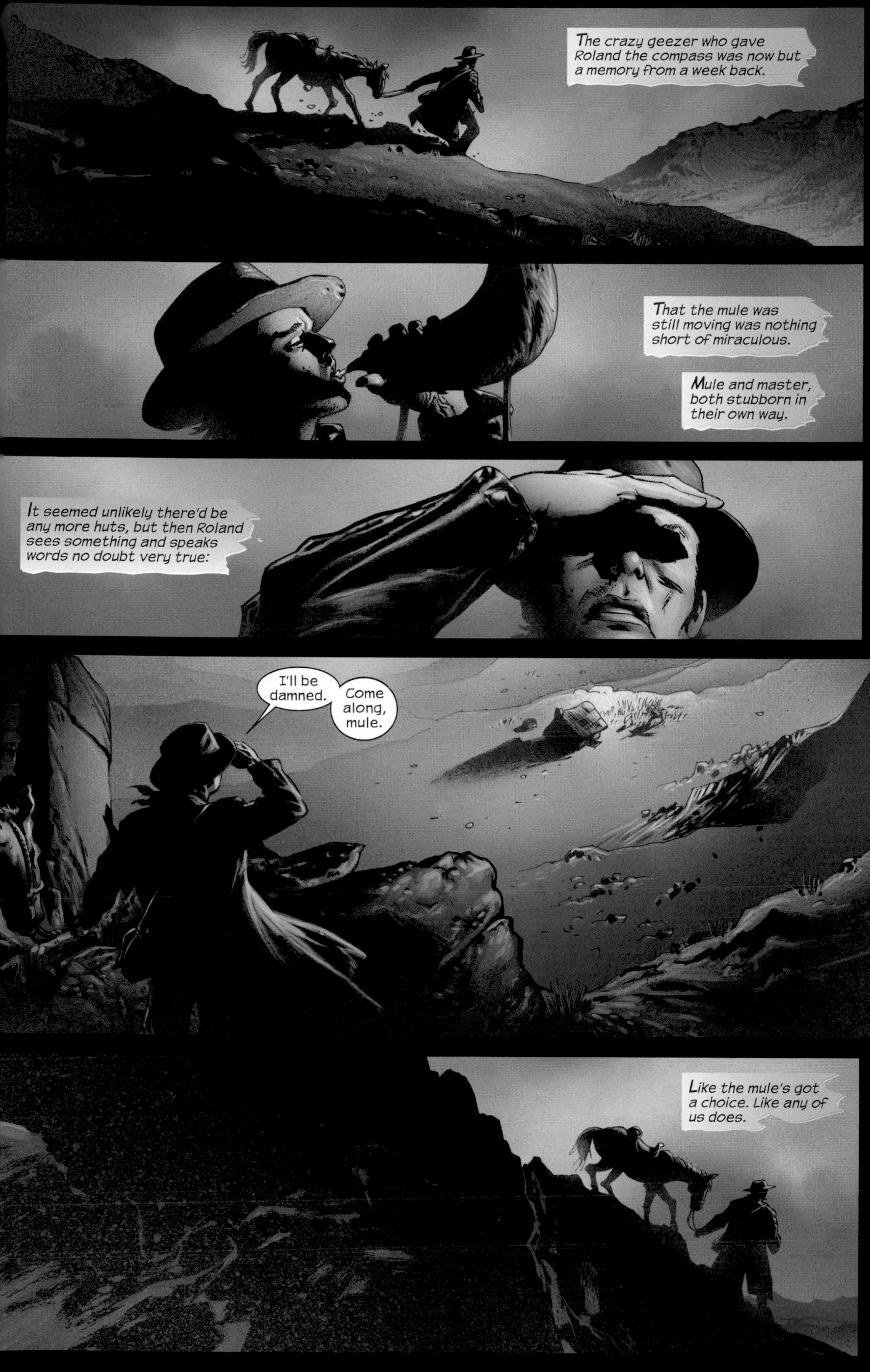
The crazy geezer who gave Roland the compass was now but a memory from a week back.
That the mule was still moving was nothing short of miraculous.
Mule and master, both stubborn in their own way.
It seemed unlikely there'd be any more huts, but then Roland sees something and speaks words no doubt very true:
I'll be damned.
Come along, mule.
Like the mule's got a choice. Like any of us does.

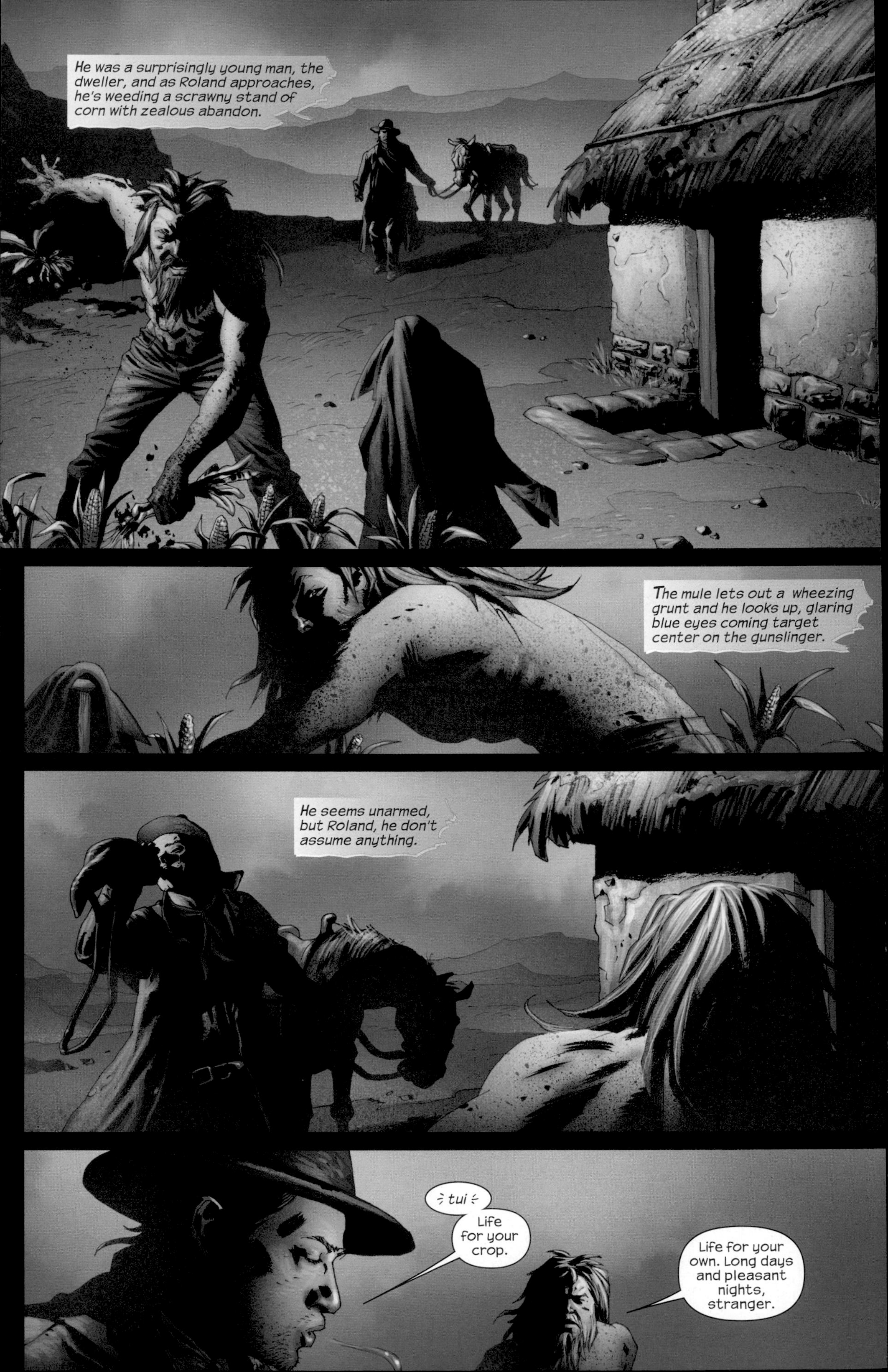
He was a surprisingly young man, the dweller, and as Roland approaches, he's weeding a scrawny stand of corn with zealous abandon.
The mule lets out a wheezing grunt and he looks up, glaring blue eyes coming target center on the gunslinger.
He seems unarmed, but Roland, he don't assume anything.
tui
Life for your crop.
Life for your own. Long days and pleasant nights, stranger.

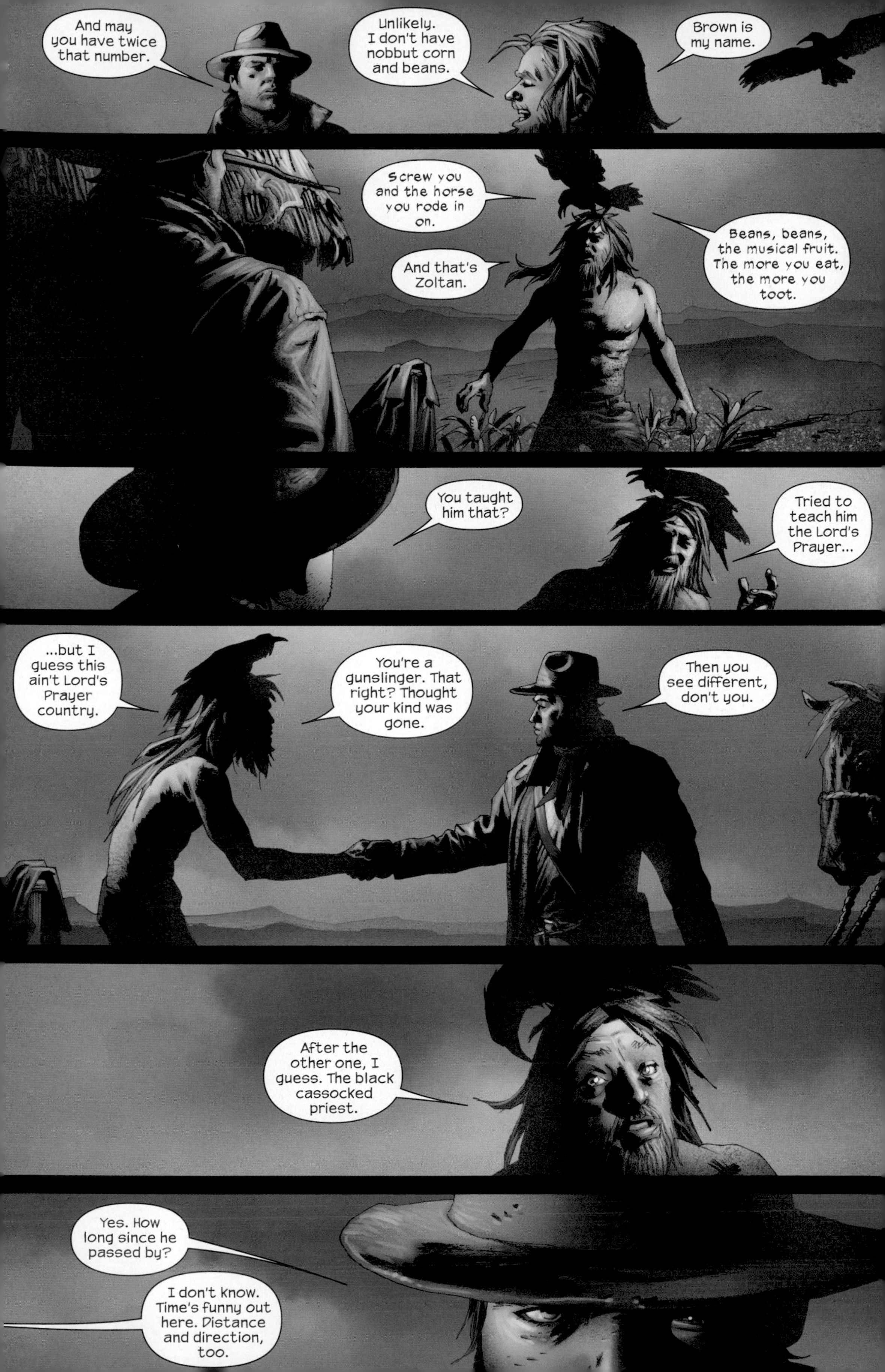
And may you have twice that number.
Unlikely. I don't have nobbut corn and beans.
Brown is my name.
Screw you and the horse you rode in on.
Beans, beans, the musical fruit. The more you eat, the more you toot.
And that's Zoltan.
You taught him that?
Tried to teach him the Lord's Prayer...
...but I guess this ain't Lord's Prayer country.
You're a gunslinger. That right? Thought your kind was gone.
Then you see different, don't you.
After the other one, I guess. The black cassocked priest.
Yes. How long since he passed by?
I don't know. Time's funny out here. Distance and direction, too.

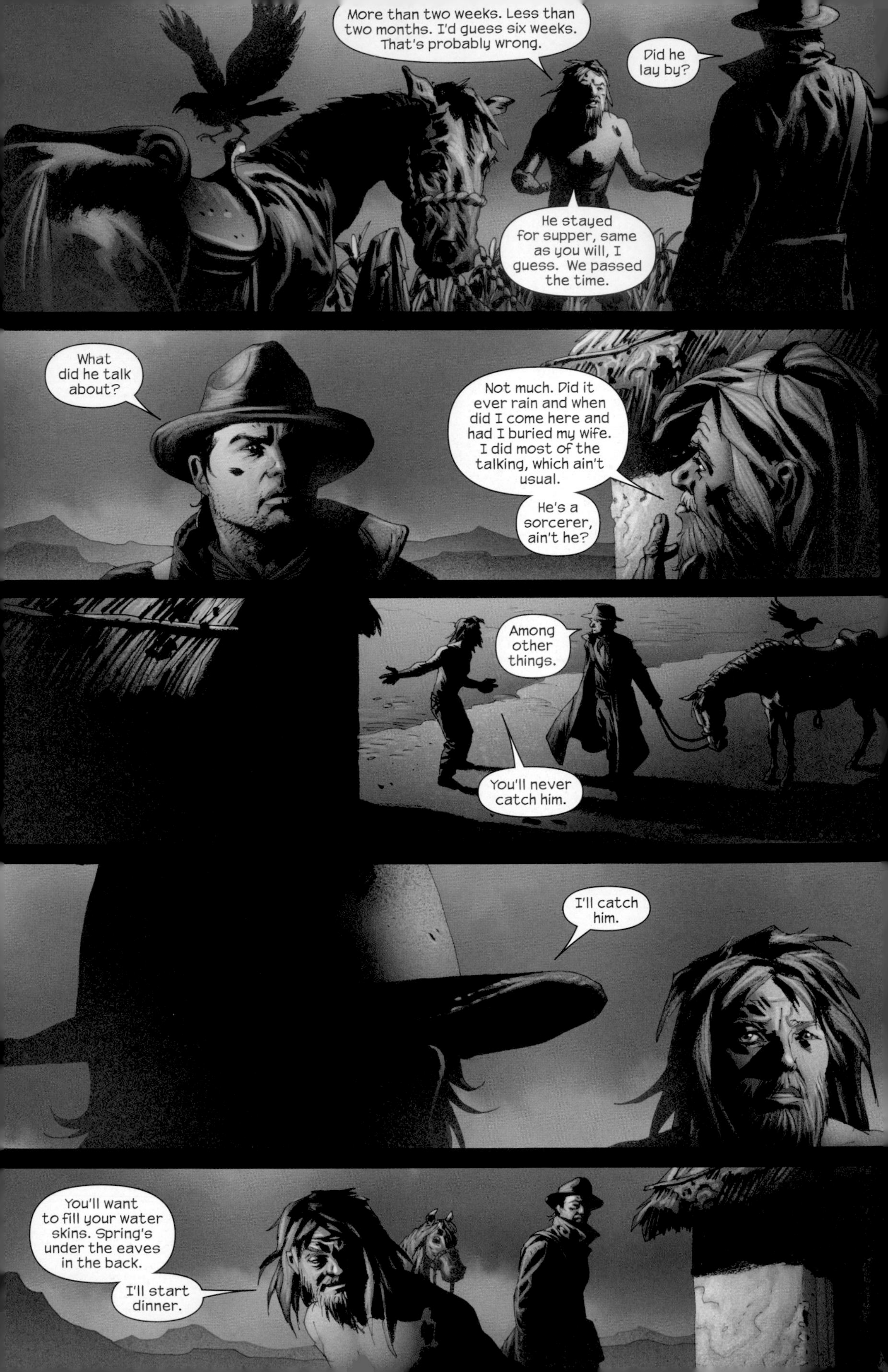
More than two weeks. Less than two months. I'd guess six weeks. That's probably wrong.
Did he lay by?
He stayed for supper, same as you will, I guess. We passed the time.
What did he talk about?
Not much. Did it ever rain and when did I come here and had I buried my wife. I did most of the talking, which ain't usual.
He's a sorcerer, ain't he?
Among other things.
You'll never catch him.
I'll catch him.
You'll want to fill your water skins. Spring's under the eaves in the back.
I'll start dinner.

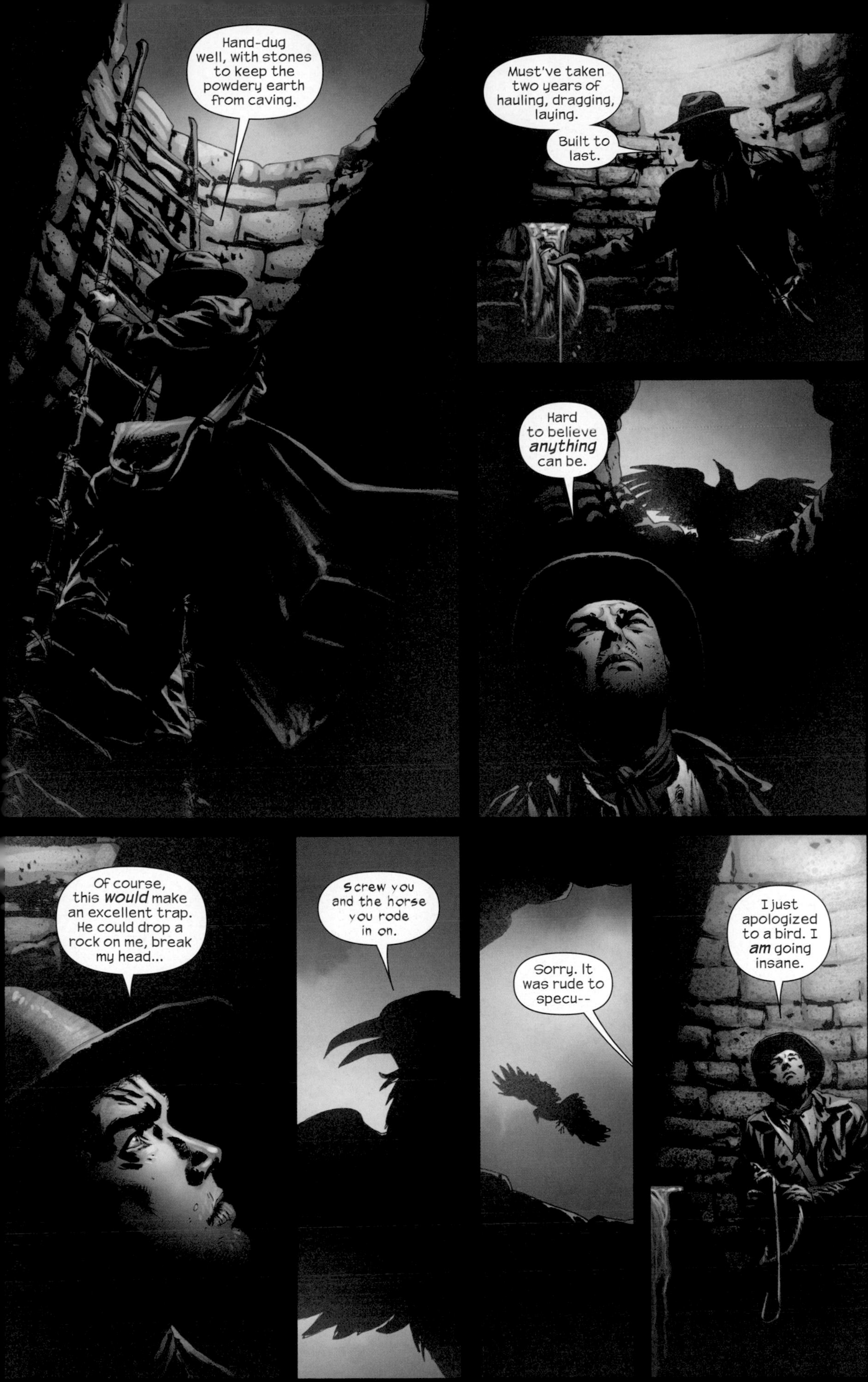
Hand-dug well, with stones to keep the powdery earth from caving.
Must've taken two years of hauling, dragging, laying.
Built to last.
Hard to believe *anything* can be.
Of course, this *would* make an excellent trap. He could drop a rock on me, break my head...
Screw you and the horse you rode in on.
Sorry. It was rude to specu--
I just apologized to a bird. I *am* going insane.

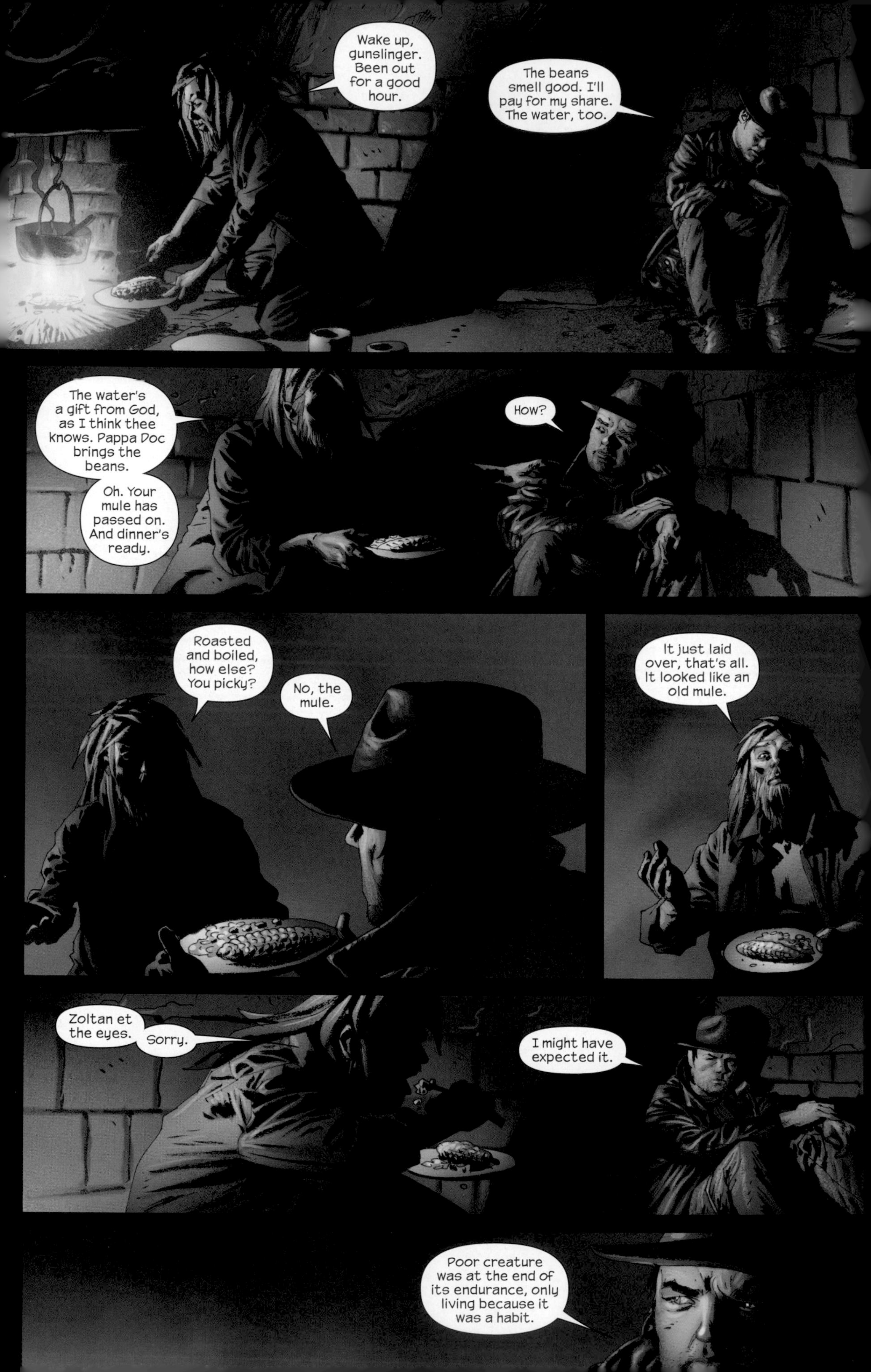
Wake up, gunslinger. Been out for a good hour.
The beans smell good. I'll pay for my share. The water, too.
The water's a gift from God, as I think thee knows. Pappa Doc brings the beans.
Oh. Your mule has passed on. And dinner's ready.
How?
Roasted and boiled, how else? You picky?
No, the mule.
It just laid over, that's all. It looked like an old mule.
Zoltan et the eyes.
Sorry.
I might have expected it.
Poor creature was at the end of its endurance, only living because it was a habit.

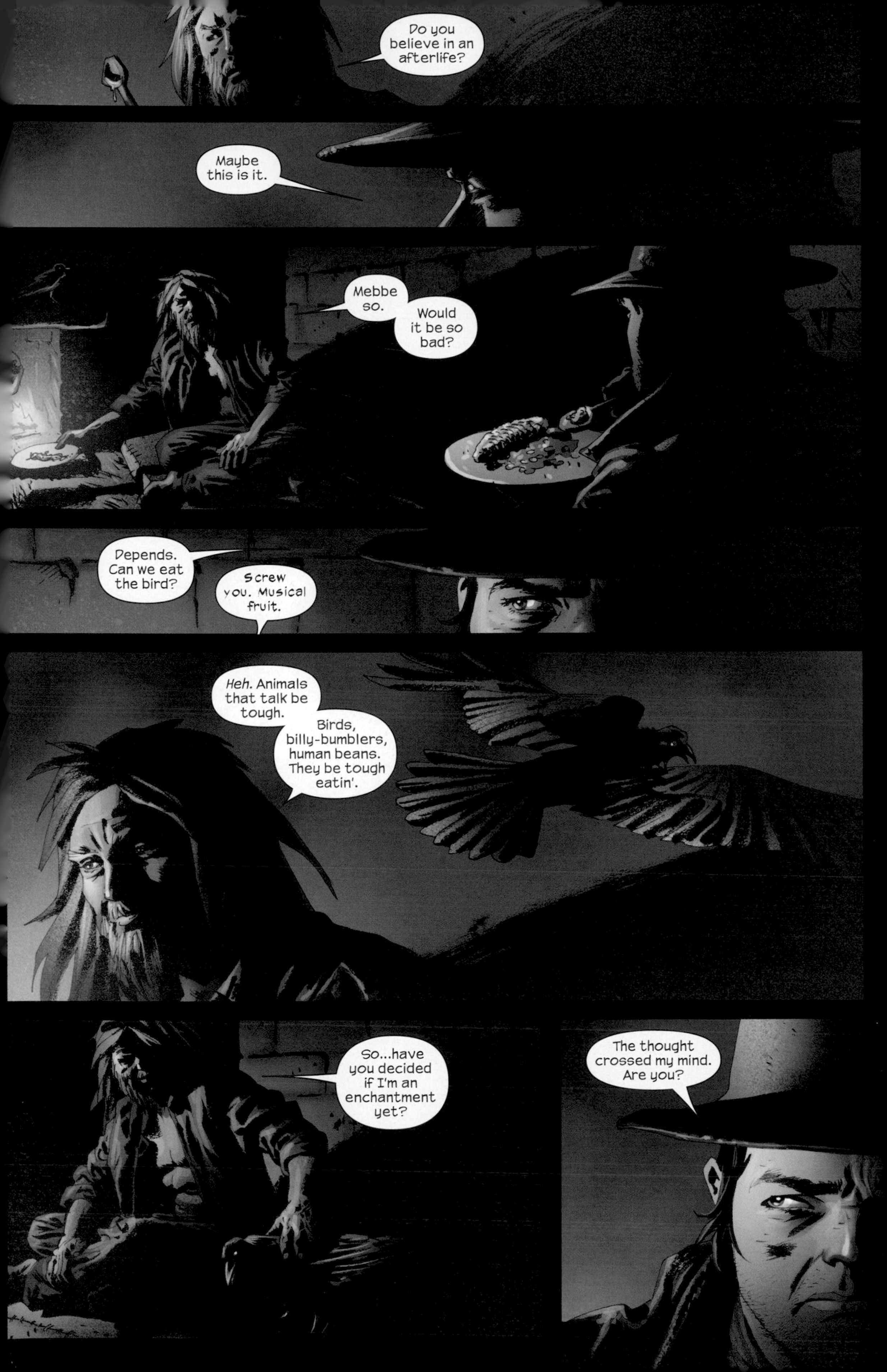
Do you believe in an afterlife?
Maybe this is it.
Mebbe so.
Would it be so bad?
Depends. Can we eat the bird?
Screw you. Musical fruit.
Heh. Animals that talk be tough.
Birds, billy-bumblers, human beans. They be tough eatin'.
So...have you decided if I'm an enchantment yet?
The thought crossed my mind. Are you?

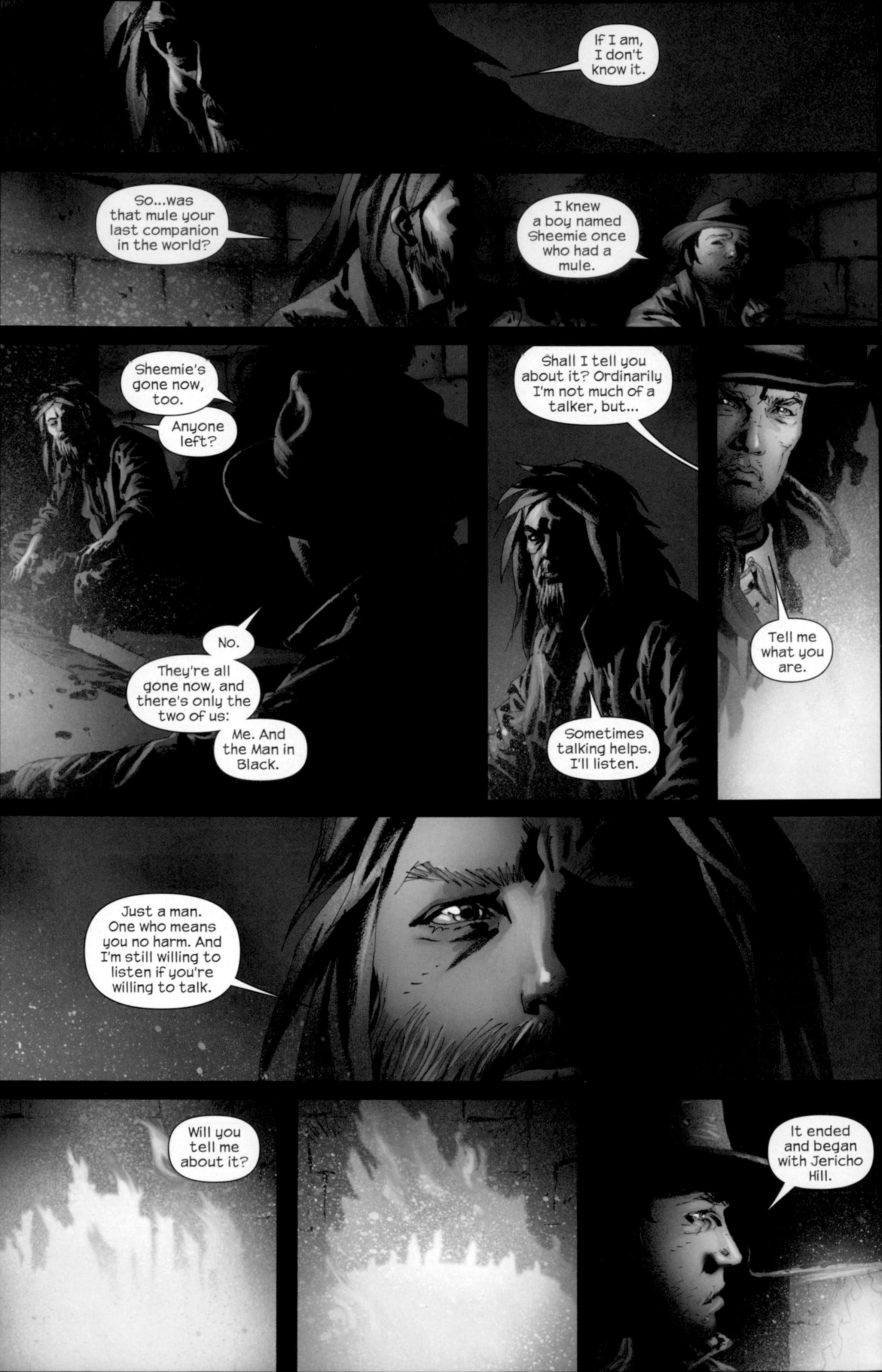
If I am, I don't know it.
So...was that mule your last companion in the world?
I knew a boy named Sheemie once who had a mule.
Sheemie's gone now, too.
Anyone left?
No.
They're all gone now, and there's only the two of us:
Me. And the Man in Black.
Shall I tell you about it? Ordinarily I'm not much of a talker, but...
Sometimes talking helps. I'll listen.
Tell me what you are.
Just a man. One who means you no harm. And I'm still willing to listen if you're willing to talk.
Will you tell me about it?
It ended and began with Jericho Hill.

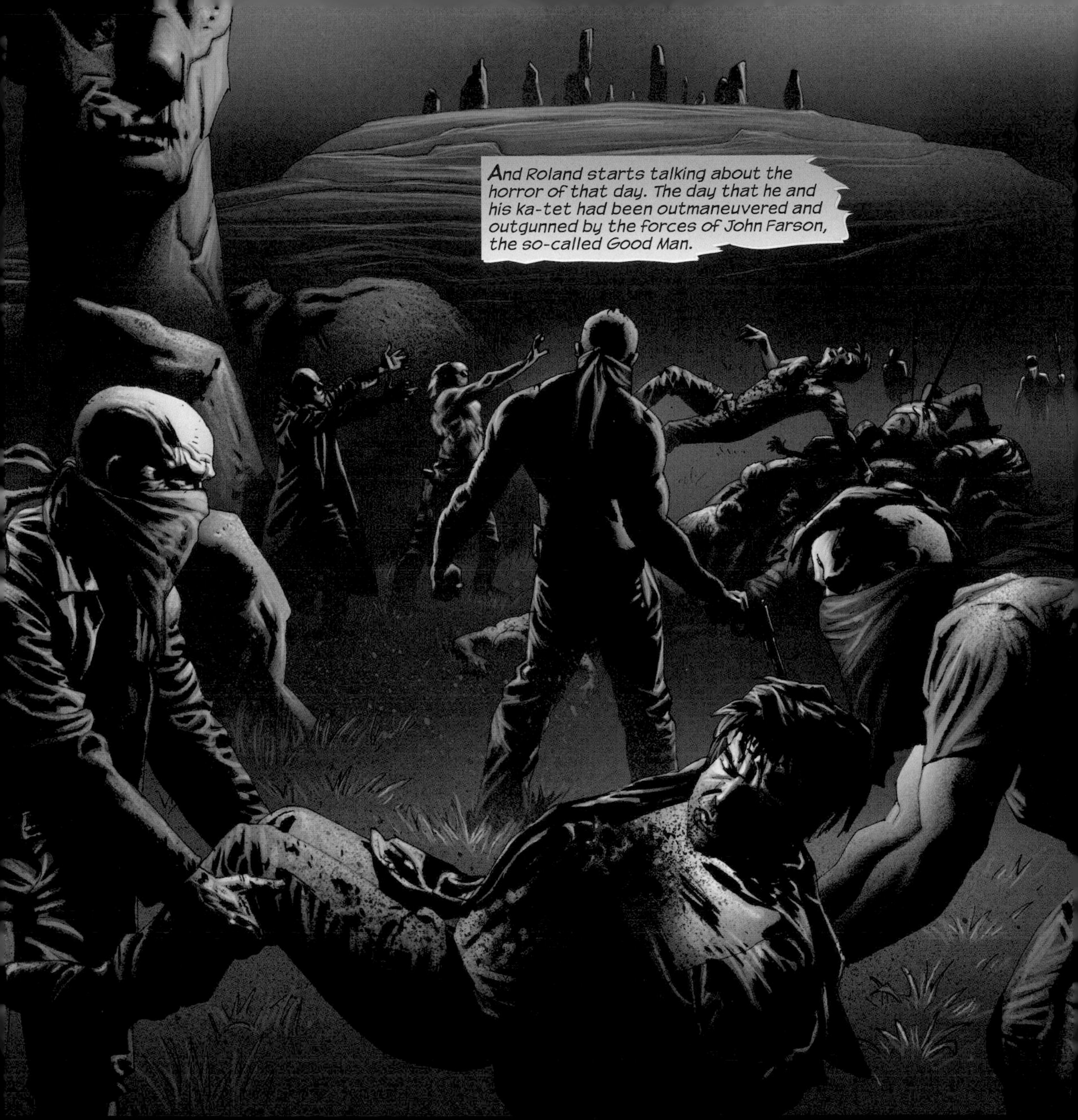
And Roland starts talking about the horror of that day. The day that he and his ka-tet had been outmaneuvered and outgunned by the forces of John Farson, the so-called Good Man.

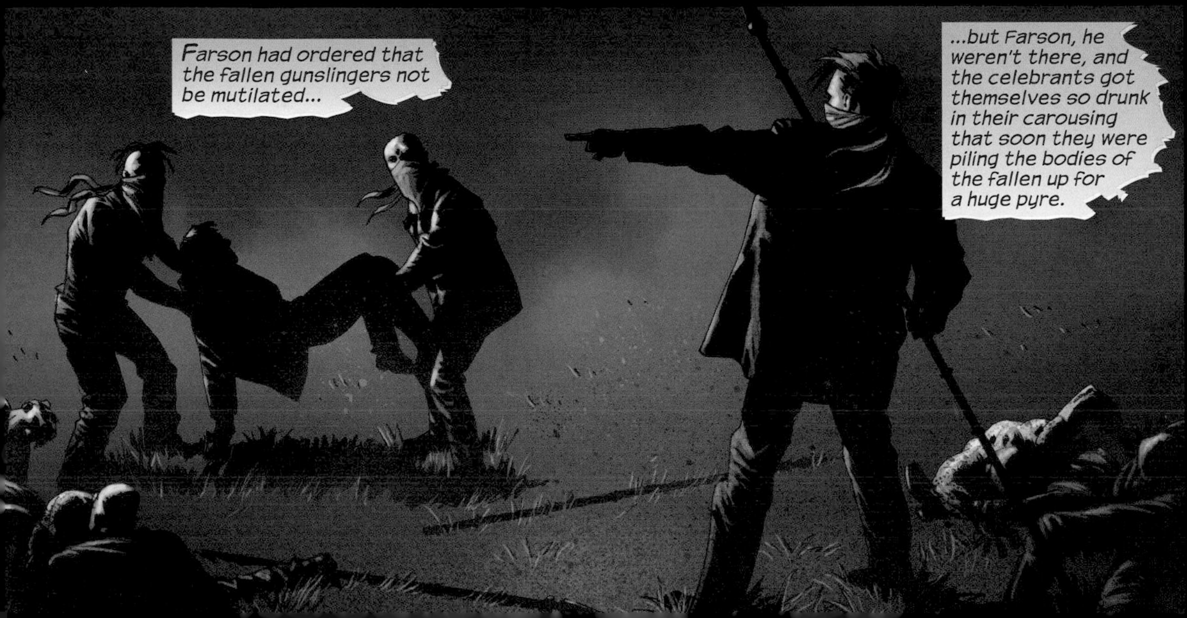
Farson had ordered that the fallen gunslingers not be mutilated...
...but Farson, he weren't there, and the celebrants got themselves so drunk in their carousing that soon they were piling the bodies of the fallen up for a huge pyre.

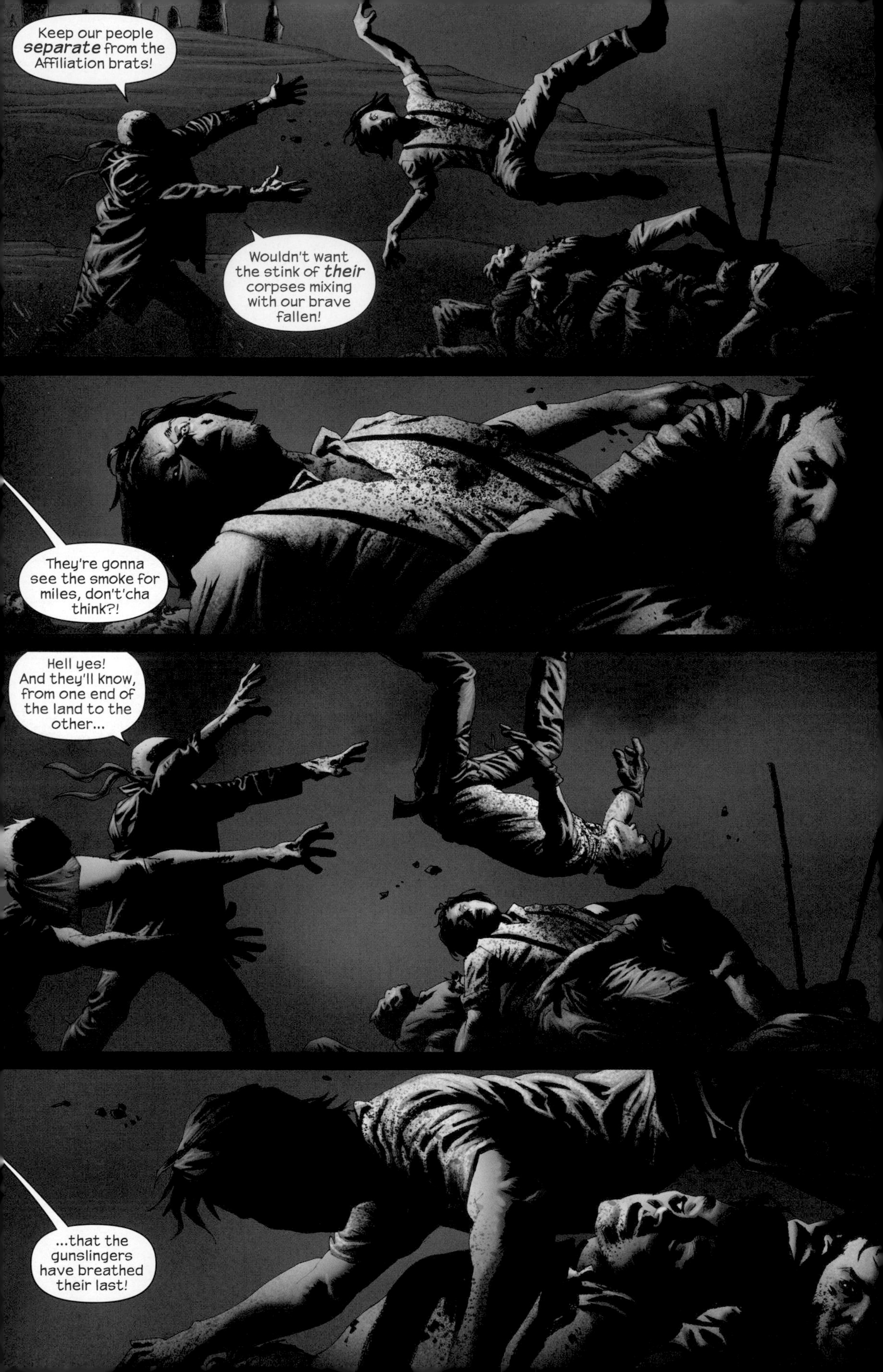
Keep our people separate from the Affiliation brats!
Wouldn't want the stink of their corpses mixing with our brave fallen!
They're gonna see the smoke for miles, don't'cha think?!
Hell yes! And they'll know, from one end of the land to the other...
...that the gunslingers have breathed their last!

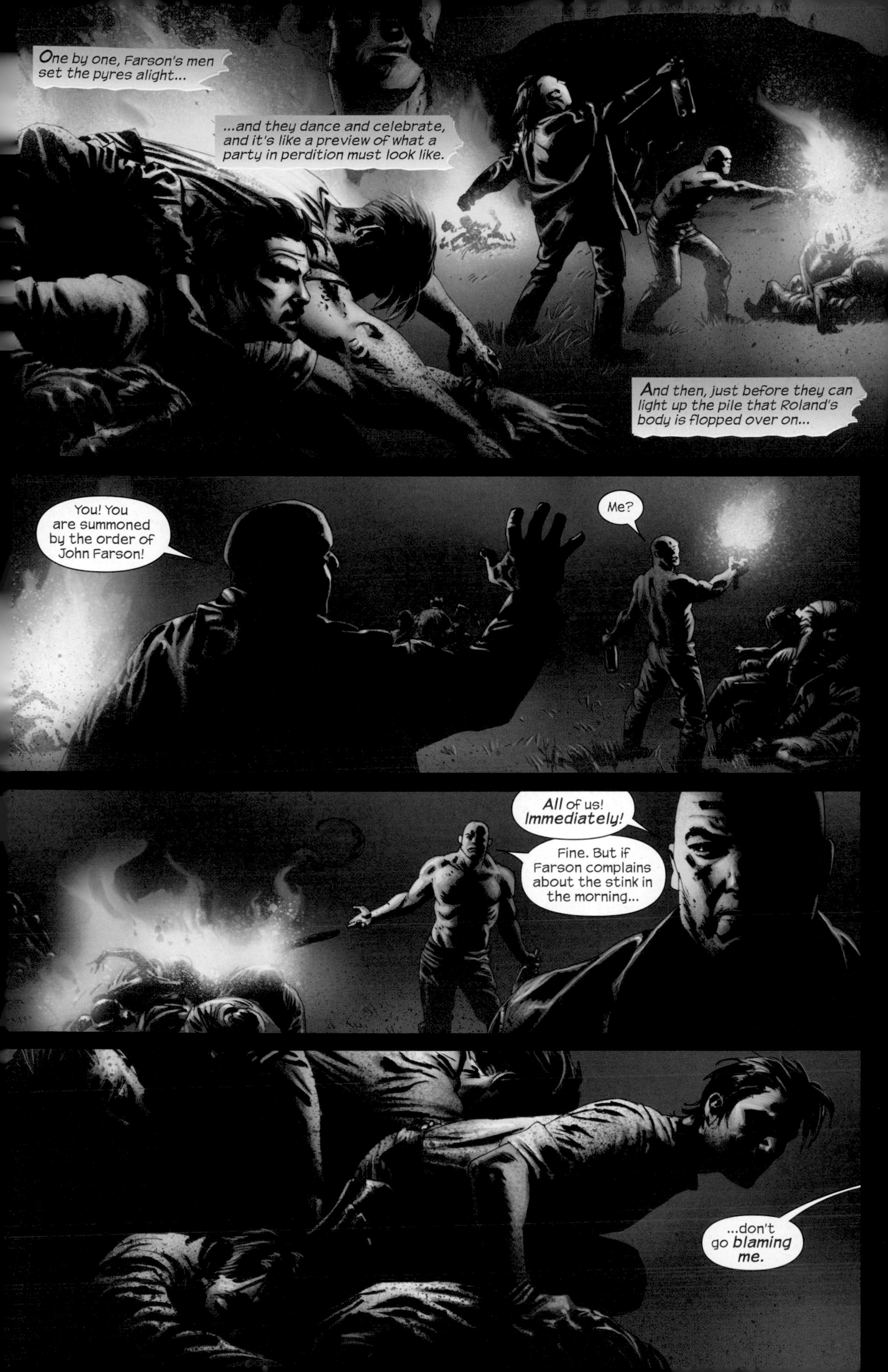
One by one, Farson's men set the pyres alight...
...and they dance and celebrate, and it's like a preview of what a party in perdition must look like.
And then, just before they can light up the pile that Roland's body is flopped over on...
You! You are summoned by the order of John Farson!
Me?
All of us! Immediately!
Fine. But if Farson complains about the stink in the morning...
...don't go blaming me.

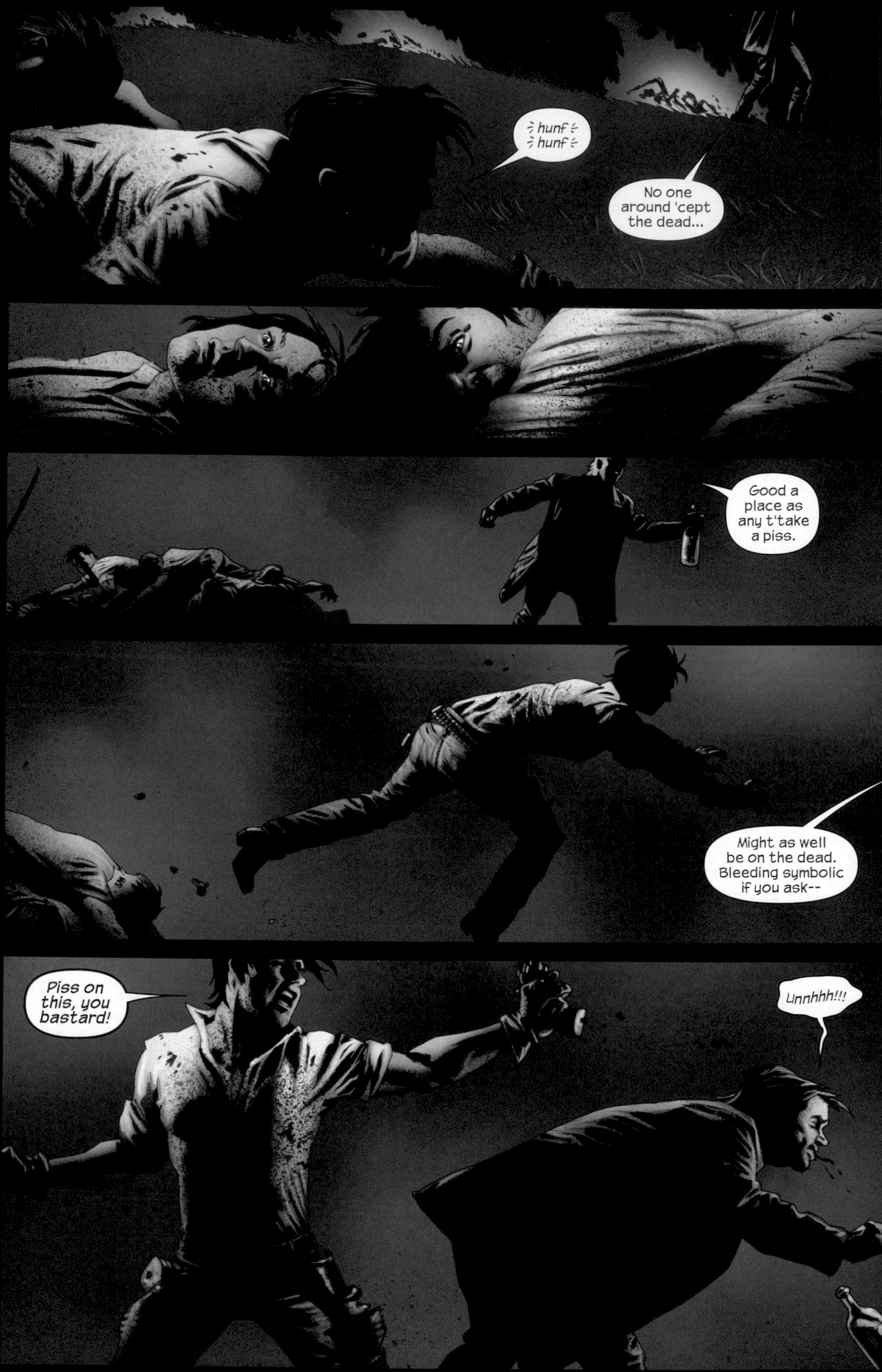
hunf hunf
No one around 'cept the dead...
Good a place as any t'take a piss.
Might as well be on the dead. Bleeding symbolic if you ask--
Piss on this, you bastard!
Unnhhh!!!

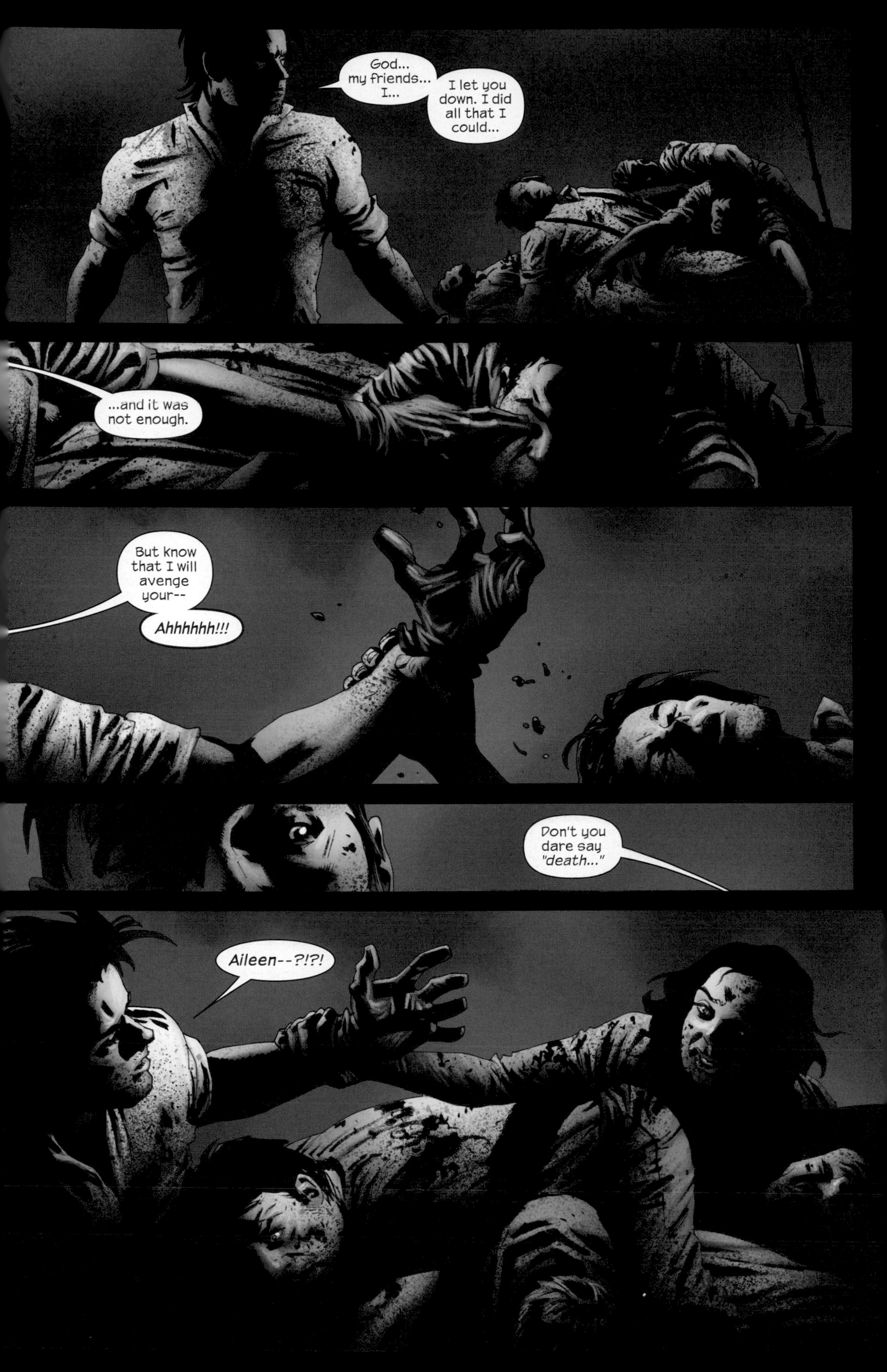
God... my friends... I...
I let you down. I did all that I could...
...and it was not enough.
But know that I will avenge your--
Ahhhhhh!!!
Don't you dare say "death..."
Aileen--?!?!

STEPHEN KING

THE DARK TOWER
~ THE GUNSLINGER ~

THE JOURNEY BEGINS
CHAPTER TWO

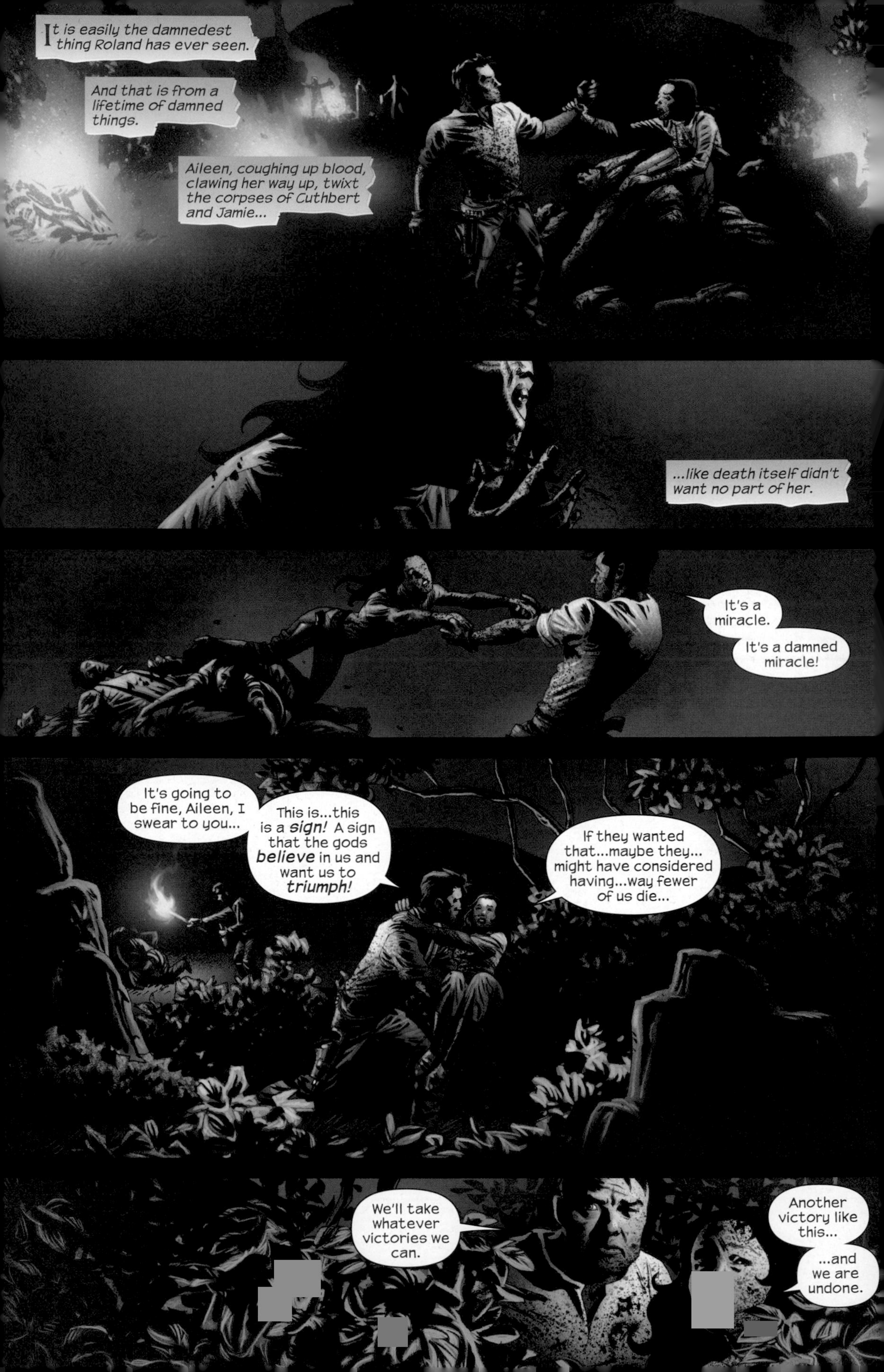
It is easily the damnedest thing Roland has ever seen.
And that is from a lifetime of damned things.
Aileen, coughing up blood, clawing her way up, twixt the corpses of Cuthbert and Jamie...
...like death itself didn't want no part of her.
It's a miracle.
It's a damned miracle!
It's going to be fine, Aileen, I swear to you...
This is...this is a sign! A sign that the gods believe in us and want us to triumph!
If they wanted that...maybe they... might have considered having...way fewer of us die...
We'll take whatever victories we can.
Another victory like this...
...and we are undone.

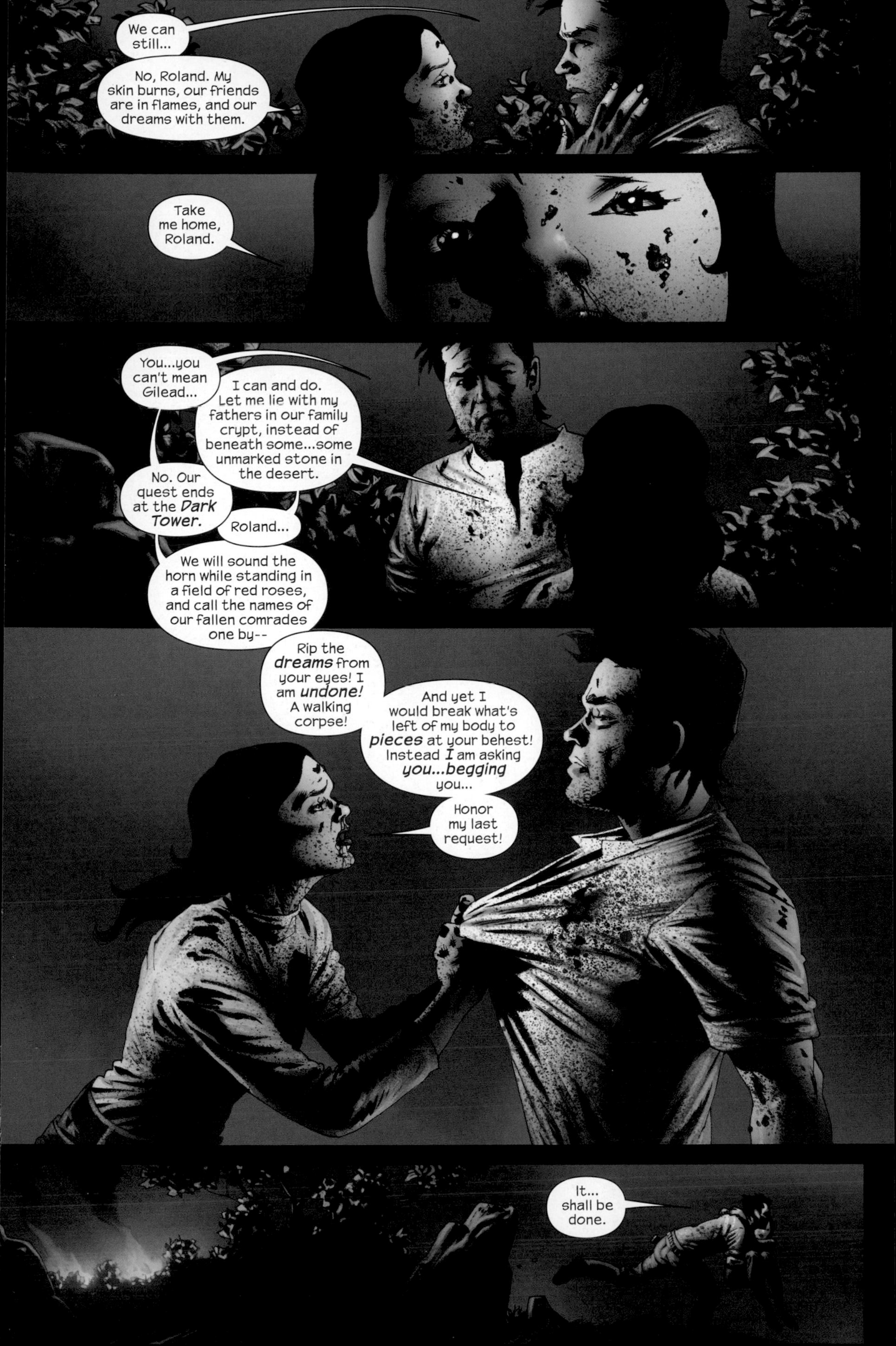
We can still...
No, Roland. My skin burns, our friends are in flames, and our dreams with them.
Take me home, Roland.
You...you can't mean Gilead...
I can and do. Let me lie with my fathers in our family crypt, instead of beneath some...some unmarked stone in the desert.
No. Our quest ends at the *Dark Tower*.
Roland...
We will sound the horn while standing in a field of red roses, and call the names of our fallen comrades one by--
Rip the ***dreams*** from your eyes! I am ***undone!*** A walking corpse!
And yet I would break what's left of my body to ***pieces*** at your behest! Instead ***I*** am asking ***you...begging*** you...
Honor my last request!
It... shall be done.

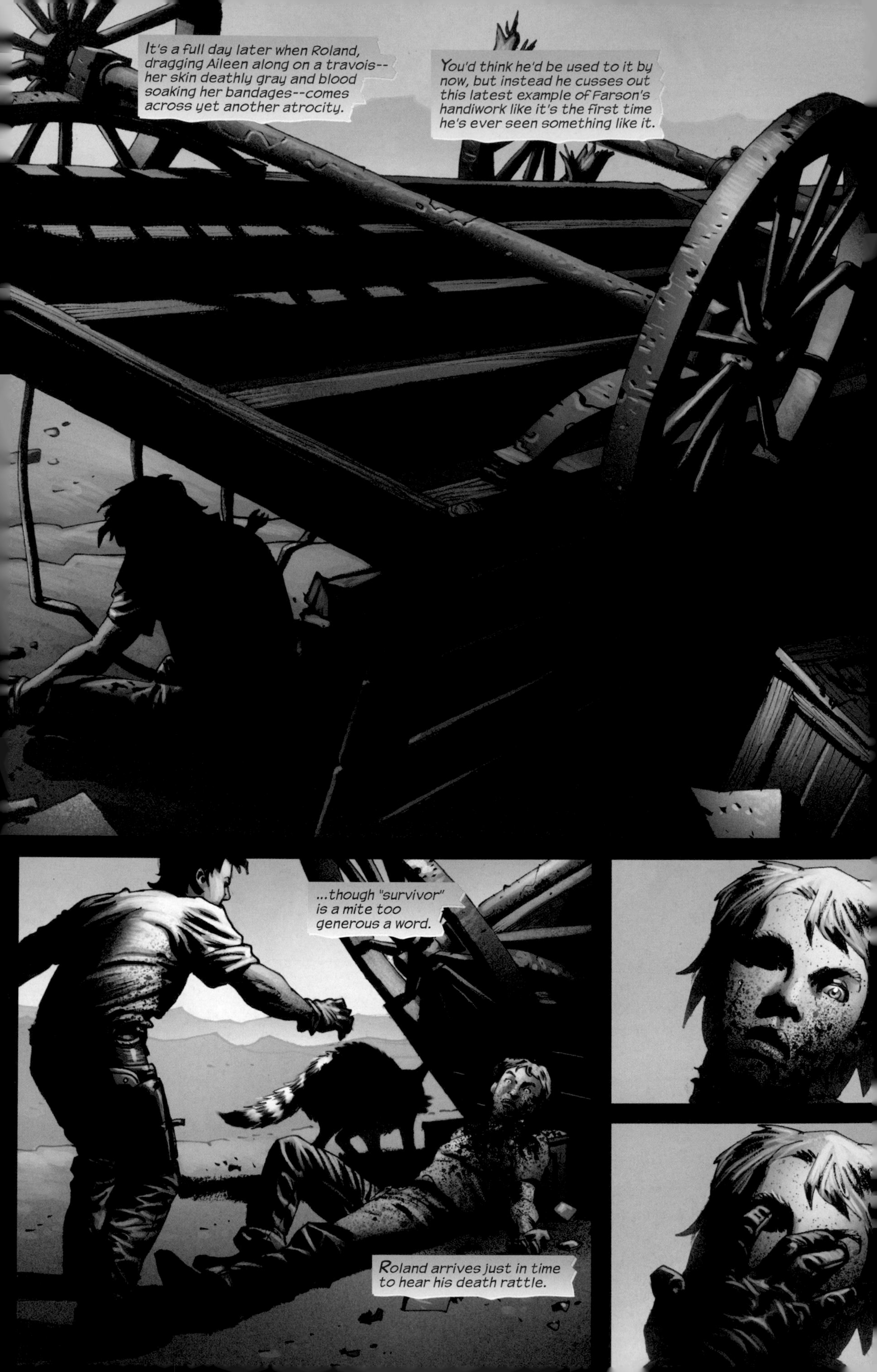
It's a full day later when Roland, dragging Aileen along on a travois-- her skin deathly gray and blood soaking her bandages--comes across yet another atrocity.
You'd think he'd be used to it by now, but instead he cusses out this latest example of Farson's handiwork like it's the first time he's ever seen something like it.
...though "survivor" is a mite too generous a word.
Roland arrives just in time to hear his death rattle.

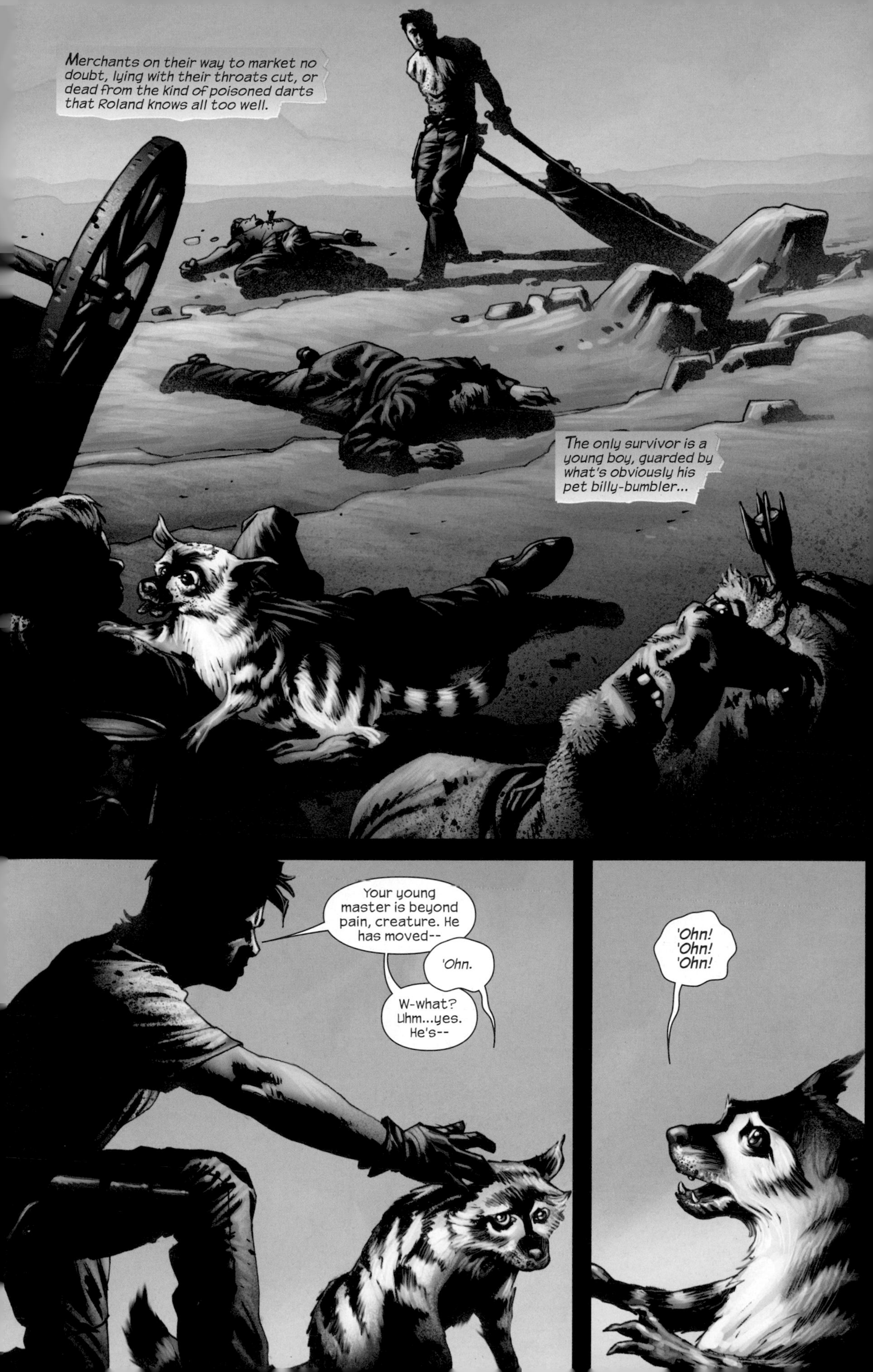
Merchants on their way to market no doubt, lying with their throats cut, or dead from the kind of poisoned darts that Roland knows all too well.
The only survivor is a young boy, guarded by what's obviously his pet billy-bumbler...
Your young master is beyond pain, creature. He has moved--
'Ohn.
W-what? Uhm...yes. He's--
'Ohn! 'Ohn! 'Ohn!

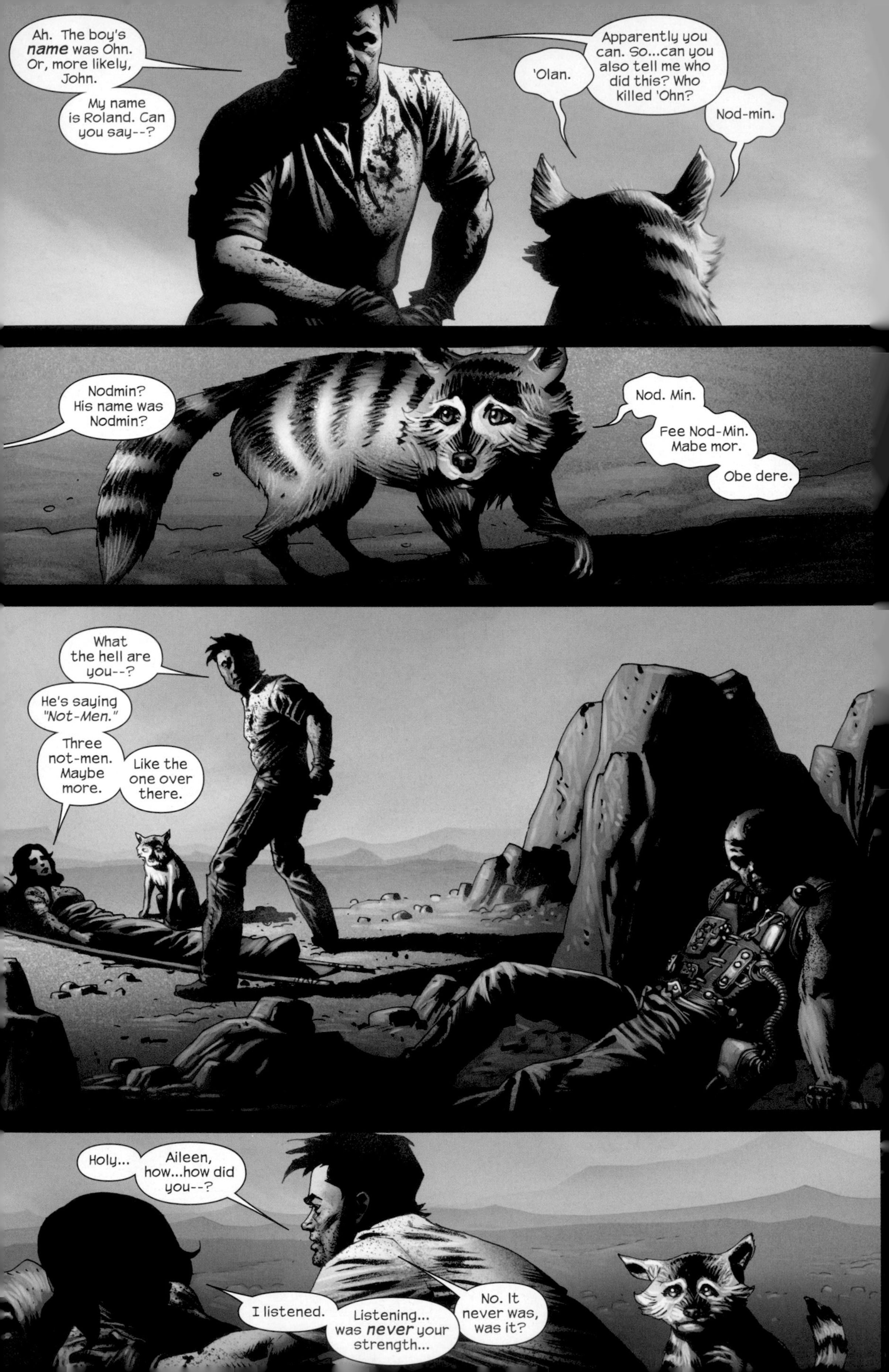
Ah. The boy's *name* was Ohn. Or, more likely, John.
My name is Roland. Can you say--?
'Olan.
Apparently you can. So...can you also tell me who did this? Who killed 'Ohn?
Nod-min.
Nodmin? His name was Nodmin?
Nod. Min.
Fee Nod-Min. Mabe mor.
Obe dere.
What the hell are you--?
He's saying "*Not-Men.*"
Three not-men. Maybe more.
Like the one over there.
Holy...
Aileen, how...how did you--?
I listened.
Listening... was *never* your strength...
No. It never was, was it?

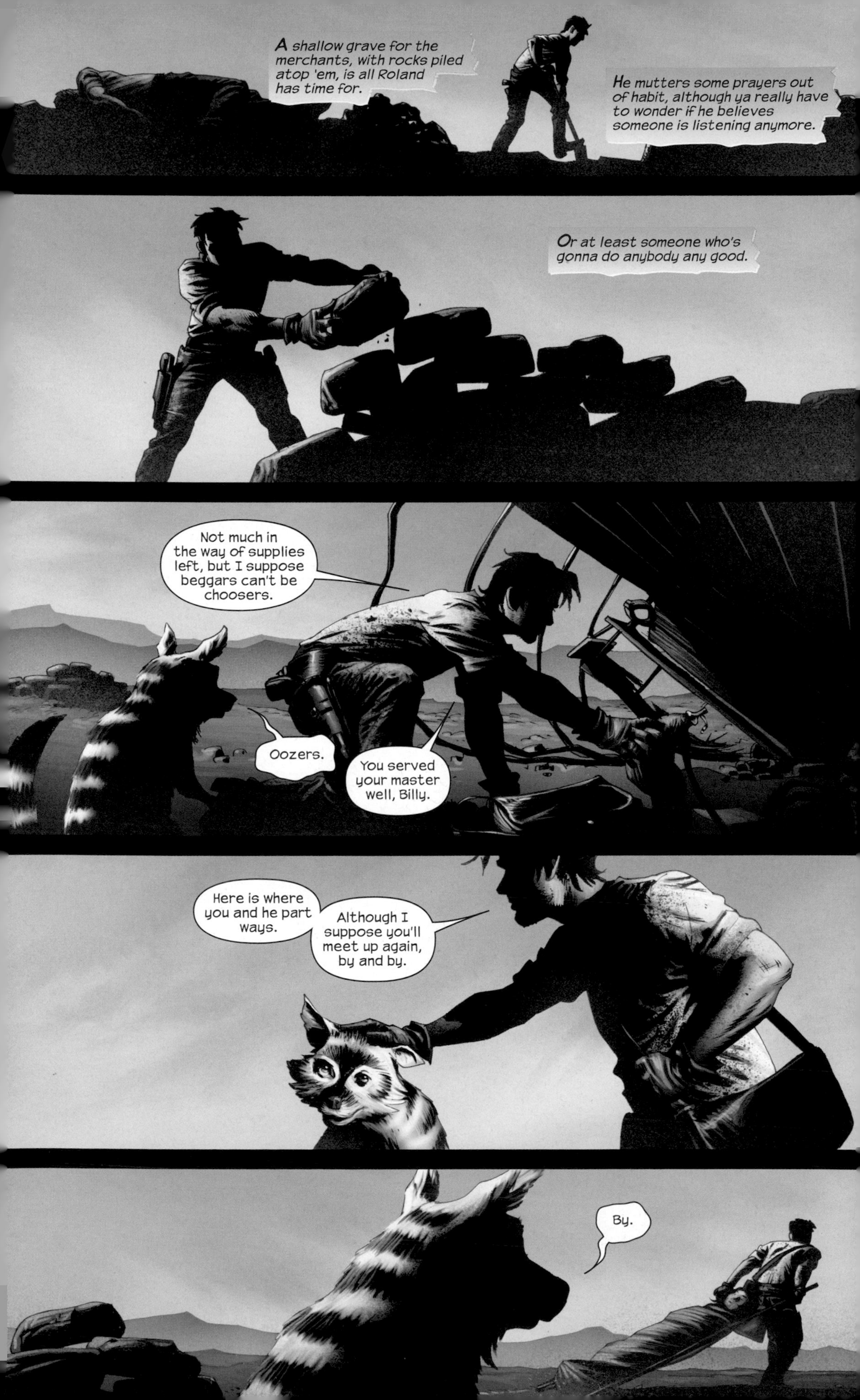
A shallow grave for the merchants, with rocks piled atop 'em, is all Roland has time for.
He mutters some prayers out of habit, although ya really have to wonder if he believes someone is listening anymore.
Or at least someone who's gonna do anybody any good.
Not much in the way of supplies left, but I suppose beggars can't be choosers.
Oozers.
You served your master well, Billy.
Here is where you and he part ways.
Although I suppose you'll meet up again, by and by.
By.

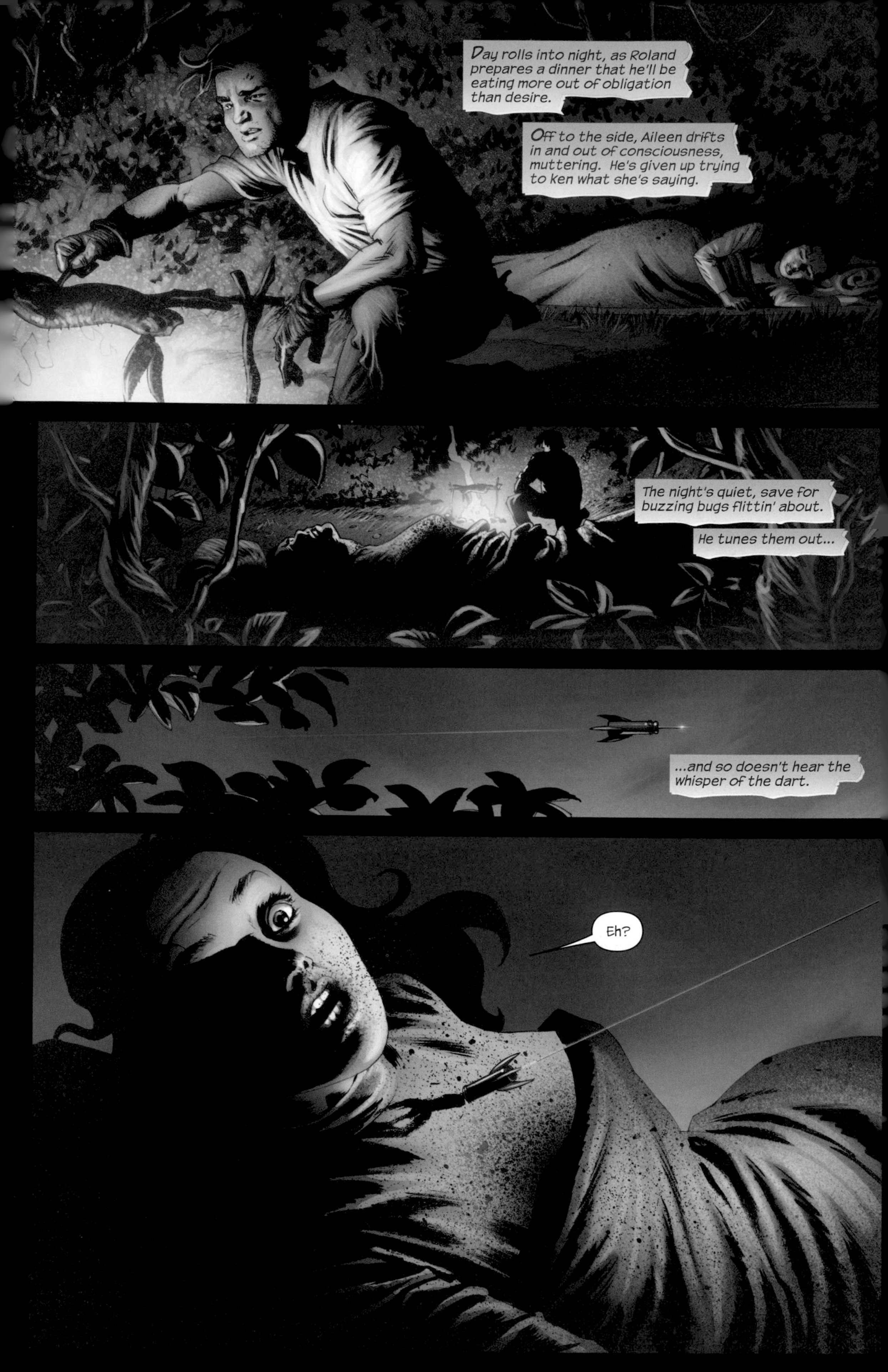
Day rolls into night, as Roland prepares a dinner that he'll be eating more out of obligation than desire.
Off to the side, Aileen drifts in and out of consciousness, muttering. He's given up trying to ken what she's saying.
The night's quiet, save for buzzing bugs flittin' about.
He tunes them out...
...and so doesn't hear the whisper of the dart.
Eh?

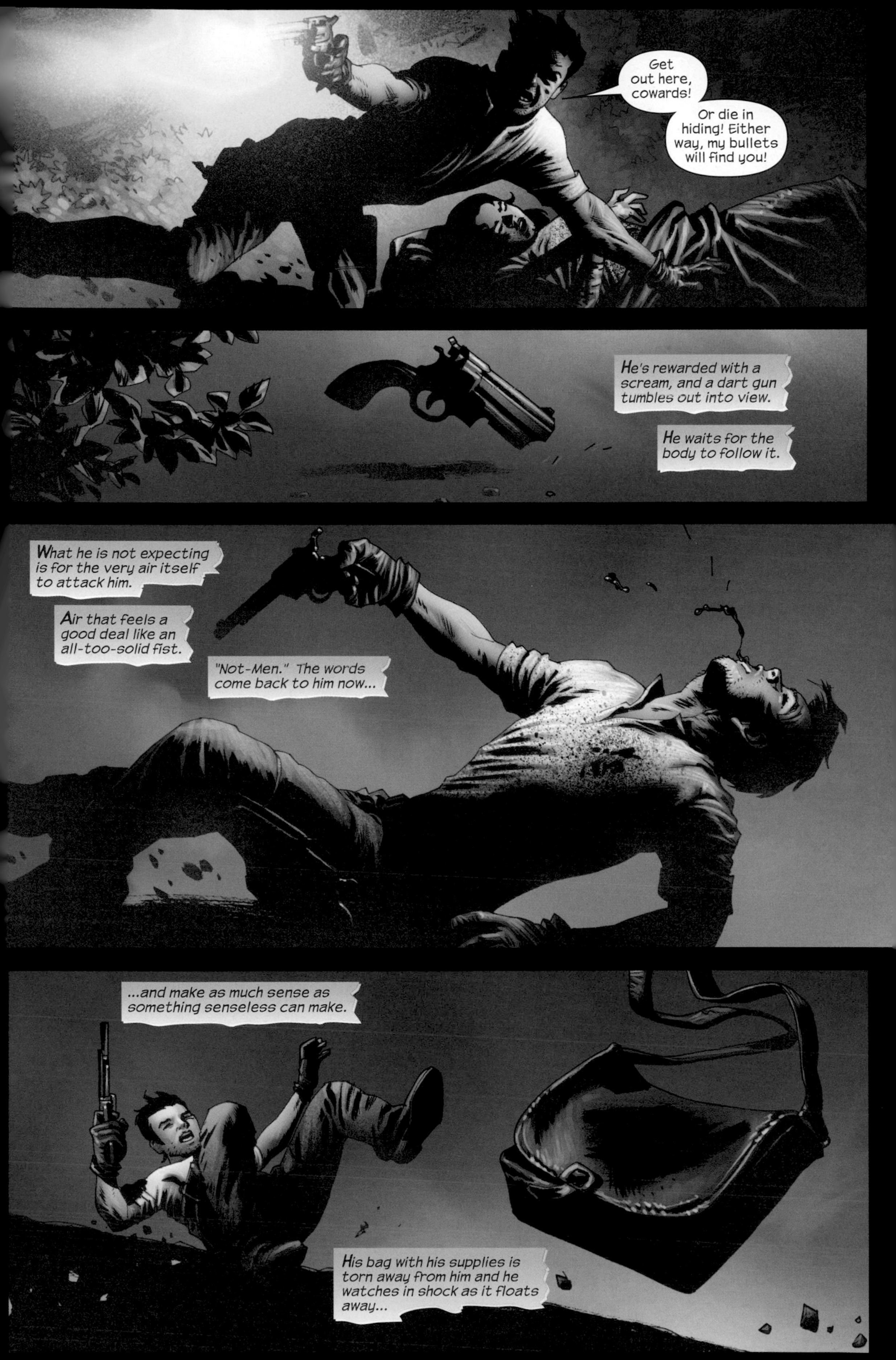
Get out here, cowards!
Or die in hiding! Either way, my bullets will find you!
He's rewarded with a scream, and a dart gun tumbles out into view.
He waits for the body to follow it.
What he is not expecting is for the very air itself to attack him.
Air that feels a good deal like an all-too-solid fist.
"Not-Men." The words come back to him now...
...and make as much sense as something senseless can make.
His bag with his supplies is torn away from him and he watches in shock as it floats away...

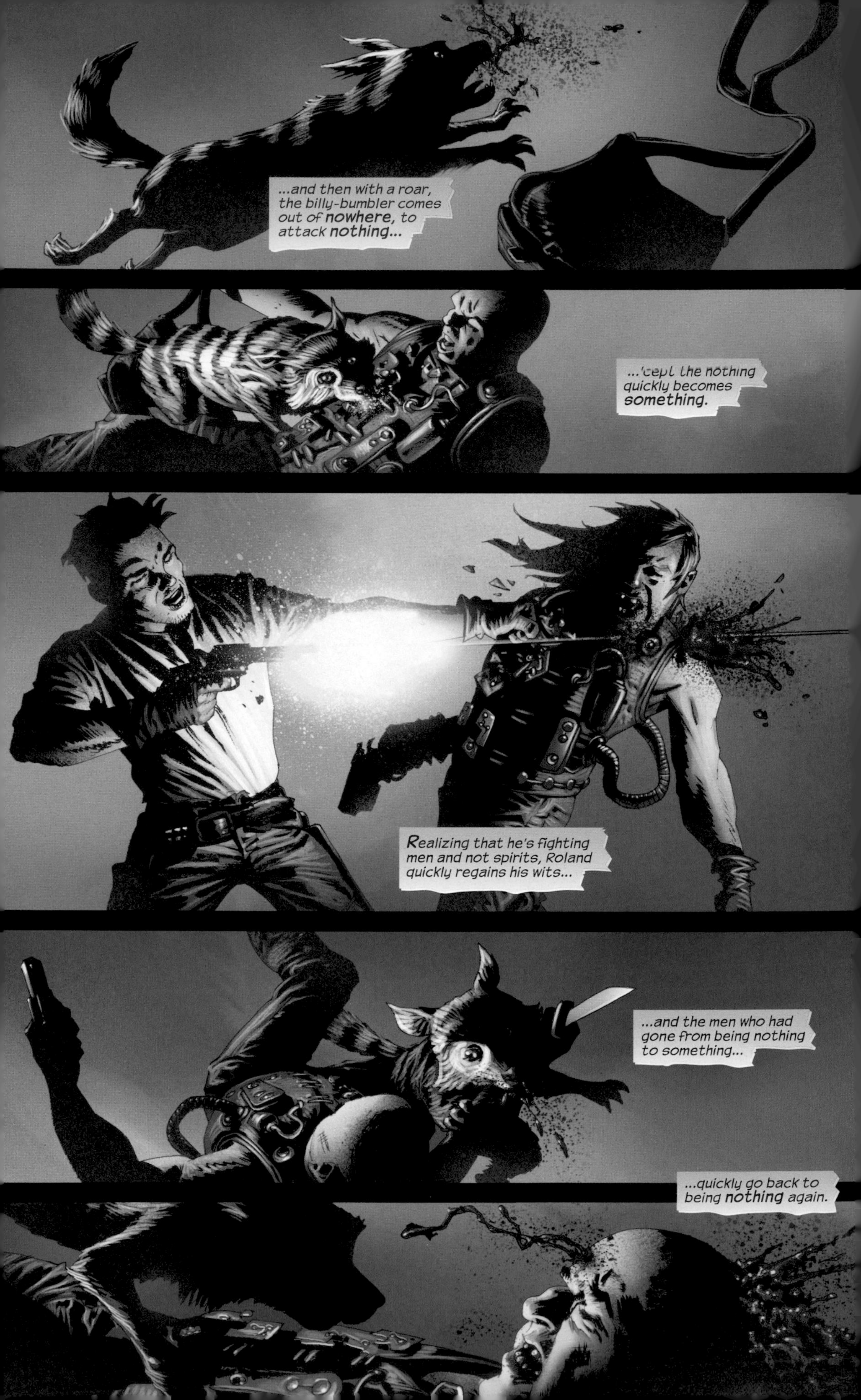
...and then with a roar, the billy-bumbler comes out of **nowhere**, to attack **nothing**...
...'cept the nothing quickly becomes **something**.
Realizing that he's fighting men and not spirits, Roland quickly regains his wits...
...and the men who had gone from being nothing to something...
...quickly go back to being **nothing** again.

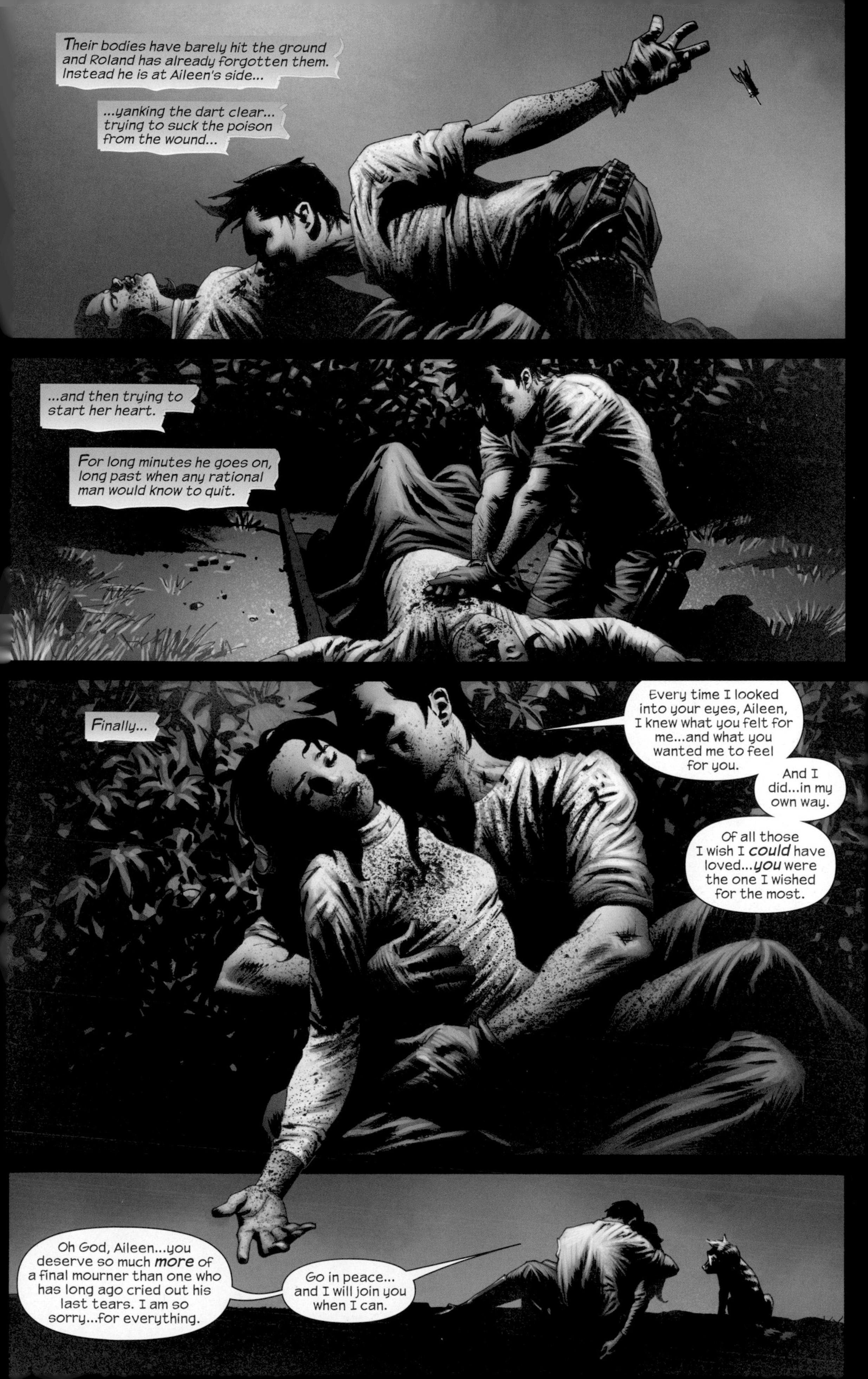
Their bodies have barely hit the ground and Roland has already forgotten them. Instead he is at Aileen's side...
...yanking the dart clear... trying to suck the poison from the wound...
...and then trying to start her heart.
For long minutes he goes on, long past when any rational man would know to quit.
Finally...
Every time I looked into your eyes, Aileen, I knew what you felt for me...and what you wanted me to feel for you.
And I did...in my own way.
Of all those I wish I could have loved...you were the one I wished for the most.
Oh God, Aileen...you deserve so much more of a final mourner than one who has long ago cried out his last tears. I am so sorry...for everything.
Go in peace... and I will join you when I can.

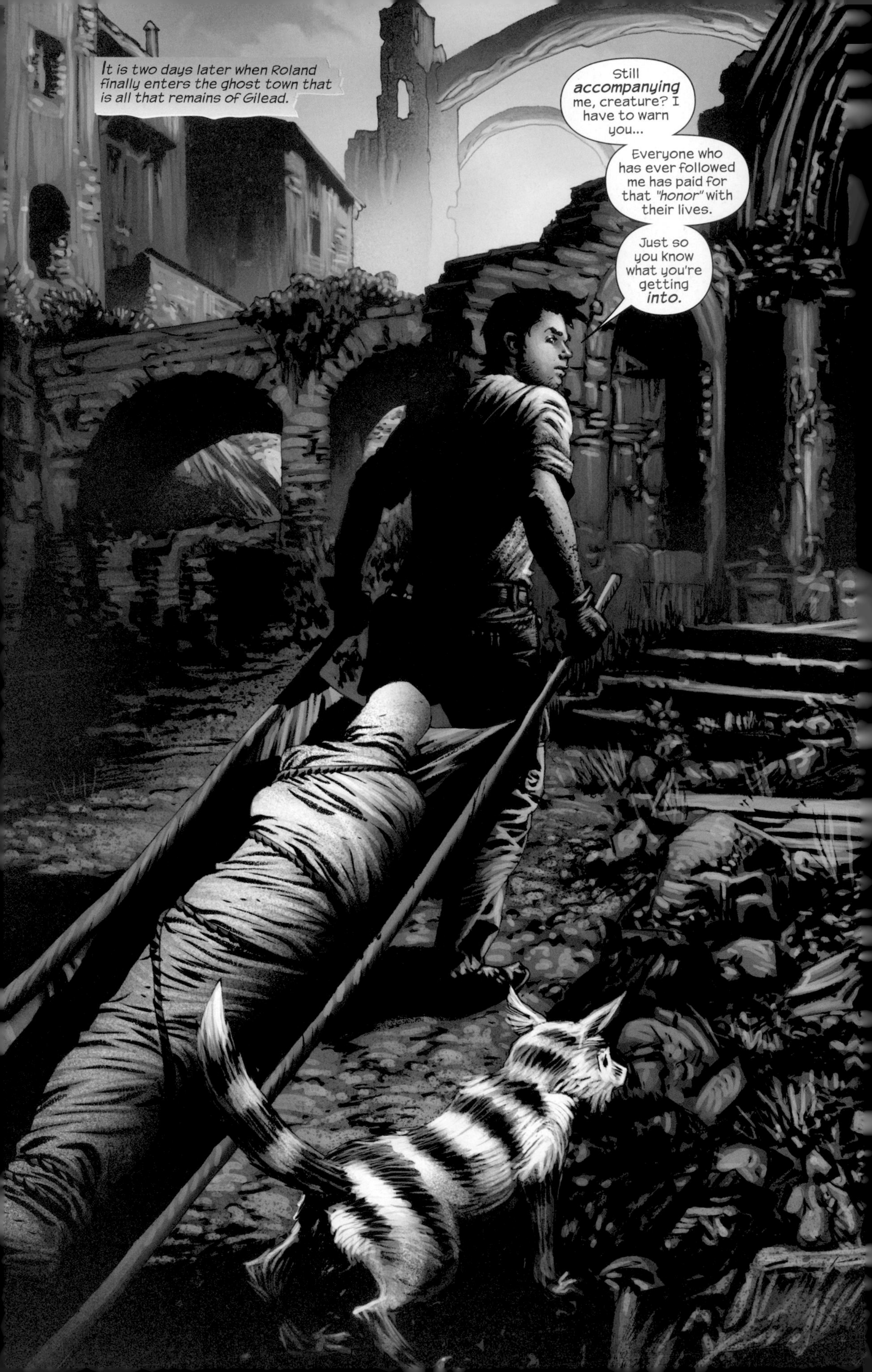
It is two days later when Roland finally enters the ghost town that is all that remains of Gilead.
Still accompanying me, creature? I have to warn you...
Everyone who has ever followed me has paid for that "honor" with their lives.
Just so you know what you're getting into.

You're not exactly seeing Gilead at its best. Once, every corner of it teemed with life.

Now it's overgrown with death.

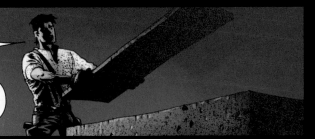

Appropriate, I guess, that I've come here. Like is drawn to like.

I *am* death and thus drawn to it.

Death to death. Ashes to ashes. Dust to dust.

Rest in the arms of Cort, who was as a father to you.

Rest, for you have *more* than earned it.

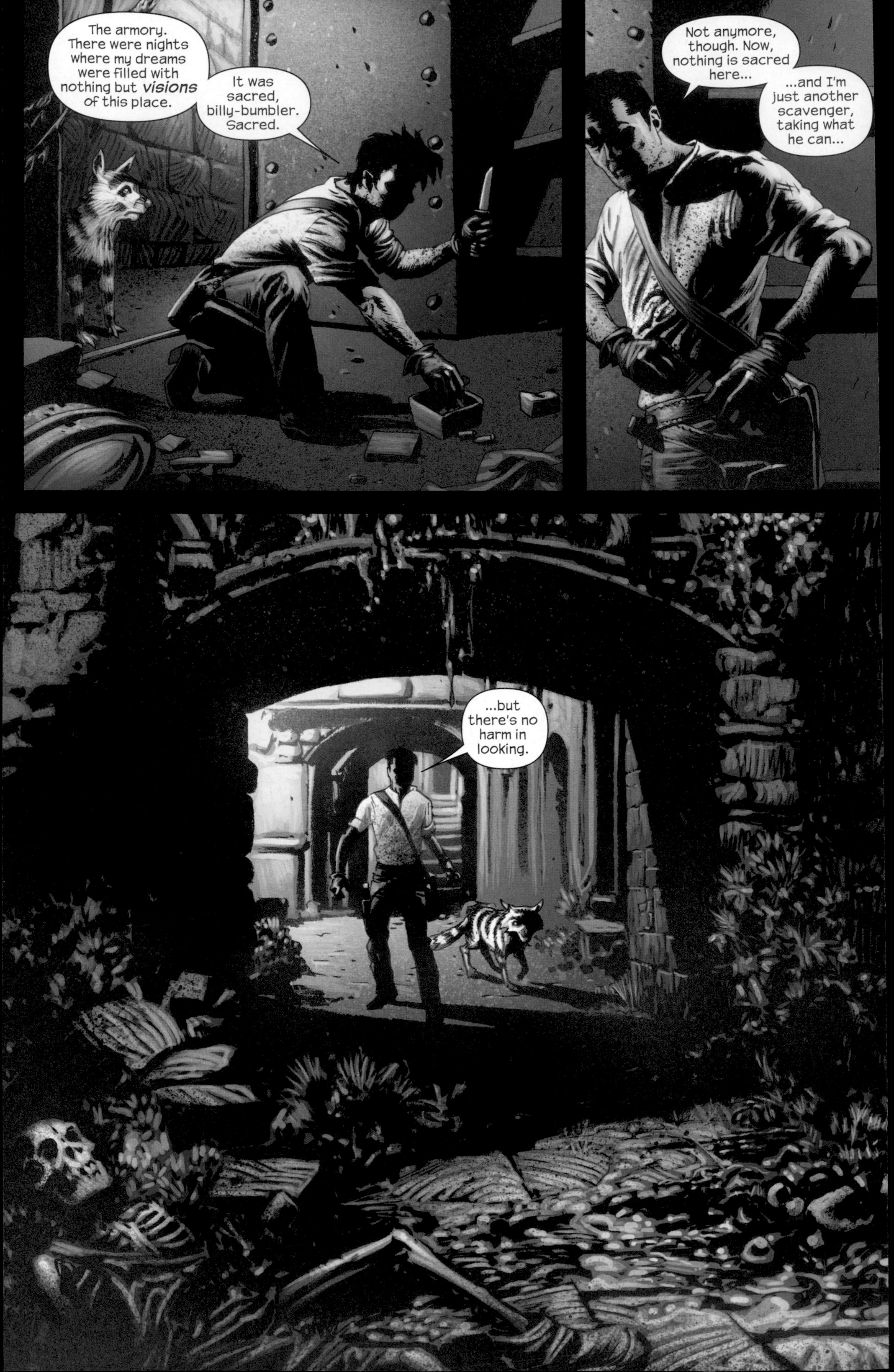
The armory. There were nights where my dreams were filled with nothing but *visions* of this place.
It was sacred, billy-bumbler. Sacred.
Not anymore, though. Now, nothing is sacred here...
...and I'm just another scavenger, taking what he can...
...but there's no harm in looking.

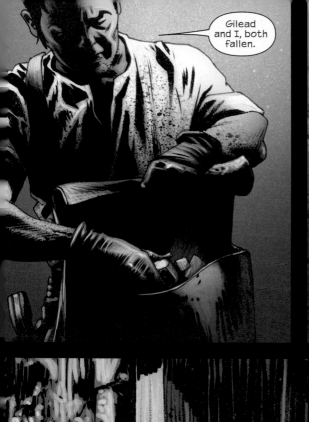

Gilead and I, both fallen.

The kitchen. The likelihood of anything useful remaining there is slim...

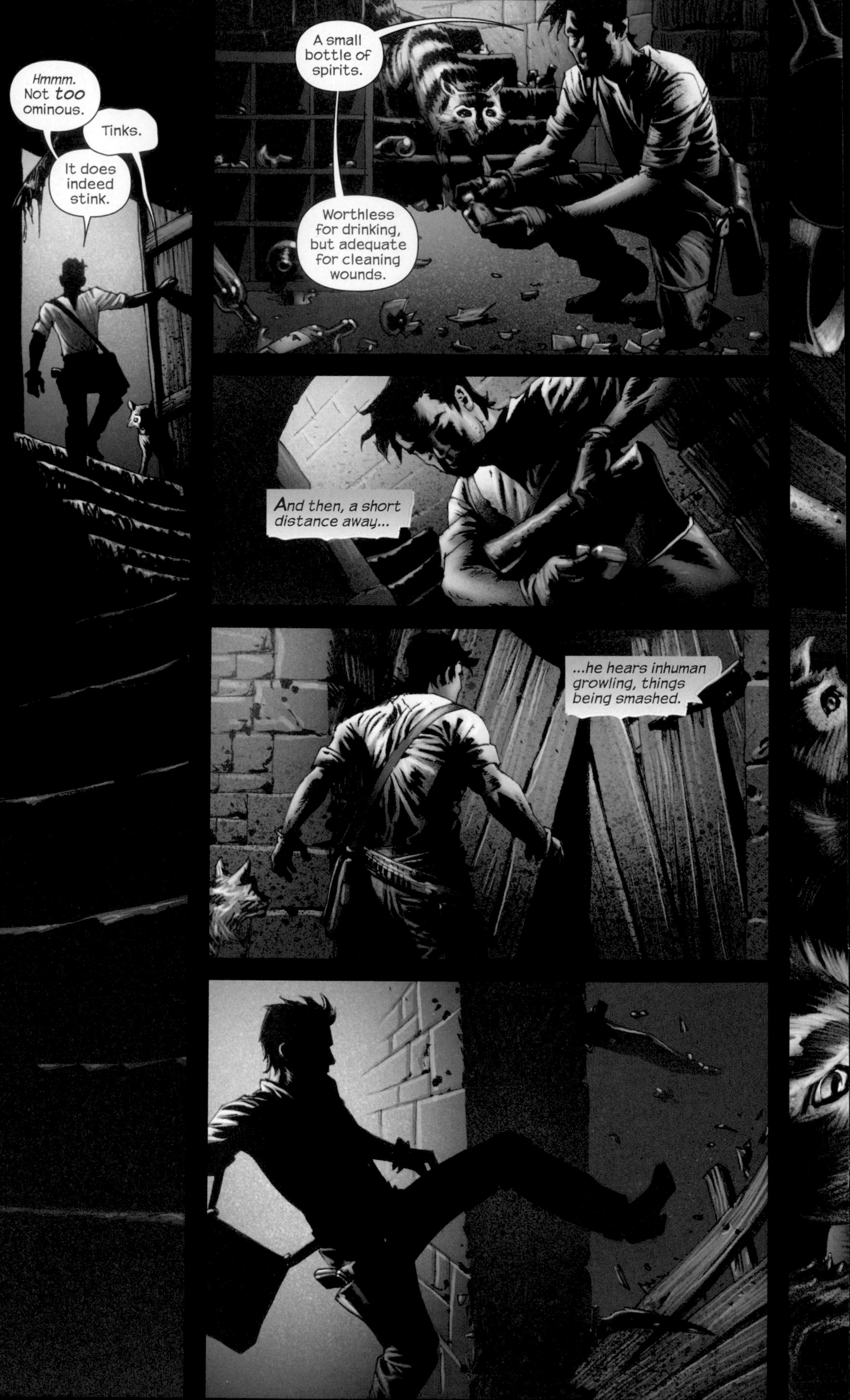

Hmmm. Not ***too*** ominous.
Tinks.
It does indeed stink.
A small bottle of spirits.
Worthless for drinking, but adequate for cleaning wounds.
And then, a short distance away...
...he hears inhuman growling, things being smashed.

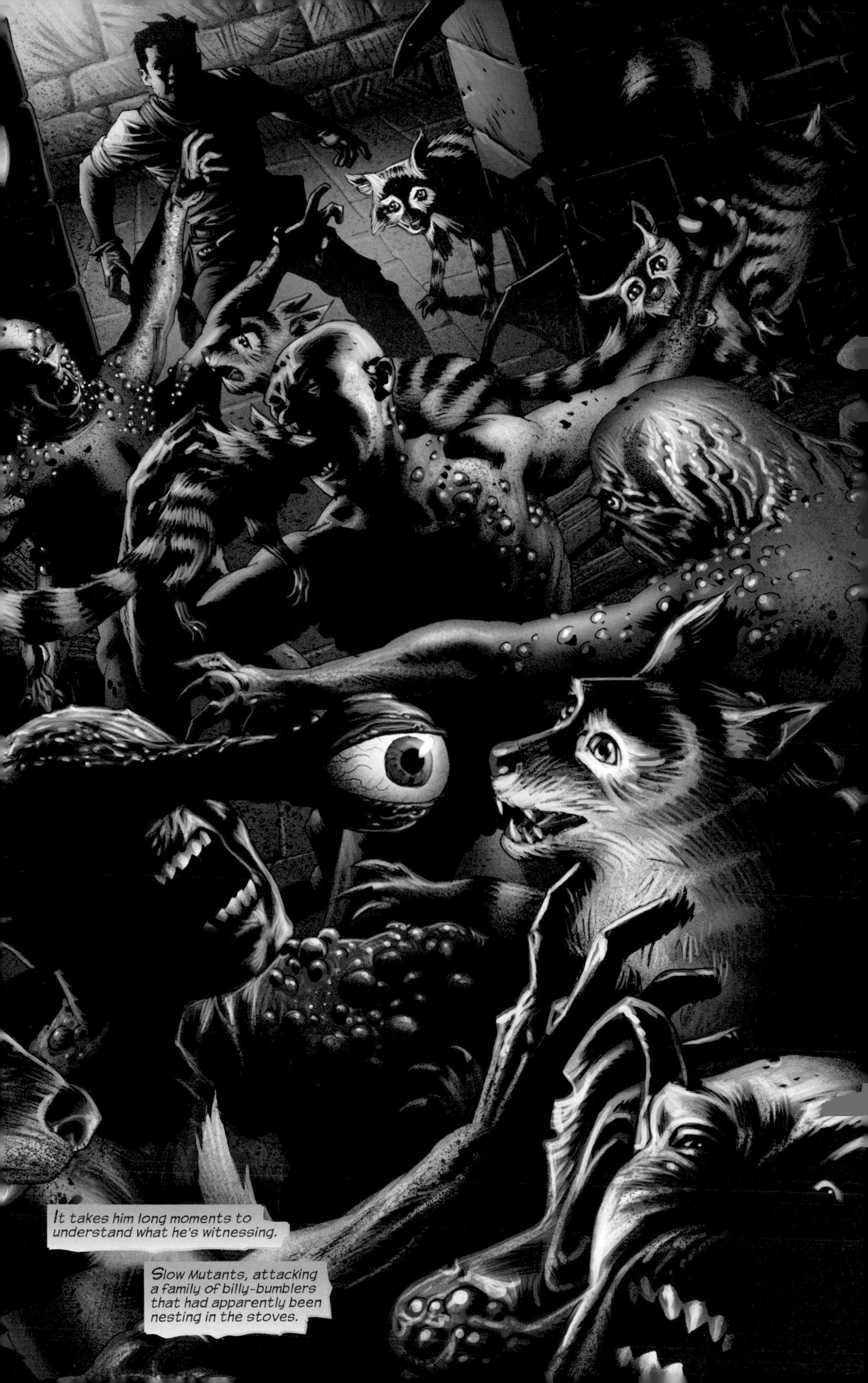
It takes him long moments to understand what he's witnessing.
Slow Mutants, attacking a family of billy-bumblers that had apparently been nesting in the stoves.

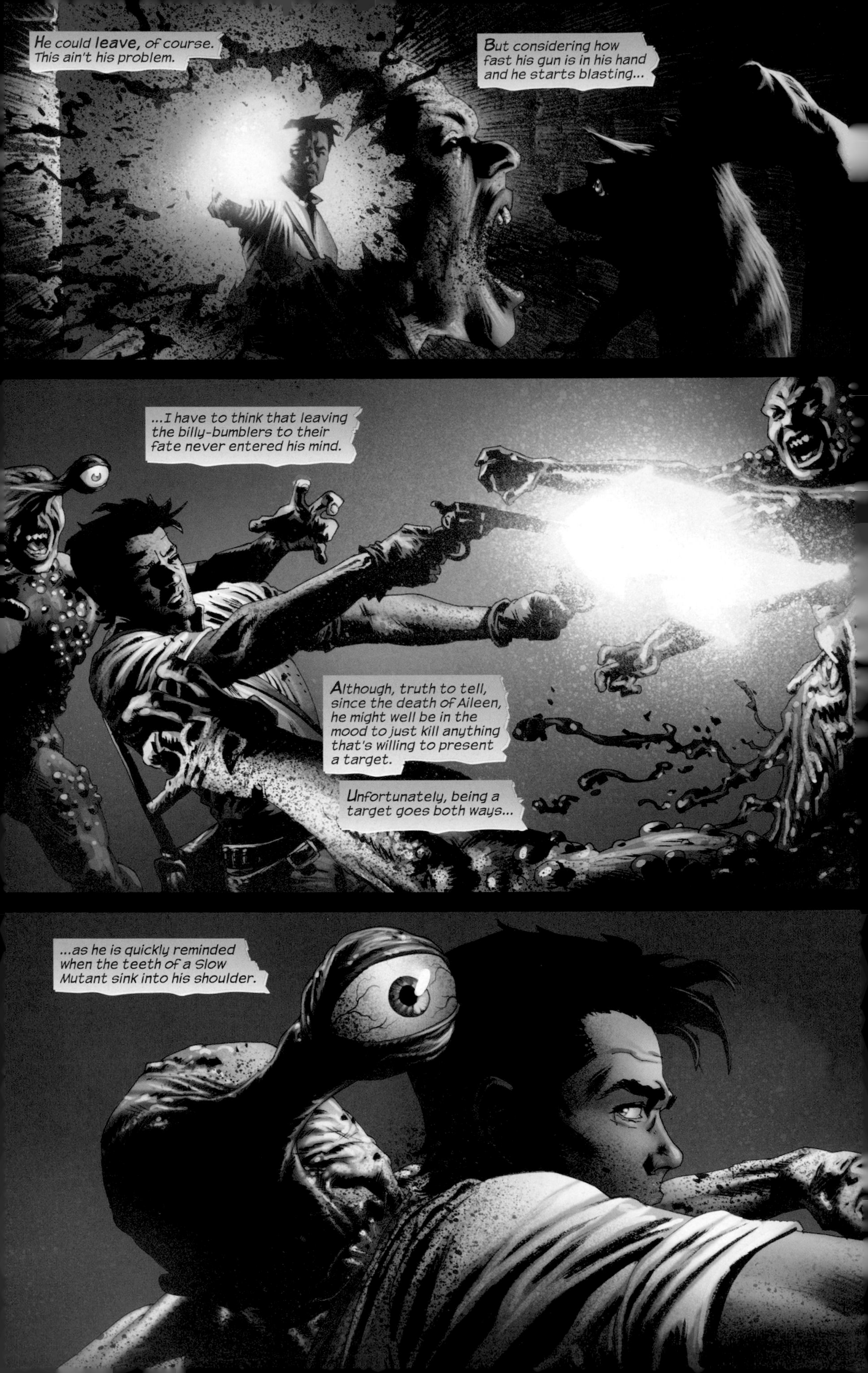
He could leave, of course. This ain't his problem.
But considering how fast his gun is in his hand and he starts blasting...
...I have to think that leaving the billy-bumblers to their fate never entered his mind.
Although, truth to tell, since the death of Aileen, he might well be in the mood to just kill anything that's willing to present a target.
Unfortunately, being a target goes both ways...
...as he is quickly reminded when the teeth of a Slow Mutant sink into his shoulder.

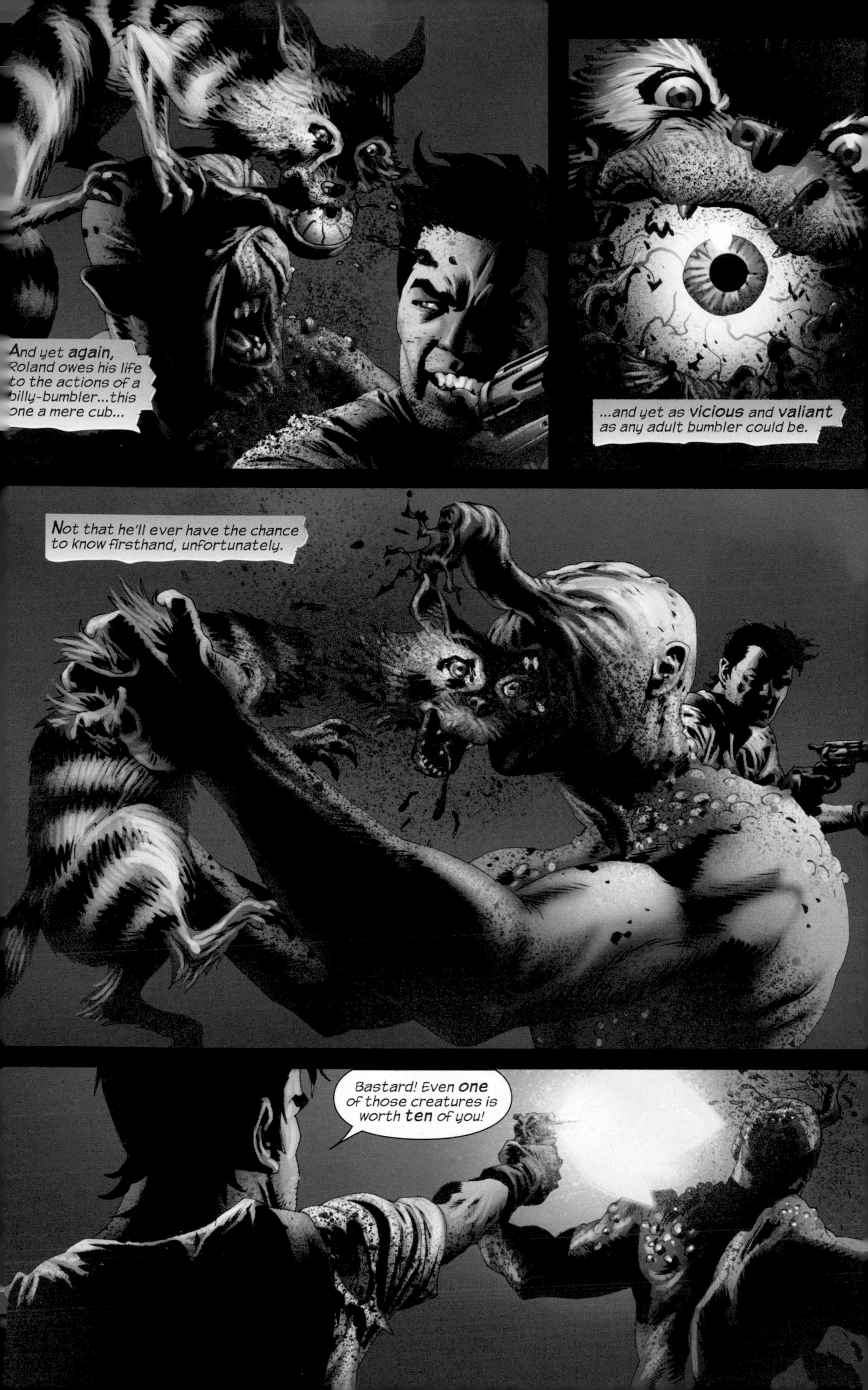
And yet again, Roland owes his life to the actions of a billy-bumbler...this one a mere cub...
...and yet as vicious and valiant as any adult bumbler could be.
Not that he'll ever have the chance to know firsthand, unfortunately.
Bastard! Even one of those creatures is worth ten of you!

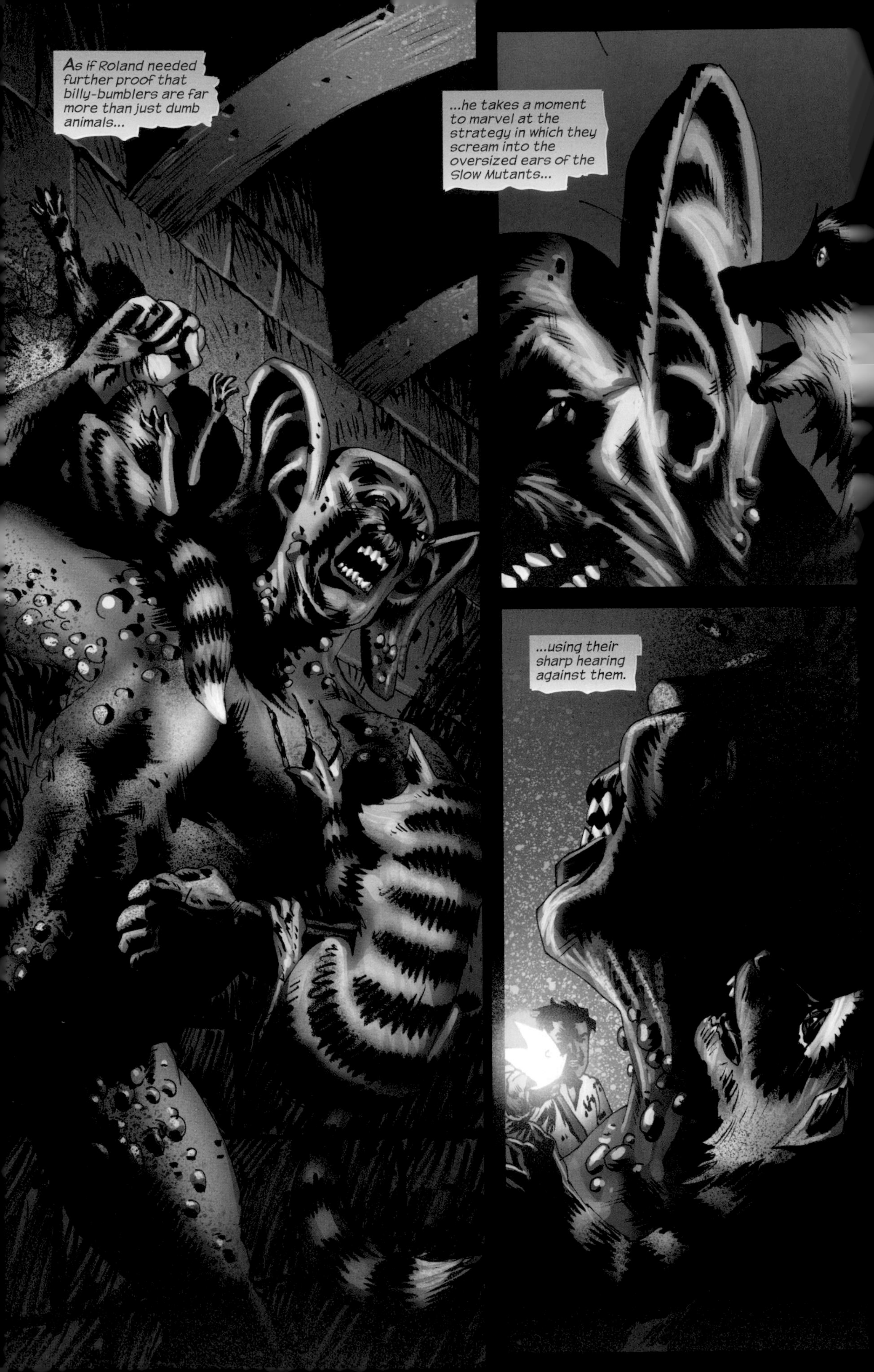
As if Roland needed further proof that billy-bumblers are far more than just dumb animals...
...he takes a moment to marvel at the strategy in which they scream into the oversized ears of the Slow Mutants...
...using their sharp hearing against them.

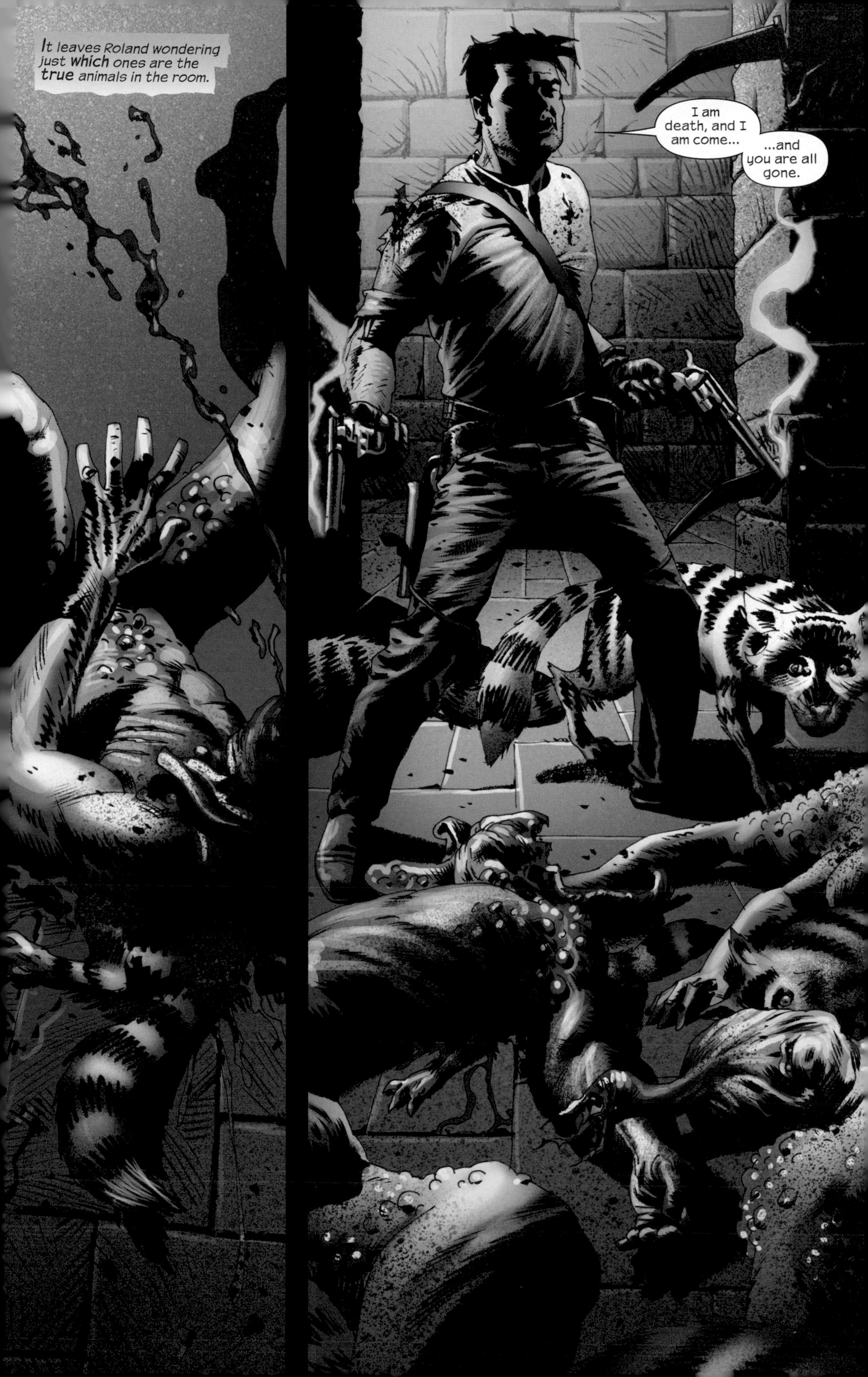
It leaves Roland wondering just which ones are the true animals in the room.
I am death, and I am come...
...and you are all gone.

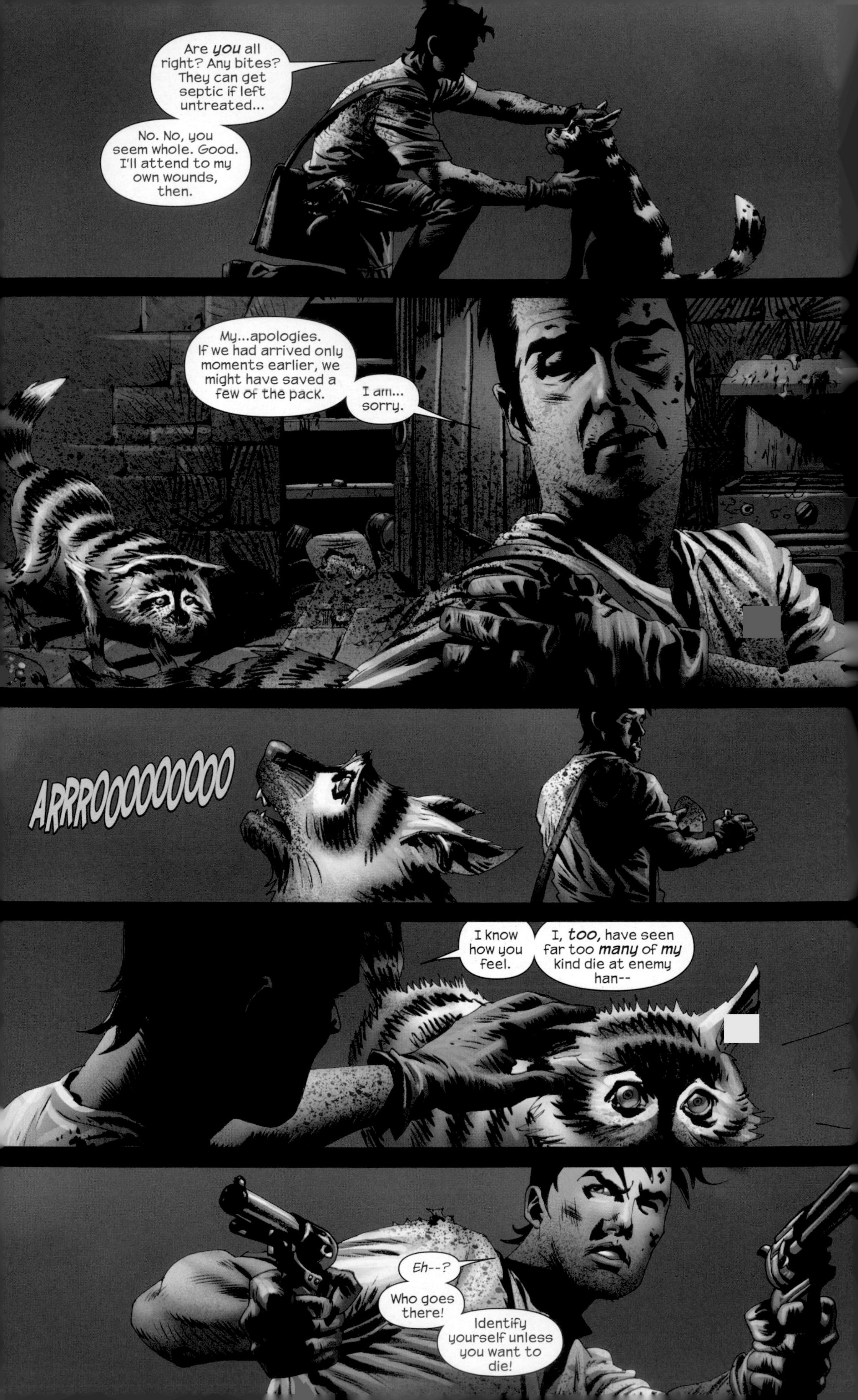

Are *you* all right? Any bites? They can get septic if left untreated...
No. No, you seem whole. Good. I'll attend to my own wounds, then.
My...apologies. If we had arrived only moments earlier, we might have saved a few of the pack.
I am... sorry.
ARRROOOOOOOOO
I know how you feel.
I, *too,* have seen far too *many* of *my* kind die at enemy han--
Eh--?
Who goes there!
Identify yourself unless you want to die!

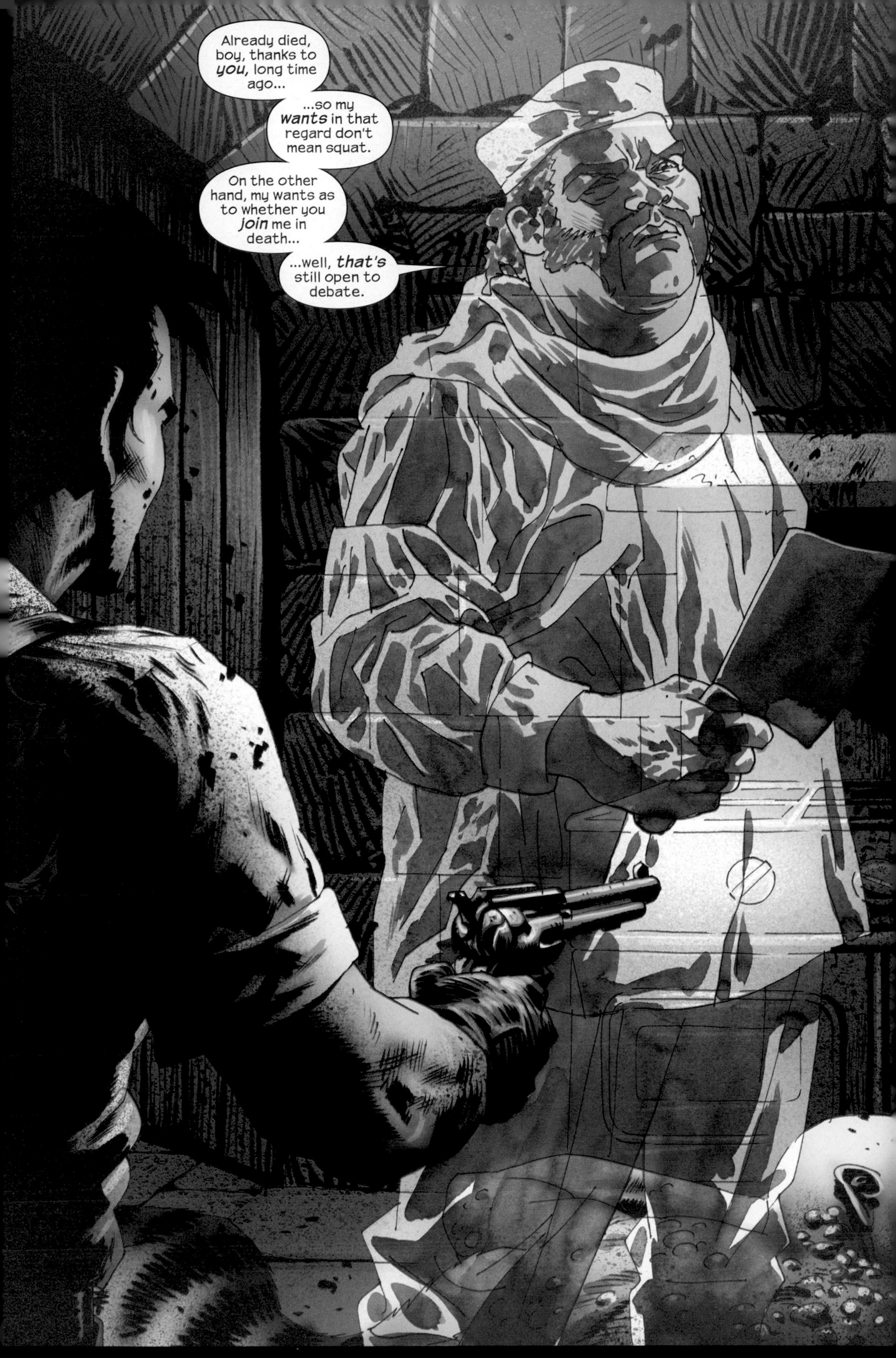
Already died, boy, thanks to *you,* long time ago...
...so my *wants* in that regard don't mean squat.
On the other hand, my wants as to whether you *join* me in death...
...well, *that's* still open to debate.

STEPHEN KING

THE DARK TOWER
~THE GUNSLINGER~

THE JOURNEY BEGINS
CHAPTER THREE

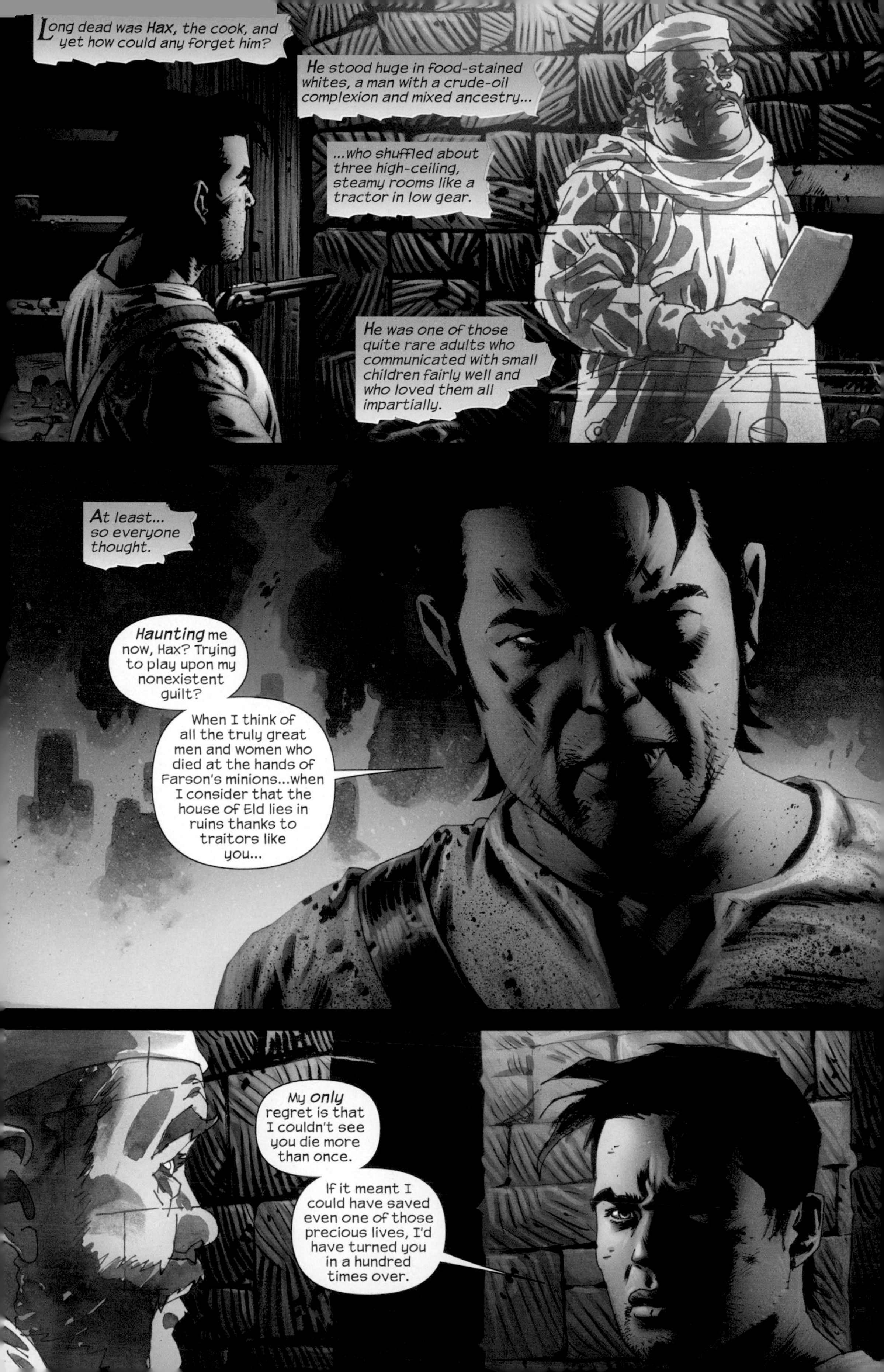
Long dead was Hax, the cook, and yet how could any forget him?
He stood huge in food-stained whites, a man with a crude-oil complexion and mixed ancestry...
...who shuffled about three high-ceiling, steamy rooms like a tractor in low gear.
He was one of those quite rare adults who communicated with small children fairly well and who loved them all impartially.
At least... so everyone thought.
Haunting me now, Hax? Trying to play upon my nonexistent guilt?
When I think of all the truly great men and women who died at the hands of Farson's minions...when I consider that the house of Eld lies in ruins thanks to traitors like you...
My only regret is that I couldn't see you die more than once.
If it meant I could have saved even one of those precious lives, I'd have turned you in a hundred times over.

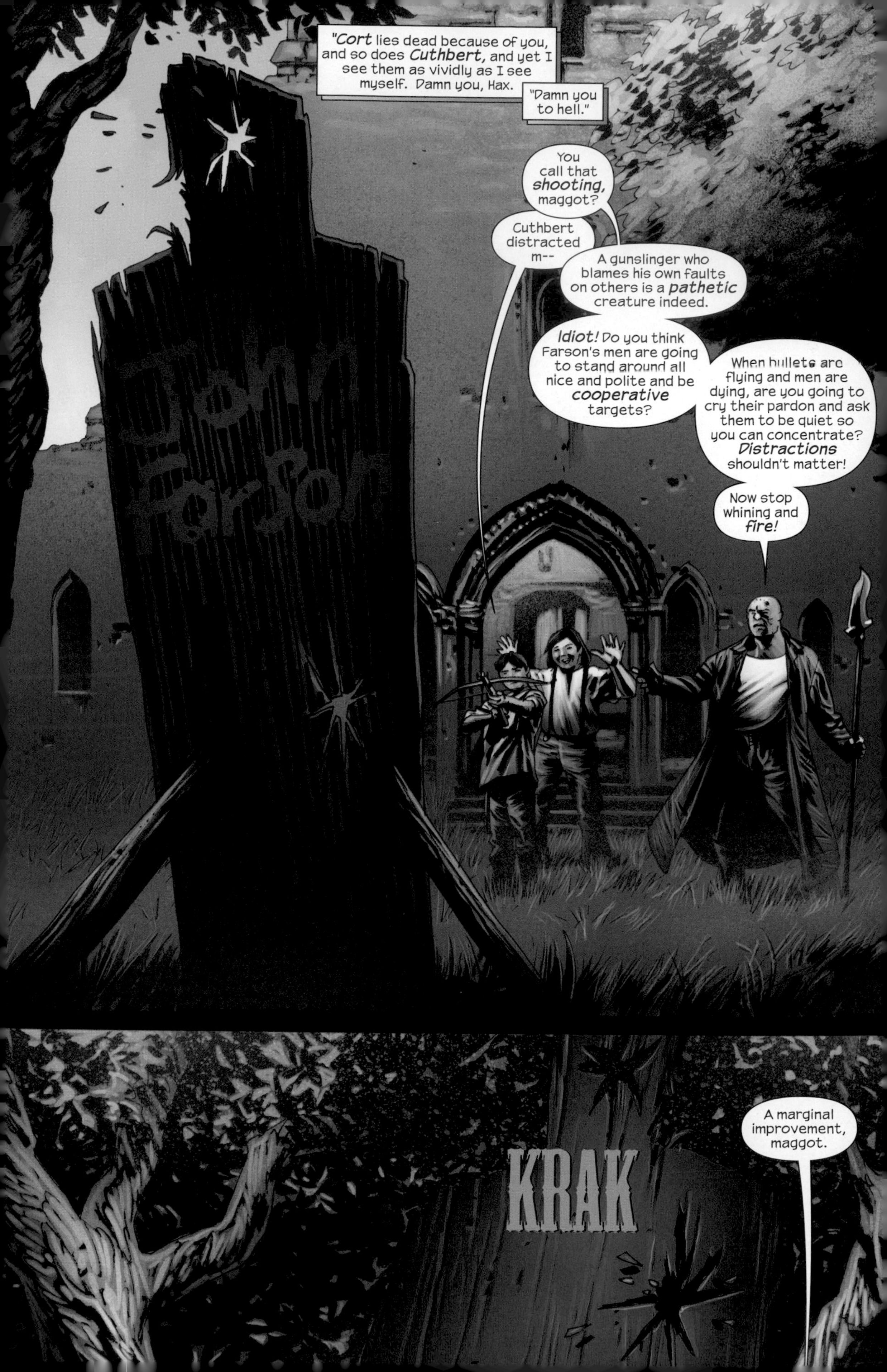
"Cort lies dead because of you, and so does Cuthbert, and yet I see them as vividly as I see myself. Damn you, Hax.
"Damn you to hell."
You call that shooting, maggot?
Cuthbert distracted m--
A gunslinger who blames his own faults on others is a pathetic creature indeed.
Idiot! Do you think Farson's men are going to stand around all nice and polite and be cooperative targets?
When bullets are flying and men are dying, are you going to cry their pardon and ask them to be quiet so you can concentrate? Distractions shouldn't matter!
Now stop whining and fire!
KRAK
A marginal improvement, maggot.

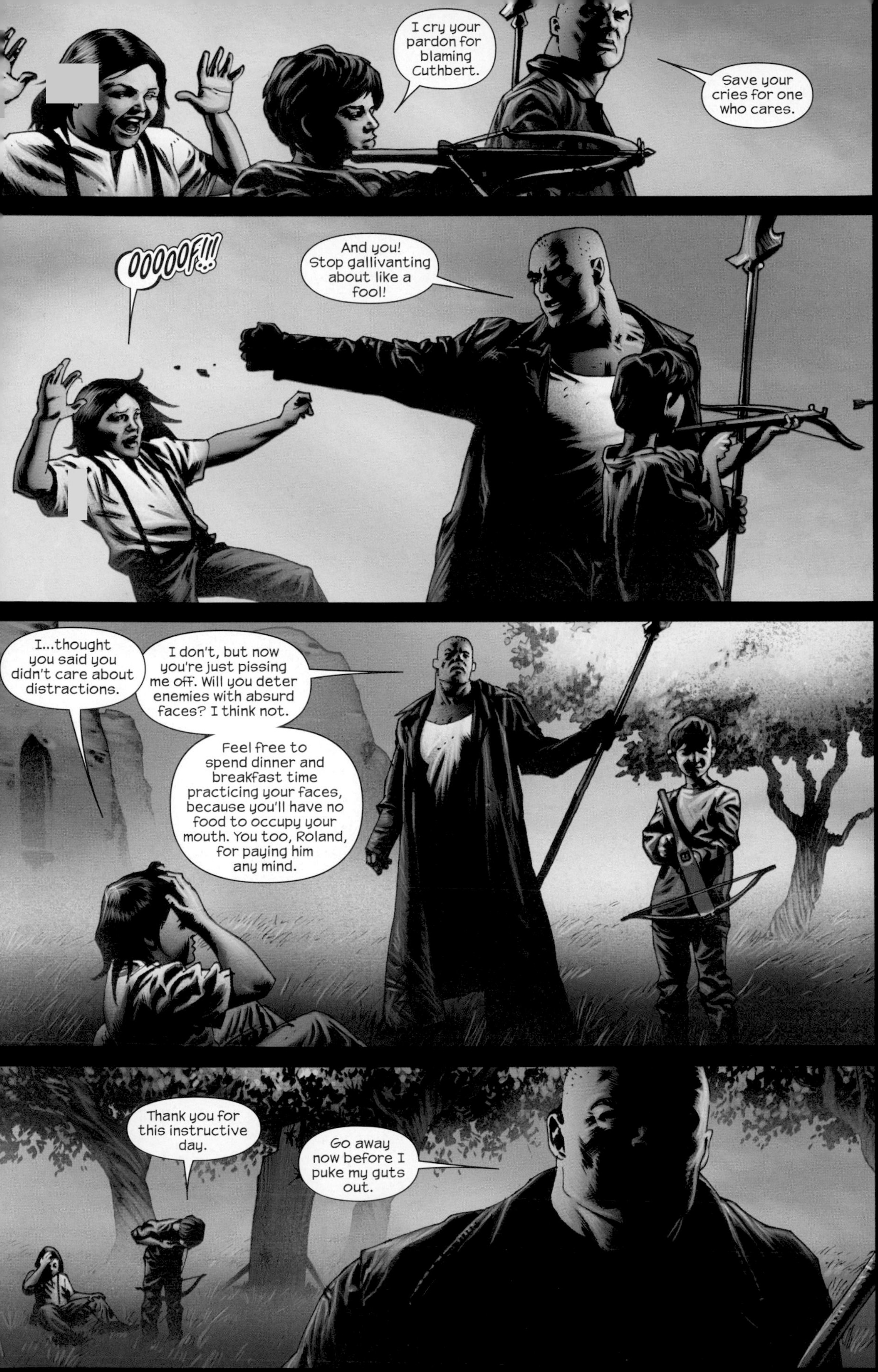
I cry your pardon for blaming Cuthbert.
Save your cries for one who cares.
OOOOOF!!!
And you! Stop gallivanting about like a fool!
I...thought you said you didn't care about distractions.
I don't, but now you're just pissing me off. Will you deter enemies with absurd faces? I think not.
Feel free to spend dinner and breakfast time practicing your faces, because you'll have no food to occupy your mouth. You too, Roland, for paying him any mind.
Thank you for this instructive day.
Go away now before I puke my guts out.

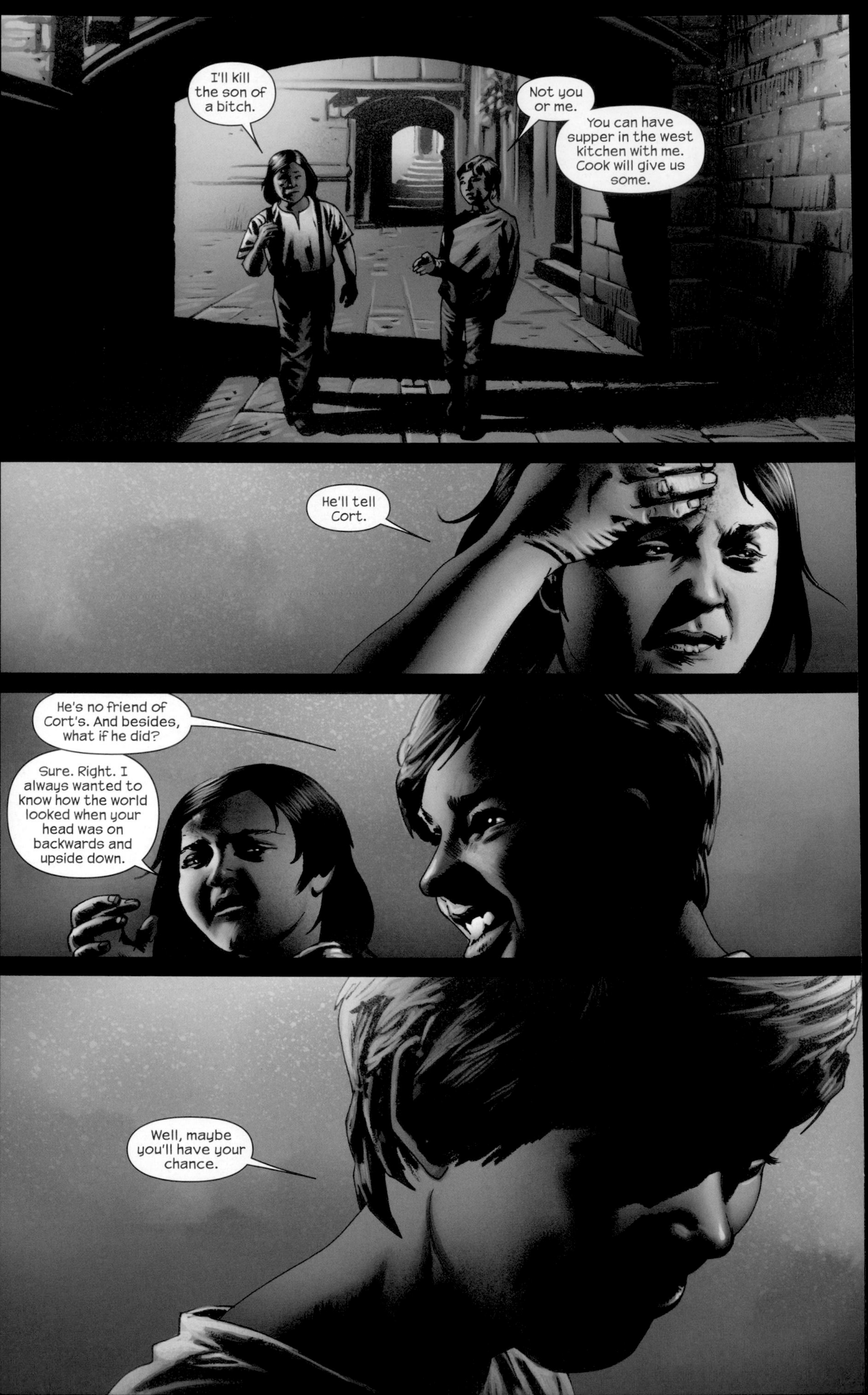

I'll kill the son of a bitch.
Not you or me.
You can have supper in the west kitchen with me. Cook will give us some.
He'll tell Cort.
He's no friend of Cort's. And besides, what if he did?
Sure. Right. I always wanted to know how the world looked when your head was on backwards and upside down.
Well, maybe you'll have your chance.

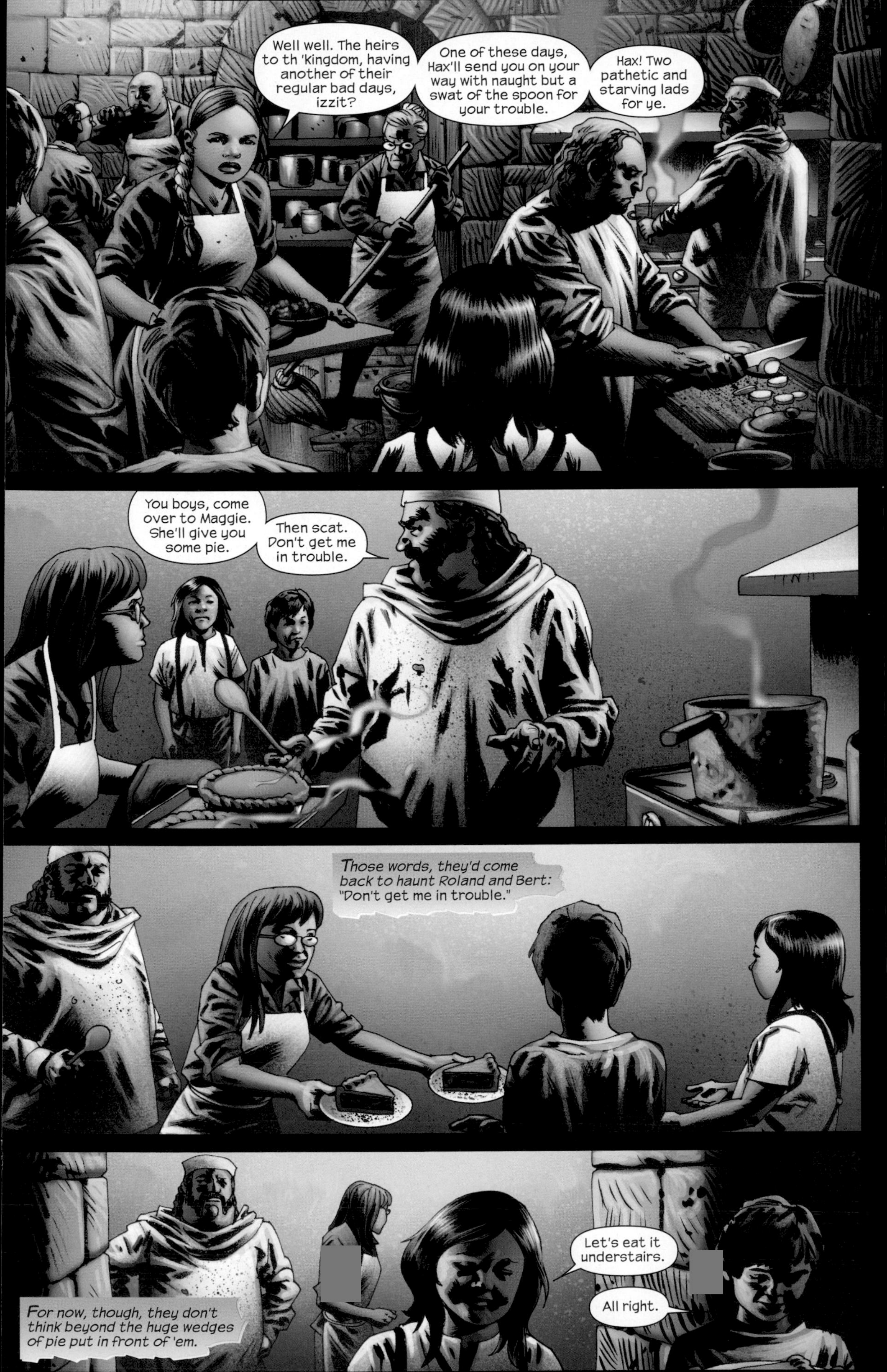
Well well. The heirs to th 'kingdom, having another of their regular bad days, izzit?
One of these days, Hax'll send you on your way with naught but a swat of the spoon for your trouble.
Hax! Two pathetic and starving lads for ye.
You boys, come over to Maggie. She'll give you some pie.
Then scat. Don't get me in trouble.
Those words, they'd come back to haunt Roland and Bert: "Don't get me in trouble."
For now, though, they don't think beyond the huge wedges of pie put in front of 'em.
Let's eat it understairs.
All right.

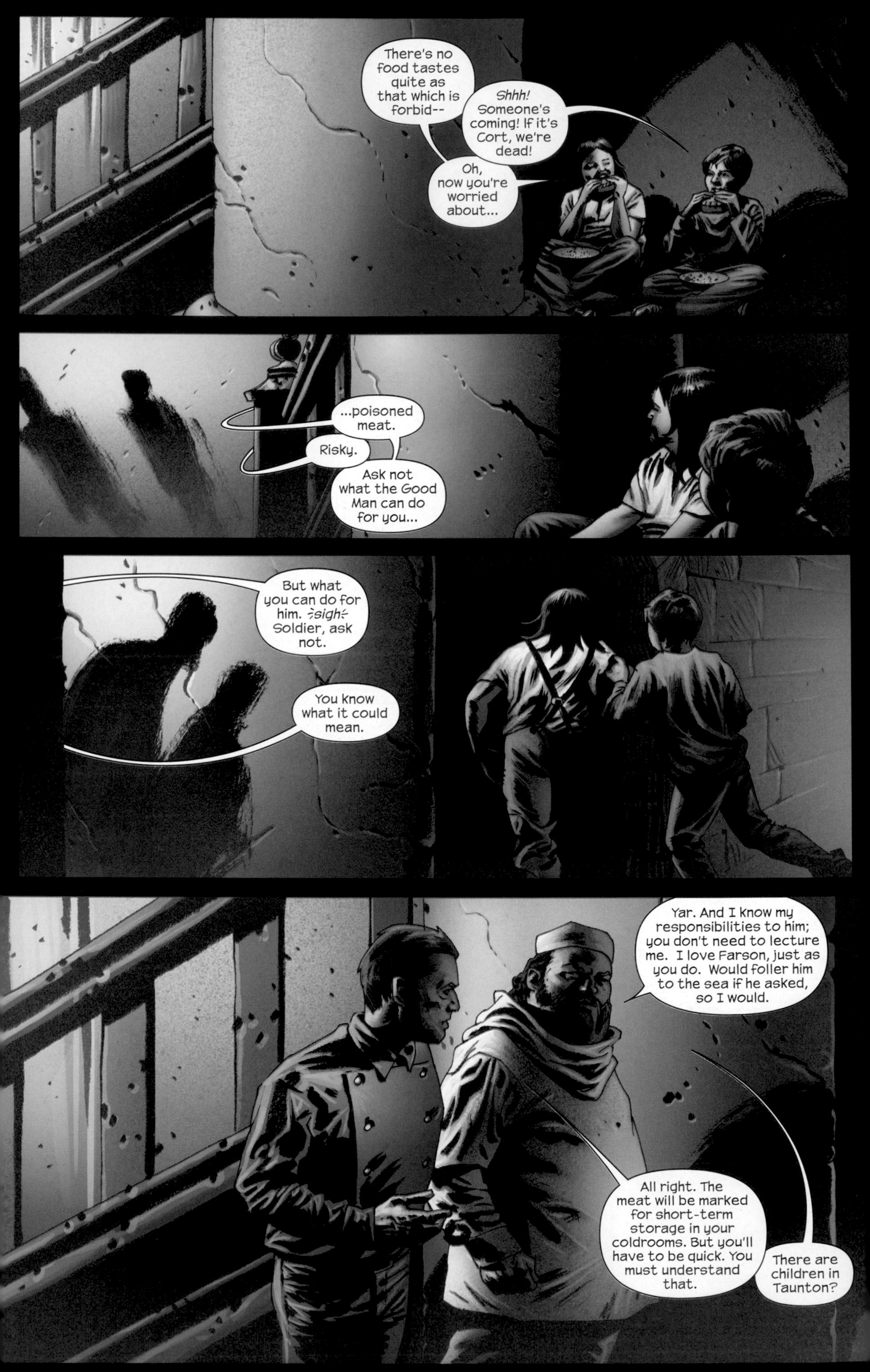
There's no food tastes quite as that which is forbid--
Shhh! Someone's coming! If it's Cort, we're dead!
Oh, now you're worried about...
...poisoned meat.
Risky.
Ask not what the Good Man can do for you...
But what you can do for him. ~sigh~ Soldier, ask not.
You know what it could mean.
Yar. And I know my responsibilities to him; you don't need to lecture me. I love Farson, just as you do. Would foller him to the sea if he asked, so I would.
All right. The meat will be marked for short-term storage in your coldrooms. But you'll have to be quick. You must understand that.
There are children in Taunton?

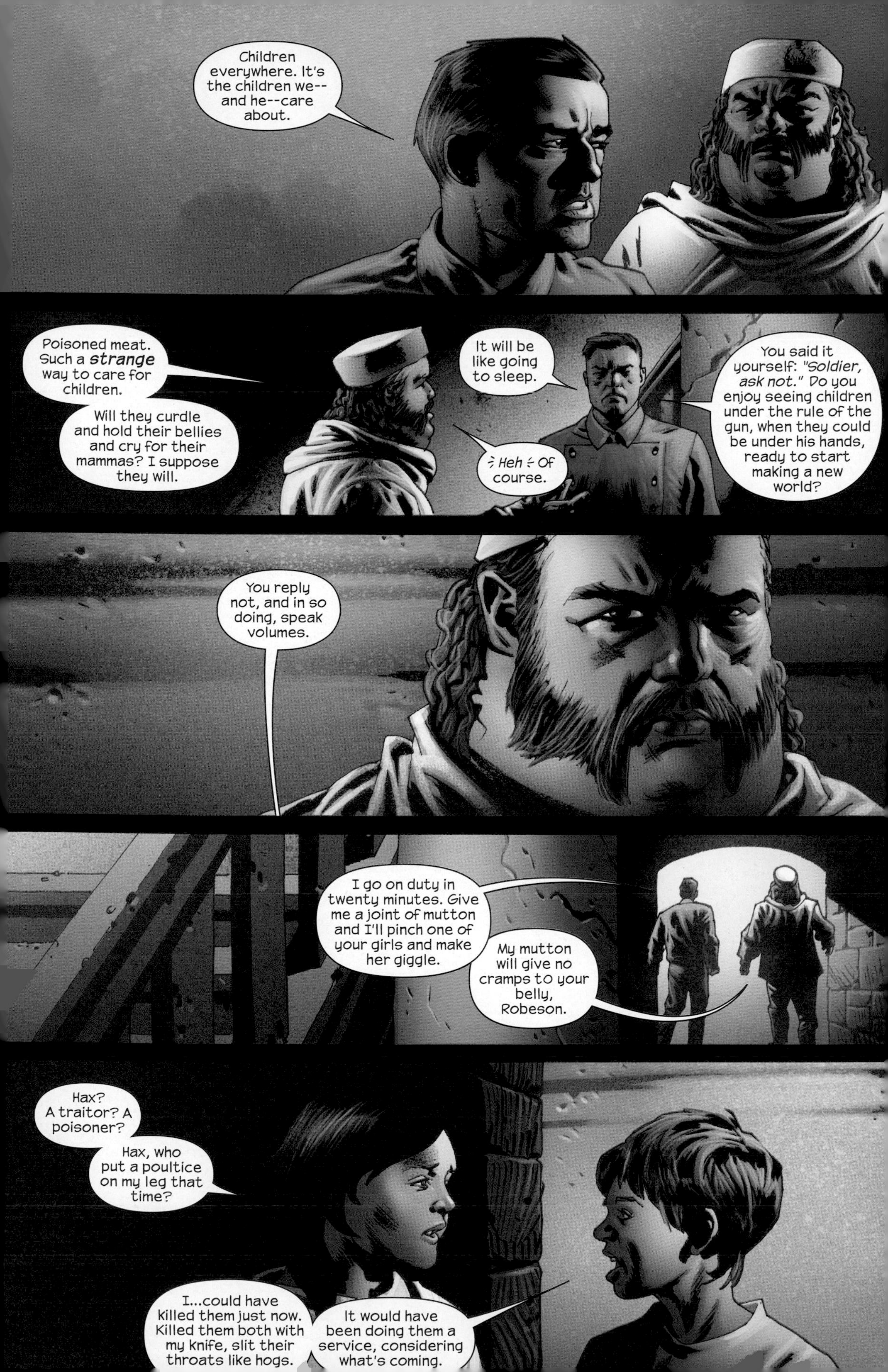
Children everywhere. It's the children we--and he--care about.
Poisoned meat. Such a **strange** way to care for children.
Will they curdle and hold their bellies and cry for their mammas? I suppose they will.
It will be like going to sleep.
~Heh~ Of course.
You said it yourself: *"Soldier, ask not."* Do you enjoy seeing children under the rule of the gun, when they could be under his hands, ready to start making a new world?
You reply not, and in so doing, speak volumes.
I go on duty in twenty minutes. Give me a joint of mutton and I'll pinch one of your girls and make her giggle.
My mutton will give no cramps to your belly, Robeson.
Hax? A traitor? A poisoner?
Hax, who put a poultice on my leg that time?
I...could have killed them just now. Killed them both with my knife, slit their throats like hogs.
It would have been doing them a service, considering what's coming.

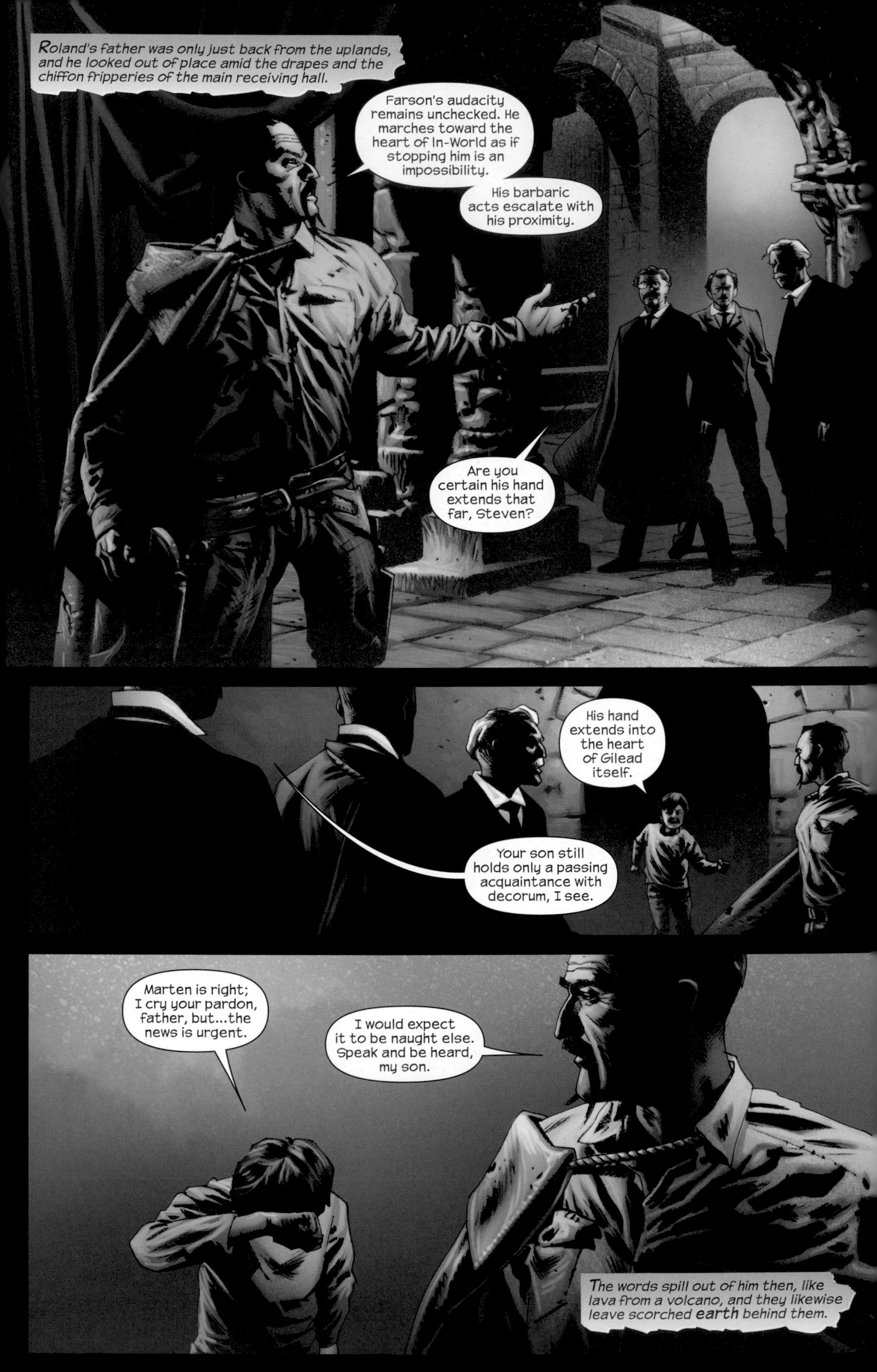
Roland's father was only just back from the uplands, and he looked out of place amid the drapes and the chiffon fripperies of the main receiving hall.
Farson's audacity remains unchecked. He marches toward the heart of In-World as if stopping him is an impossibility.
His barbaric acts escalate with his proximity.
Are you certain his hand extends that far, Steven?
His hand extends into the heart of Gilead itself.
Your son still holds only a passing acquaintance with decorum, I see.
Marten is right; I cry your pardon, father, but...the news is urgent.
I would expect it to be naught else. Speak and be heard, my son.
The words spill out of him then, like lava from a volcano, and they likewise leave scorched earth behind them.

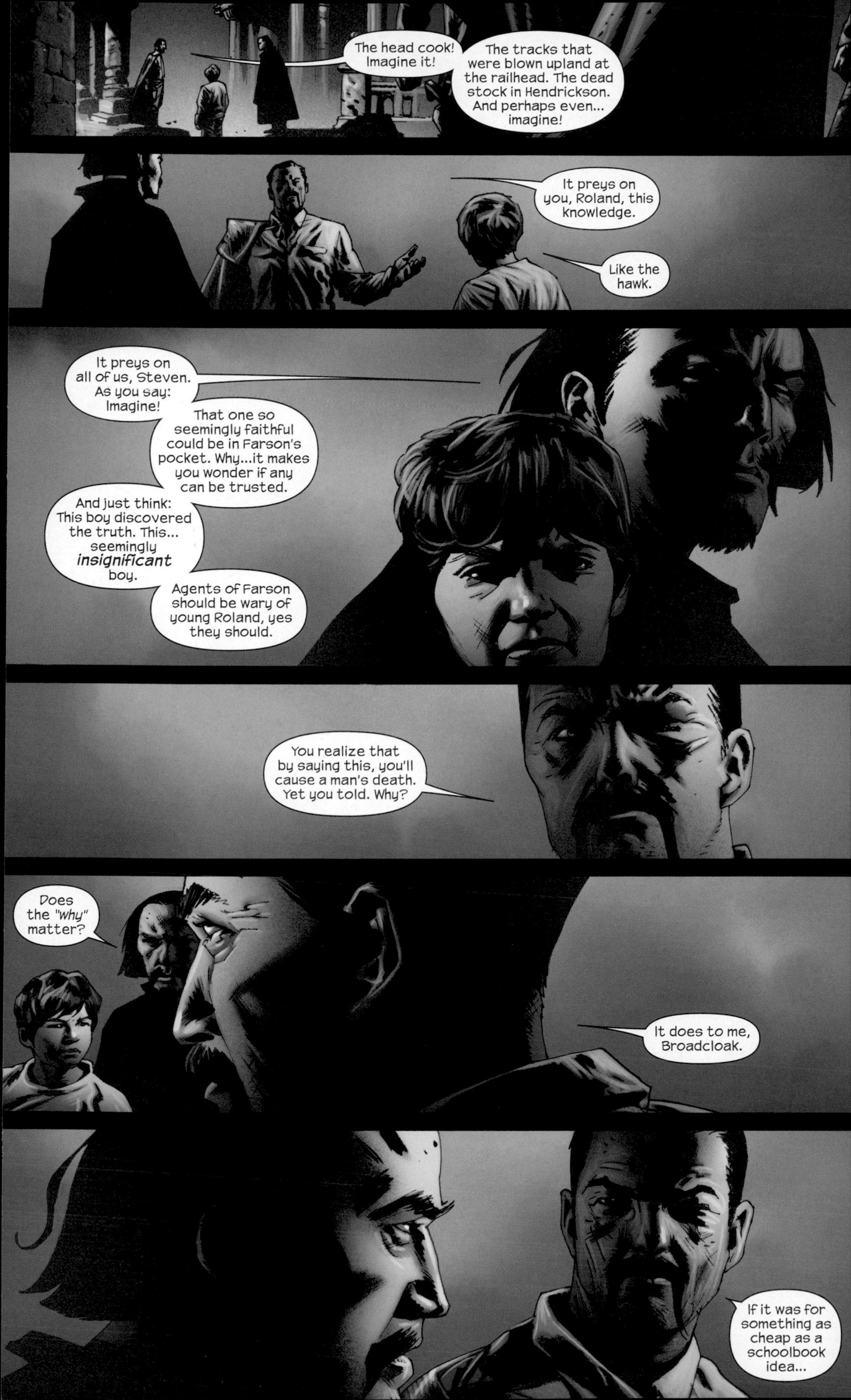

The head cook! Imagine it!
The tracks that were blown upland at the railhead. The dead stock in Hendrickson. And perhaps even... imagine!
It preys on you, Roland, this knowledge.
Like the hawk.
It preys on all of us, Steven. As you say: Imagine!
That one so seemingly faithful could be in Farson's pocket. Why...it makes you wonder if any can be trusted.
And just think: This boy discovered the truth. This... seemingly *insignificant* boy.
Agents of Farson should be wary of young Roland, yes they should.
You realize that by saying this, you'll cause a man's death. Yet you told. Why?
Does the "*why*" matter?
It does to me, Broadcloak.
If it was for something as cheap as a schoolbook idea...

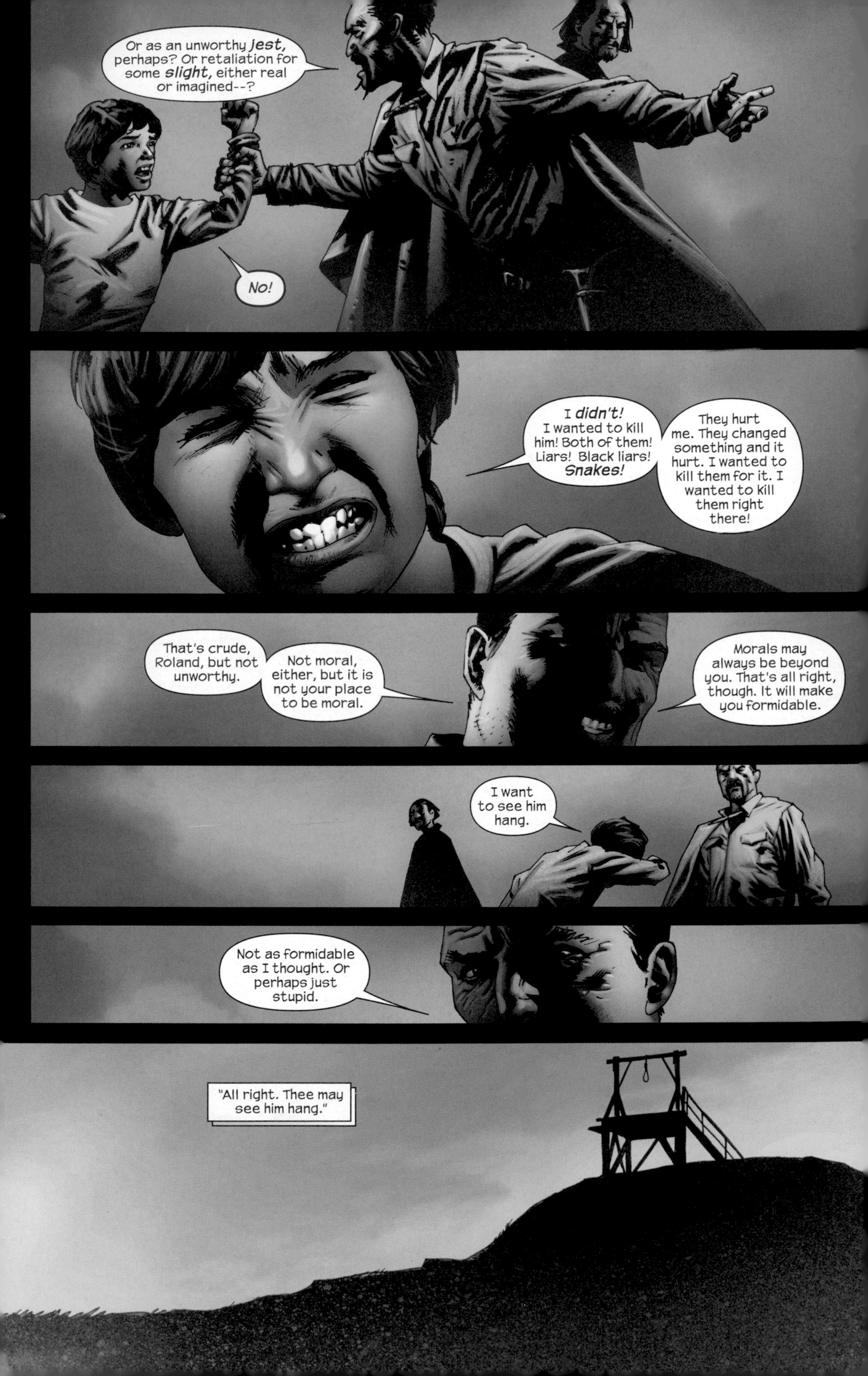
Or as an unworthy jest, perhaps? Or retaliation for some slight, either real or imagined--?
No!
I didn't! I wanted to kill him! Both of them! Liars! Black liars! Snakes!
They hurt me. They changed something and it hurt. I wanted to kill them for it. I wanted to kill them right there!
That's crude, Roland, but not unworthy.
Not moral, either, but it is not your place to be moral.
Morals may always be beyond you. That's all right, though. It will make you formidable.
I want to see him hang.
Not as formidable as I thought. Or perhaps just stupid.
"All right. Thee may see him hang."

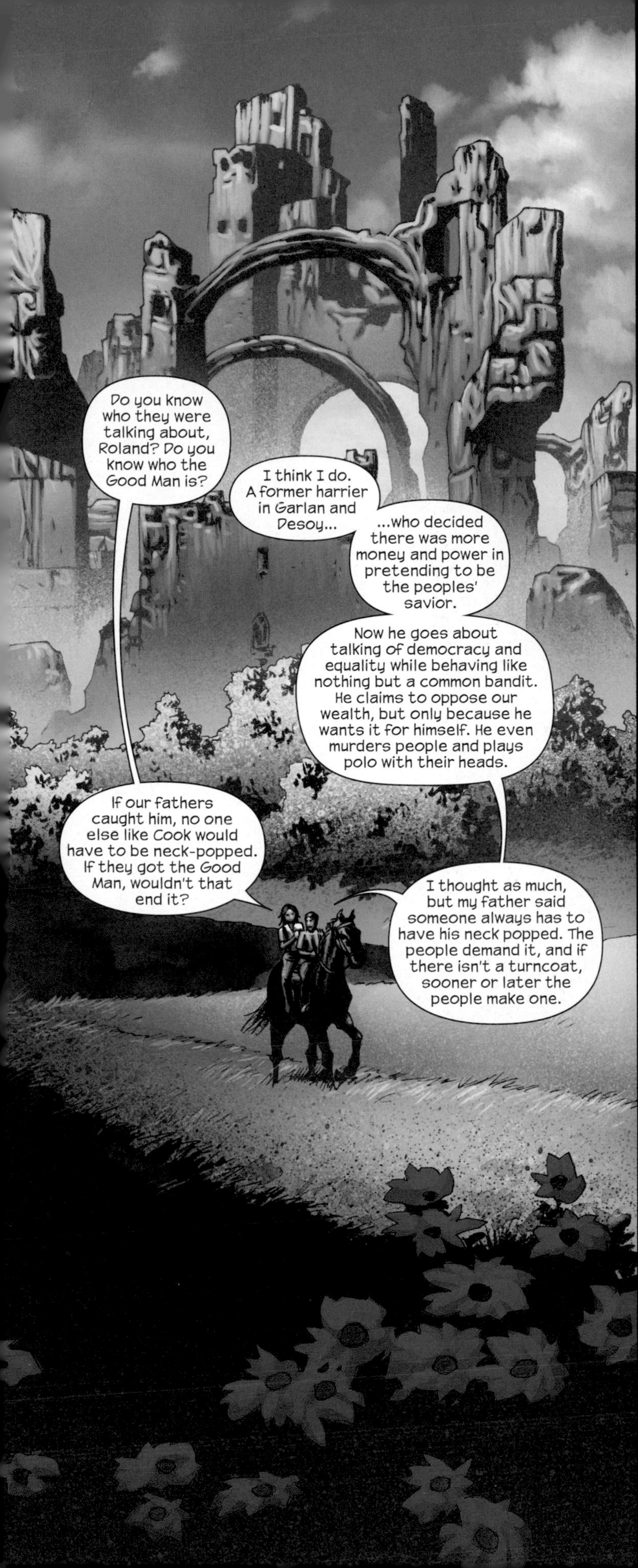
Do you know who they were talking about, Roland? Do you know who the Good Man is?
I think I do. A former harrier in Garlan and Desoy...
...who decided there was more money and power in pretending to be the peoples' savior.
Now he goes about talking of democracy and equality while behaving like nothing but a common bandit. He claims to oppose our wealth, but only because he wants it for himself. He even murders people and plays polo with their heads.
If our fathers caught him, no one else like Cook would have to be neck-popped. If they got the Good Man, wouldn't that end it?
I thought as much, but my father said someone always has to have his neck popped. The people demand it, and if there isn't a turncoat, sooner or later the people make one.
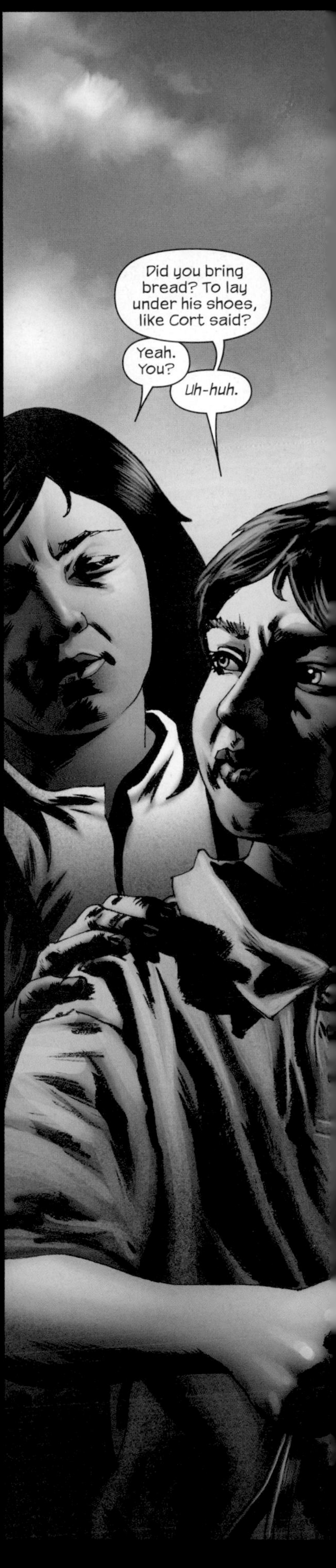
Did you bring bread? To lay under his shoes, like Cort said?
Yeah. You?
Uh-huh.

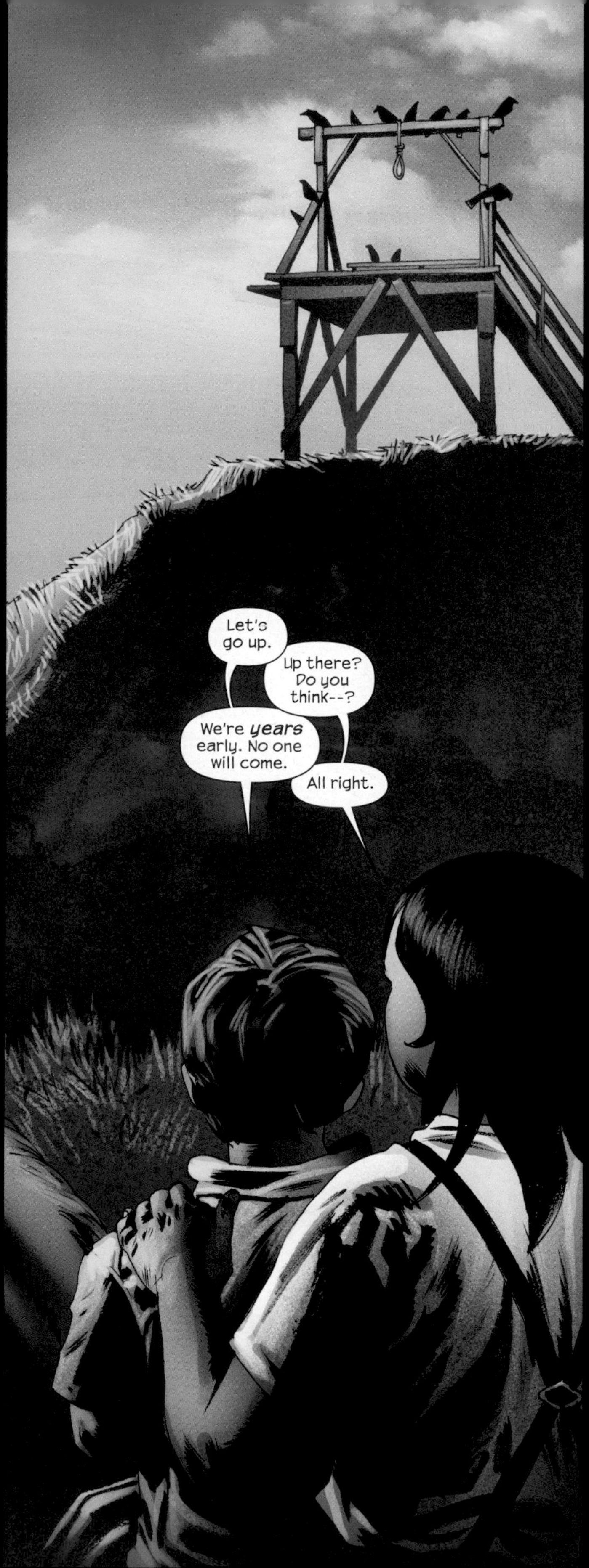
Let's go up.
Up there? Do you think--?
We're *years* early. No one will come.
All right.

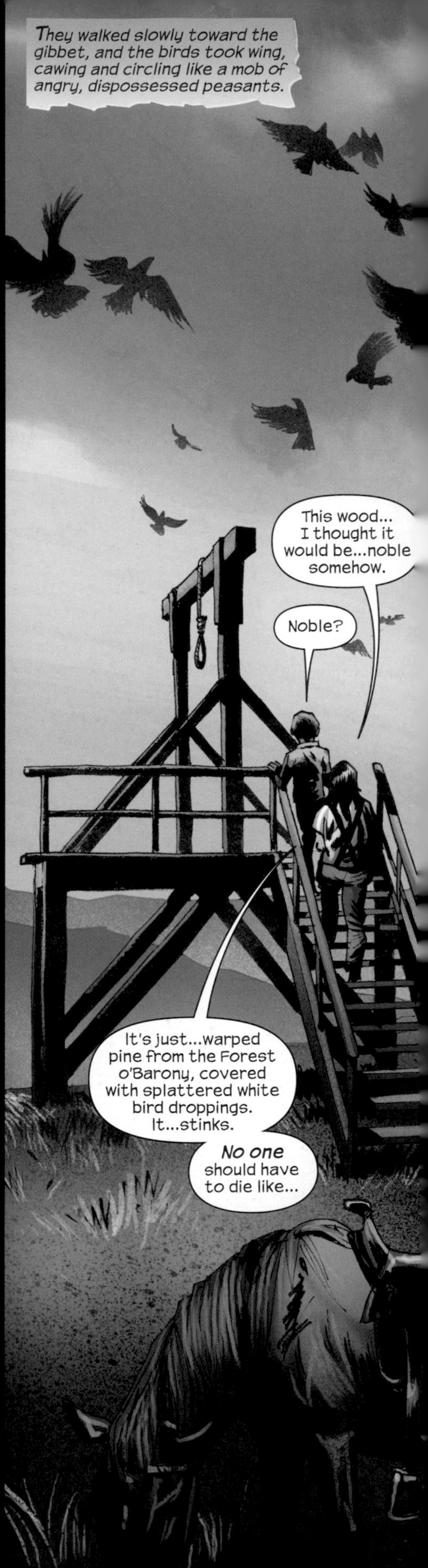
They walked slowly toward the gibbet, and the birds took wing, cawing and circling like a mob of angry, dispossessed peasants.
This wood... I thought it would be...noble somehow.
Noble?
It's just...warped pine from the Forest O'Barony, covered with splattered white bird droppings. It...stinks.
No one should have to die like...

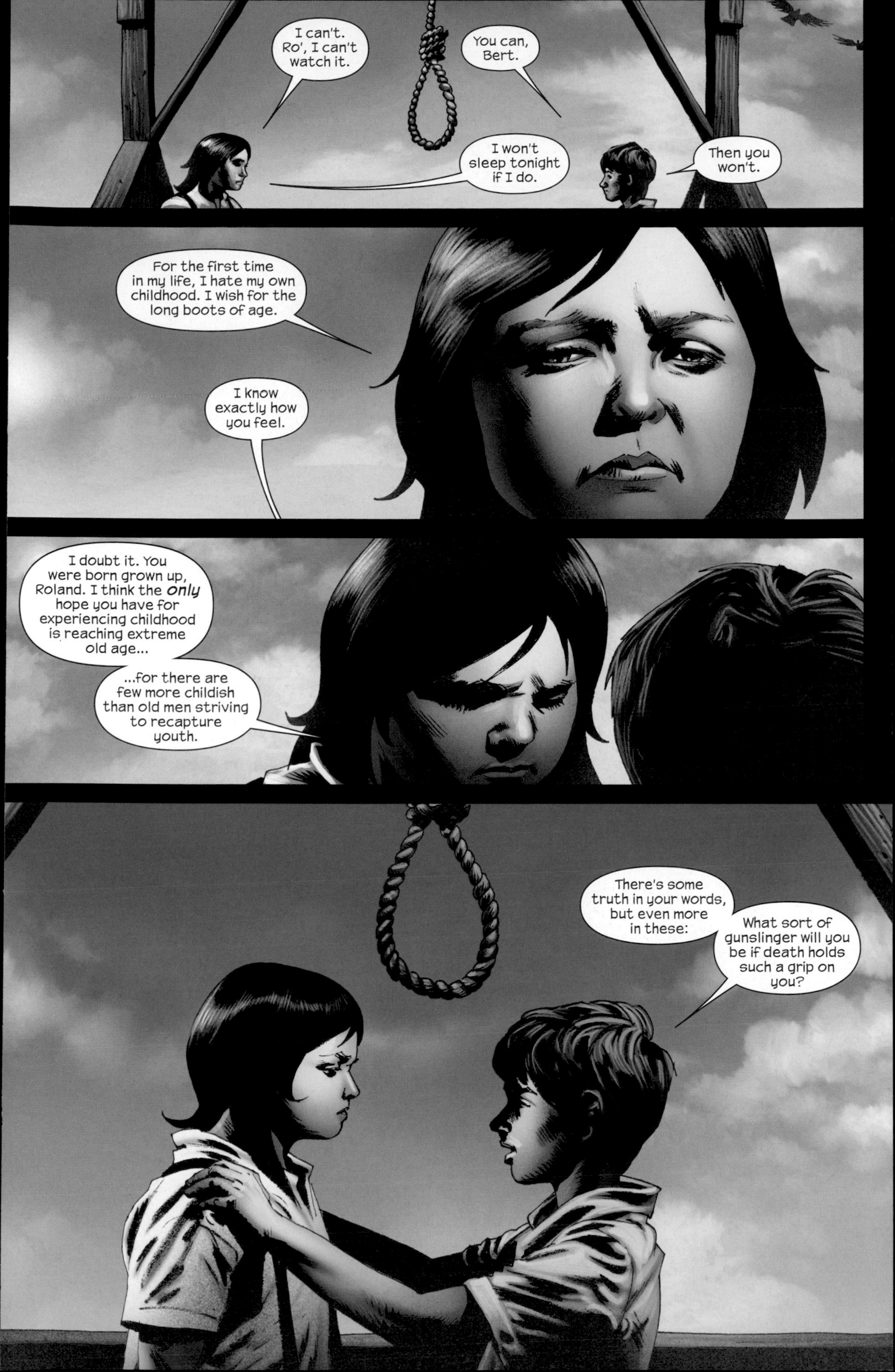
I can't. Ro', I can't watch it.
You can, Bert.
I won't sleep tonight if I do.
Then you won't.
For the first time in my life, I hate my own childhood. I wish for the long boots of age.
I know exactly how you feel.
I doubt it. You were born grown up, Roland. I think the *only* hope you have for experiencing childhood is reaching extreme old age...
...for there are few more childish than old men striving to recapture youth.
There's some truth in your words, but even more in these:
What sort of gunslinger will you be if death holds such a grip on you?

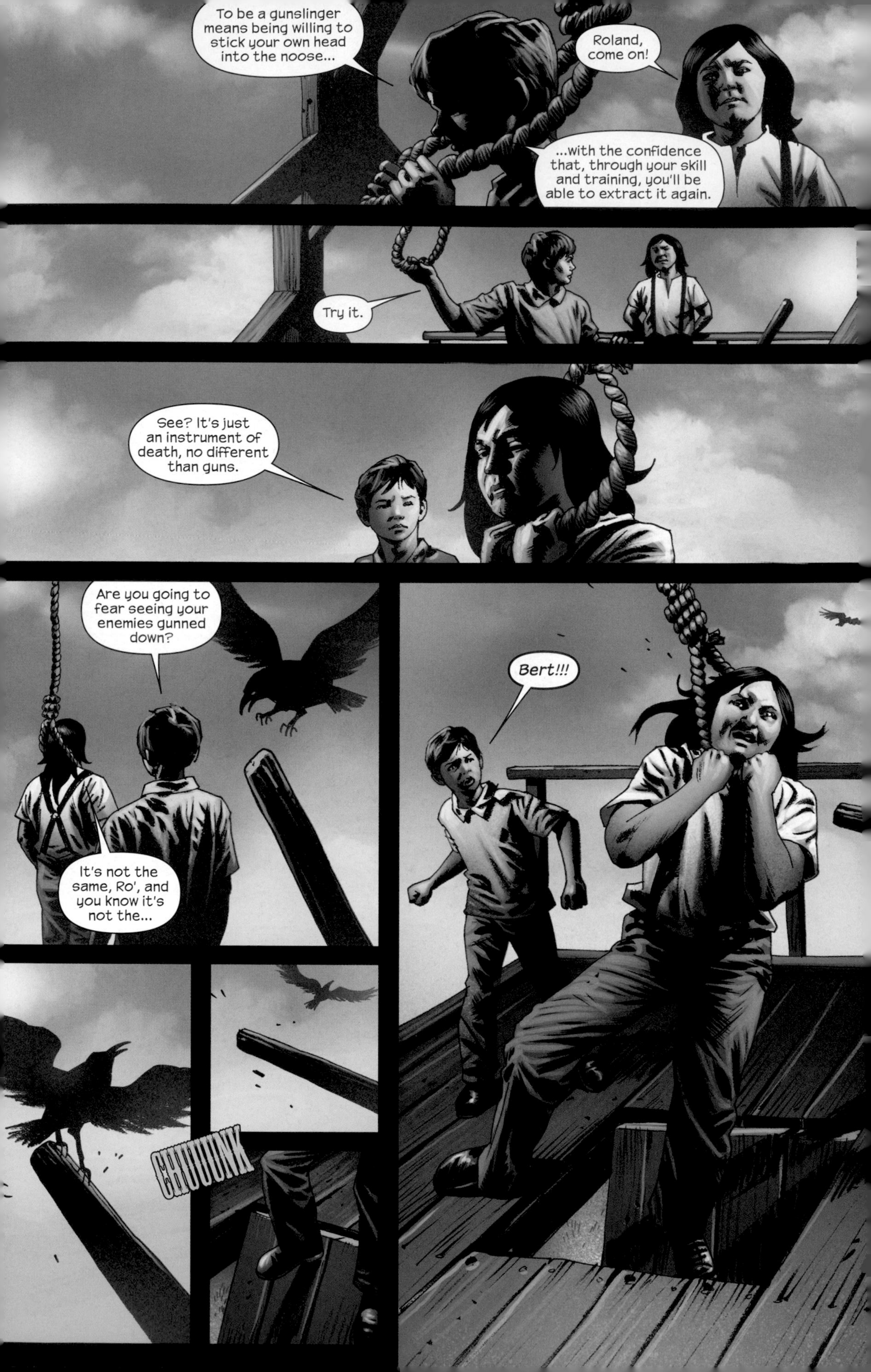
To be a gunslinger means being willing to stick your own head into the noose...
Roland, come on!
...with the confidence that, through your skill and training, you'll be able to extract it again.
Try it.
See? It's just an instrument of death, no different than guns.
Are you going to fear seeing your enemies gunned down?
It's not the same, Ro', and you know it's not the...
CHUUUNK
Bert!!!

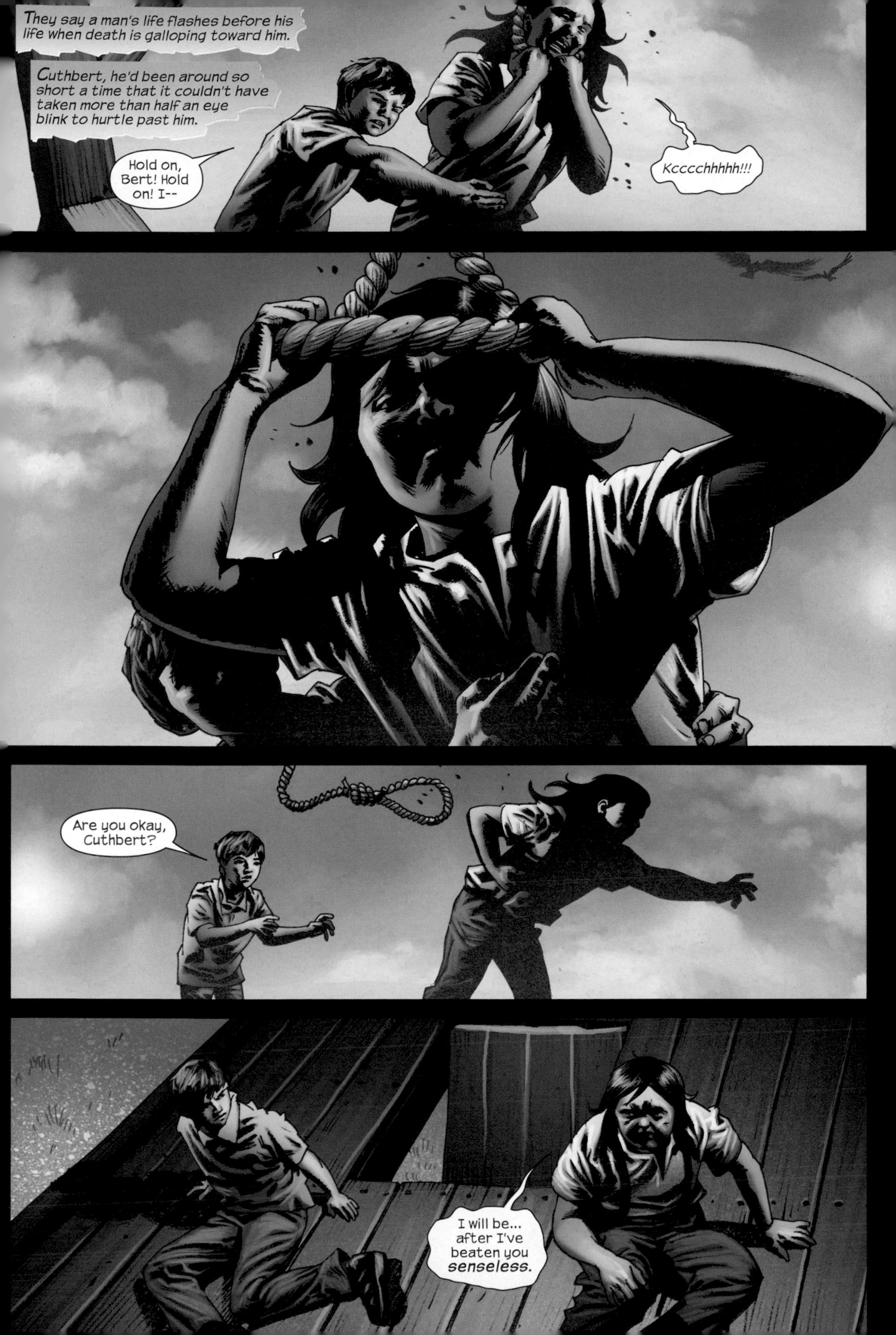
They say a man's life flashes before his life when death is galloping toward him.
Cuthbert, he'd been around so short a time that it couldn't have taken more than half an eye blink to hurtle past him.
Hold on, Bert! Hold on! I--
Kccccchhhhh!!!
Are you okay, Cuthbert?
I will be... after I've beaten you senseless.

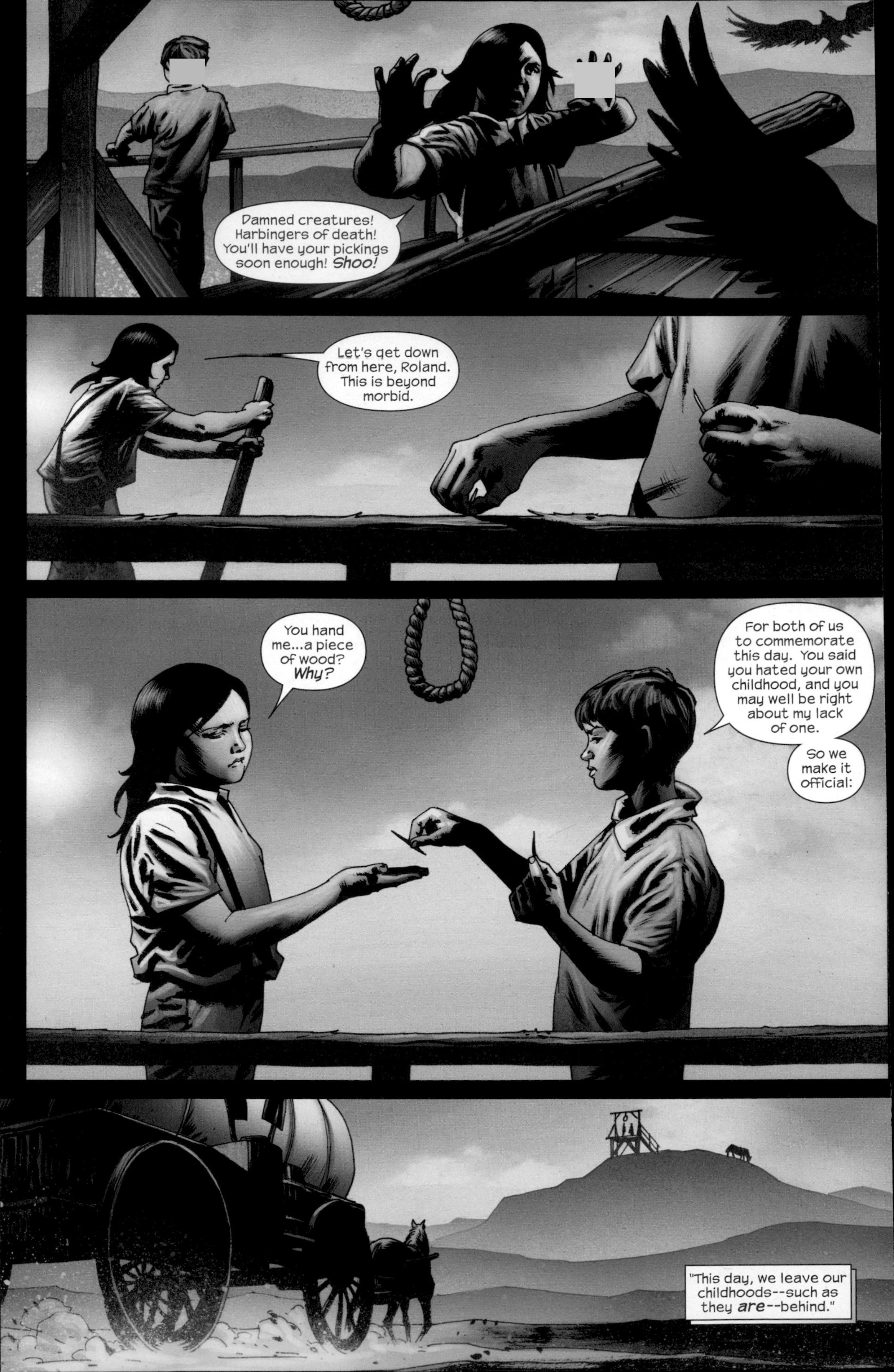
Damned creatures! Harbingers of death! You'll have your pickings soon enough! Shoo!
Let's get down from here, Roland. This is beyond morbid.
You hand me...a piece of wood? Why?
For both of us to commemorate this day. You said you hated your own childhood, and you may well be right about my lack of one.
So we make it official:
"This day, we leave our childhoods--such as they are--behind."

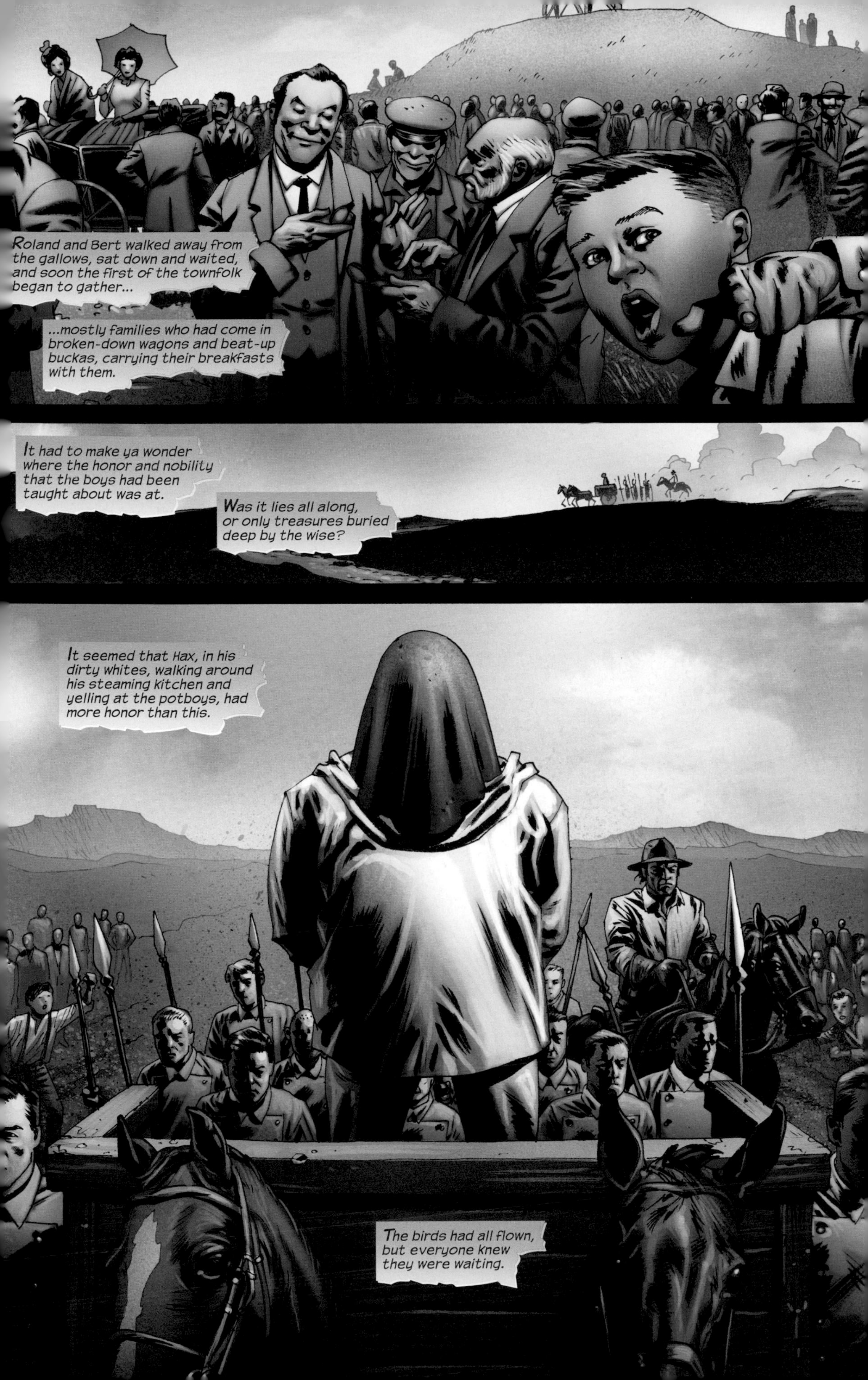
Roland and Bert walked away from the gallows, sat down and waited, and soon the first of the townfolk began to gather...
...mostly families who had come in broken-down wagons and beat-up buckas, carrying their breakfasts with them.
It had to make ya wonder where the honor and nobility that the boys had been taught about was at.
Was it lies all along, or only treasures buried deep by the wise?
It seemed that Hax, in his dirty whites, walking around his steaming kitchen and yelling at the potboys, had more honor than this.
The birds had all flown, but everyone knew they were waiting.

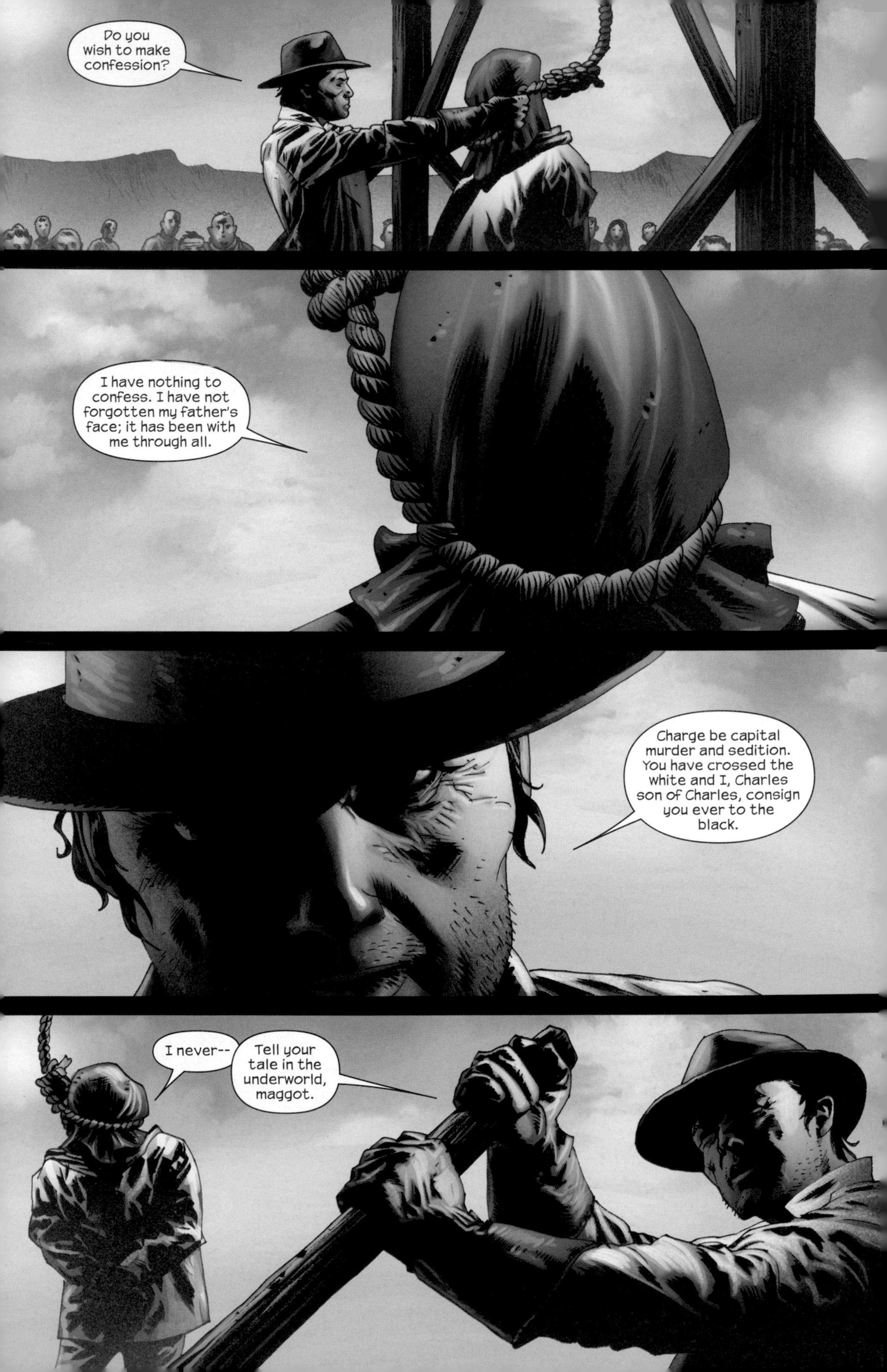
Do you wish to make confession?
I have nothing to confess. I have not forgotten my father's face; it has been with me through all.
Charge be capital murder and sedition. You have crossed the white and I, Charles son of Charles, consign you ever to the black.
I never--
Tell your tale in the underworld, maggot.

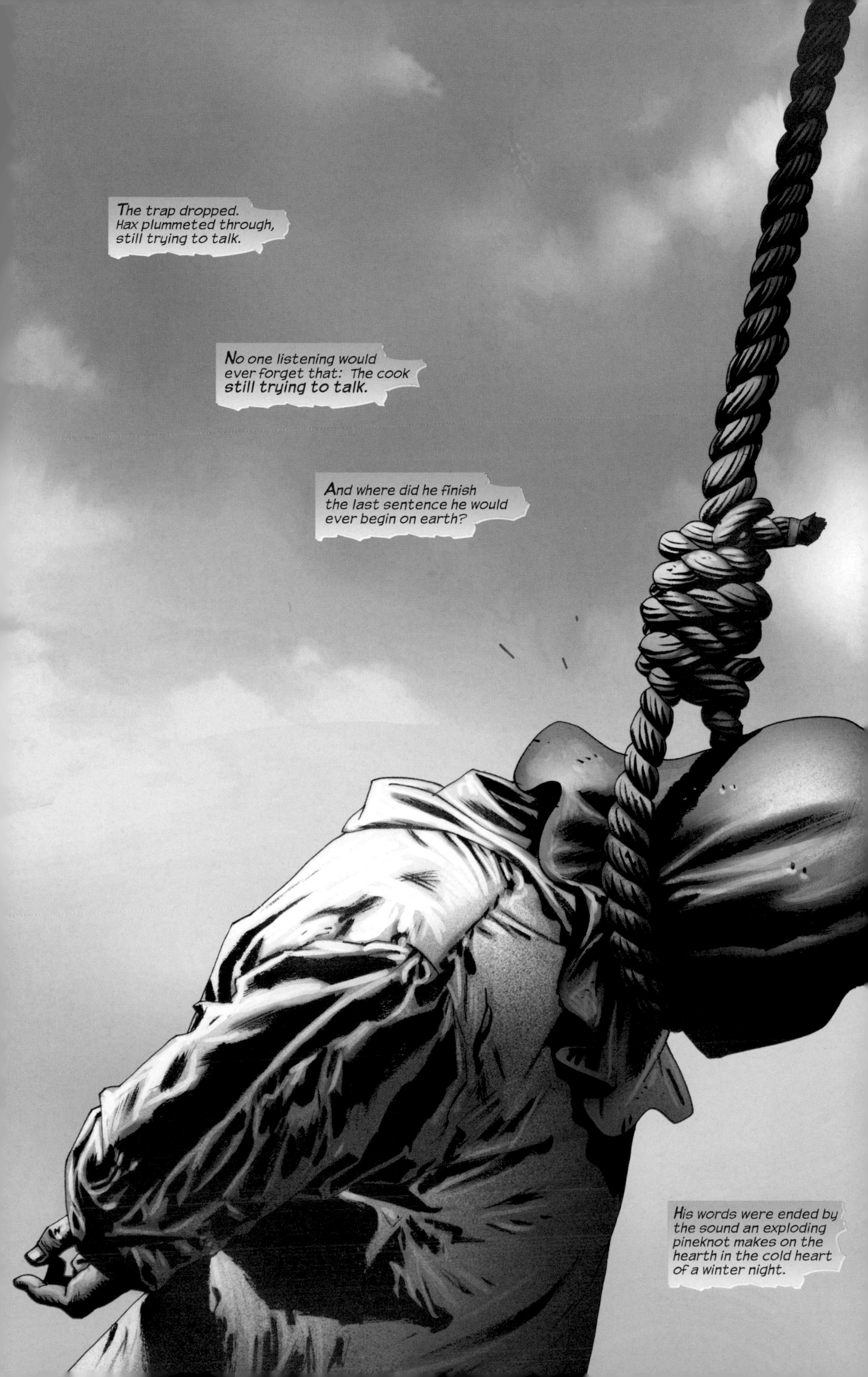
The trap dropped. Hax plummeted through, still trying to talk.
No one listening would ever forget that: The cook still trying to talk.
And where did he finish the last sentence he would ever begin on earth?
His words were ended by the sound an exploding pineknot makes on the hearth in the cold heart of a winter night.

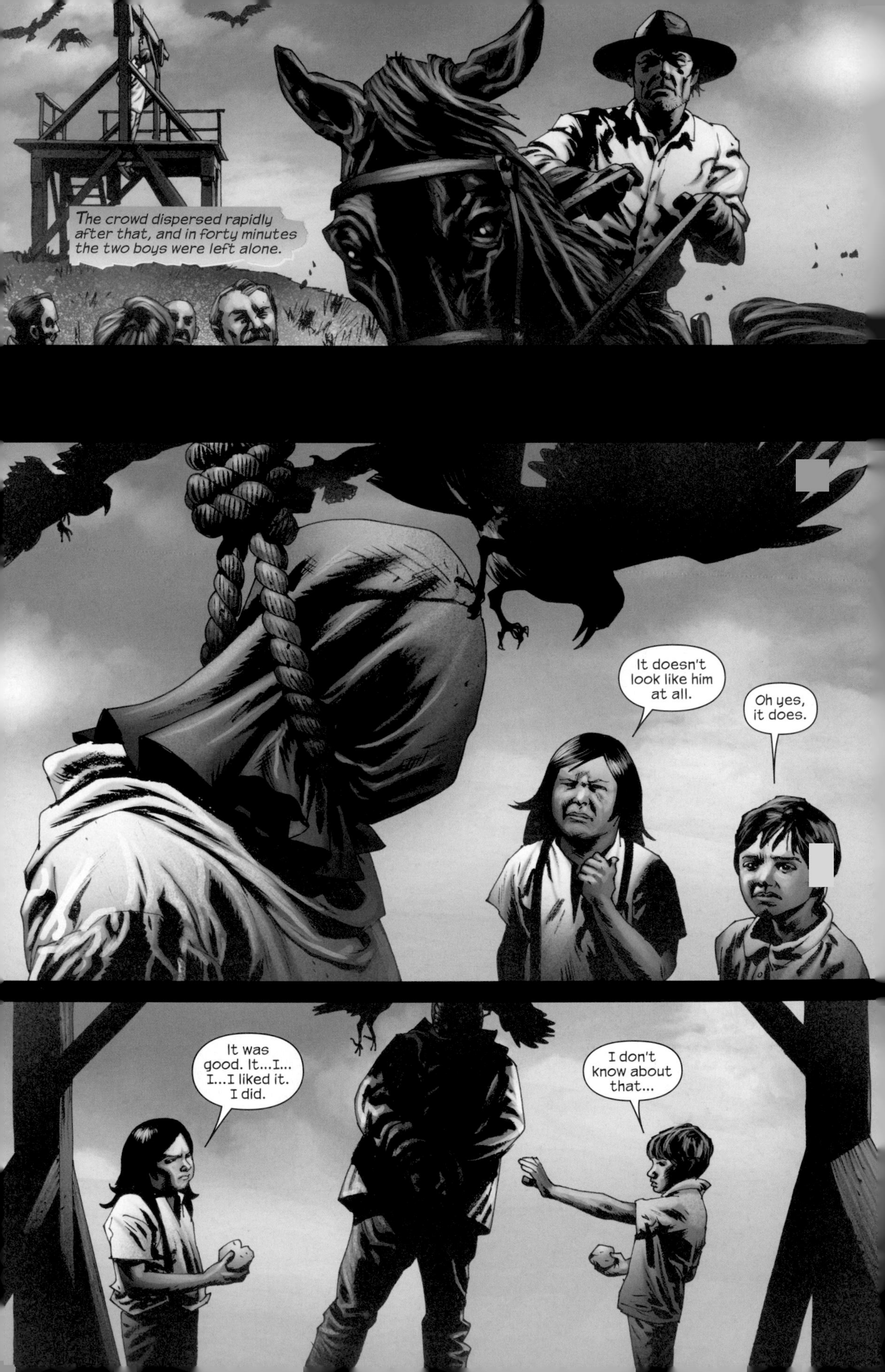
The crowd dispersed rapidly after that, and in forty minutes the two boys were left alone.
It doesn't look like him at all.
Oh yes, it does.
It was good. It...I... I...I liked it. I did.
I don't know about that...

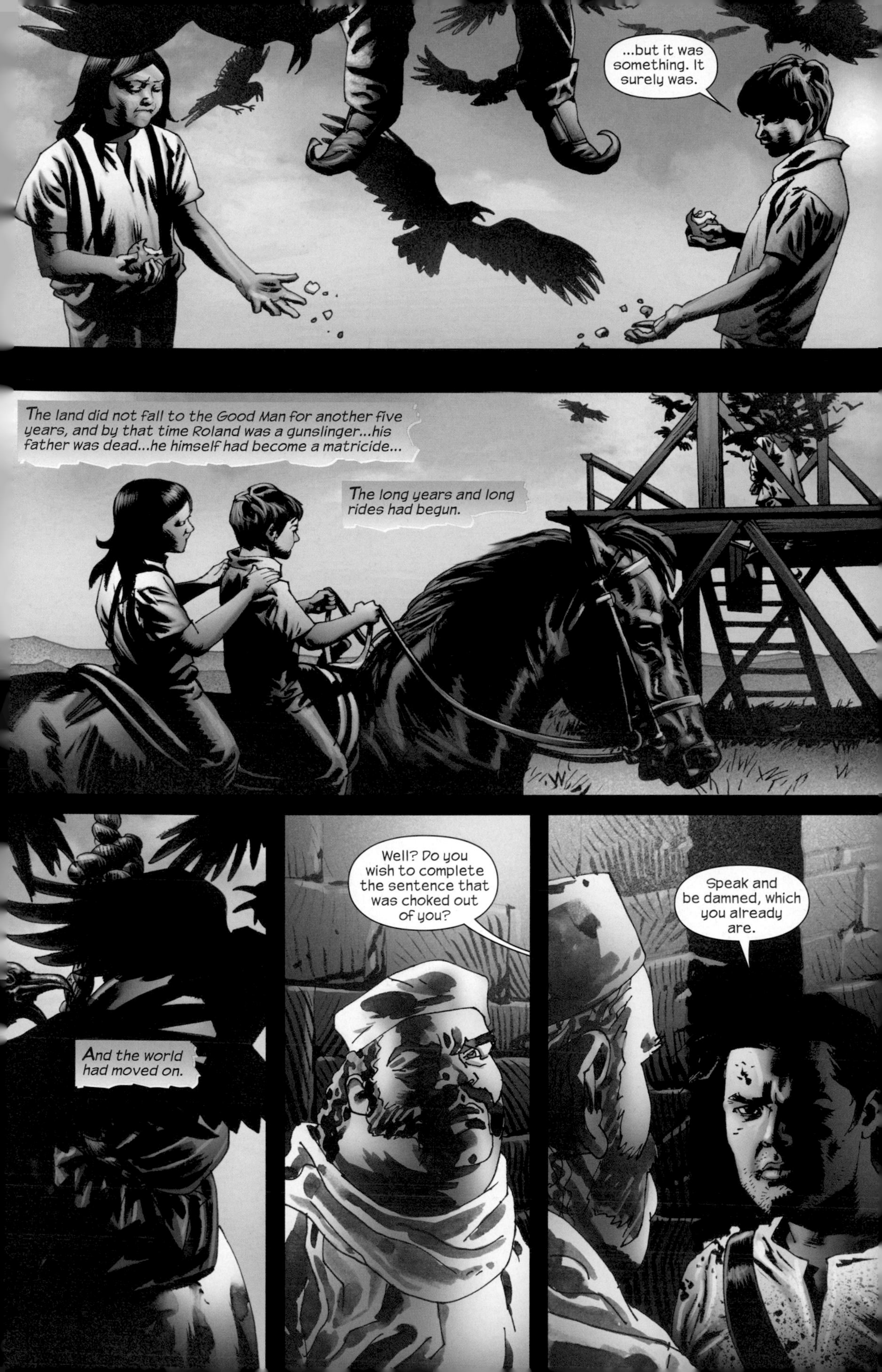
...but it was something. It surely was.
The land did not fall to the Good Man for another five years, and by that time Roland was a gunslinger...his father was dead...he himself had become a matricide...
The long years and long rides had begun.
And the world had moved on.
Well? Do you wish to complete the sentence that was choked out of you?
Speak and be damned, which you already are.

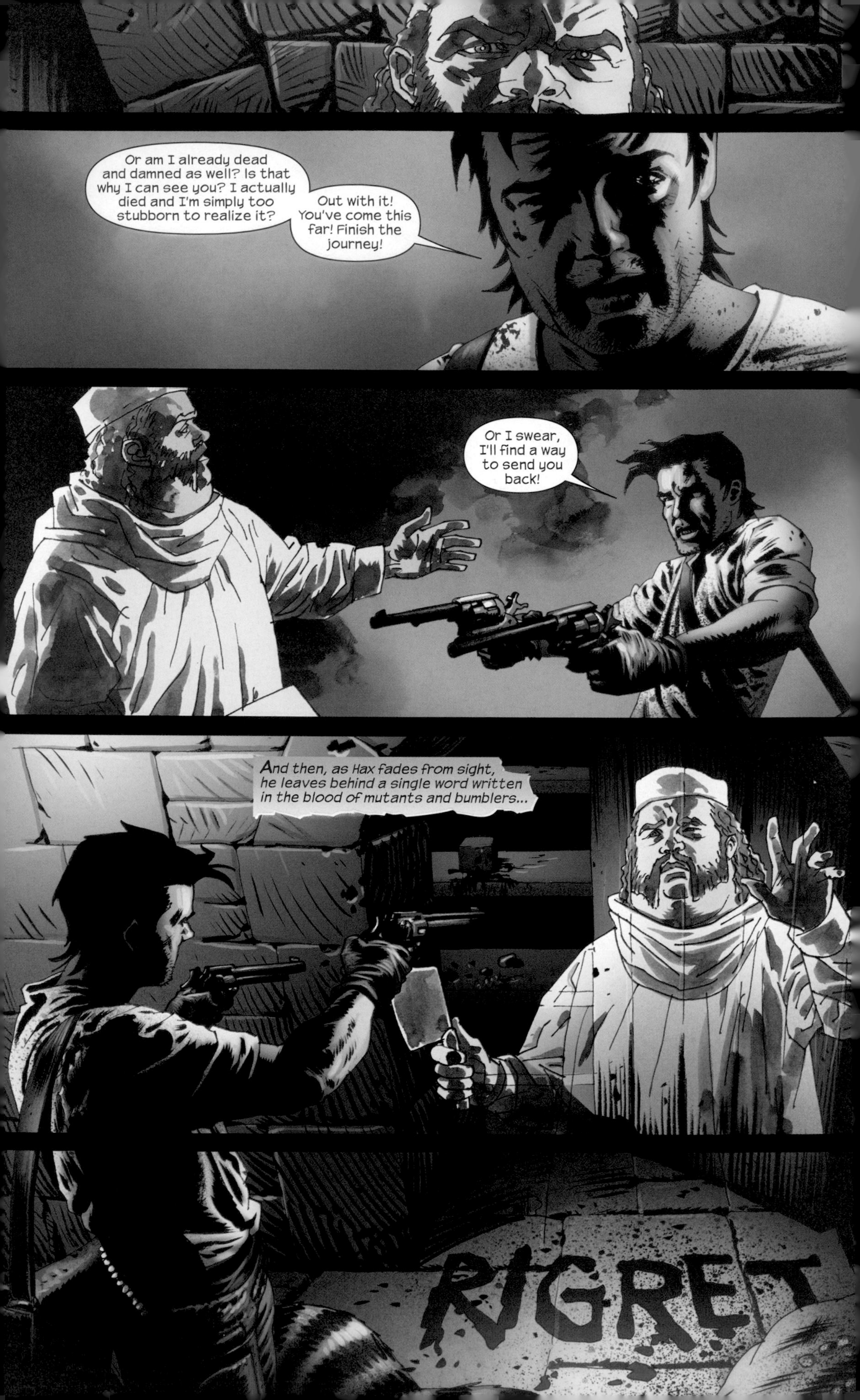
Or am I already dead and damned as well? Is that why I can see you? I actually died and I'm simply too stubborn to realize it?
Out with it! You've come this far! Finish the journey!
Or I swear, I'll find a way to send you back!
And then, as Hax fades from sight, he leaves behind a single word written in the blood of mutants and bumblers...
RIGRET

STEPHEN KING

THE DARK TOWER
~THE GUNSLINGER~

THE JOURNEY BEGINS
CHAPTER FOUR

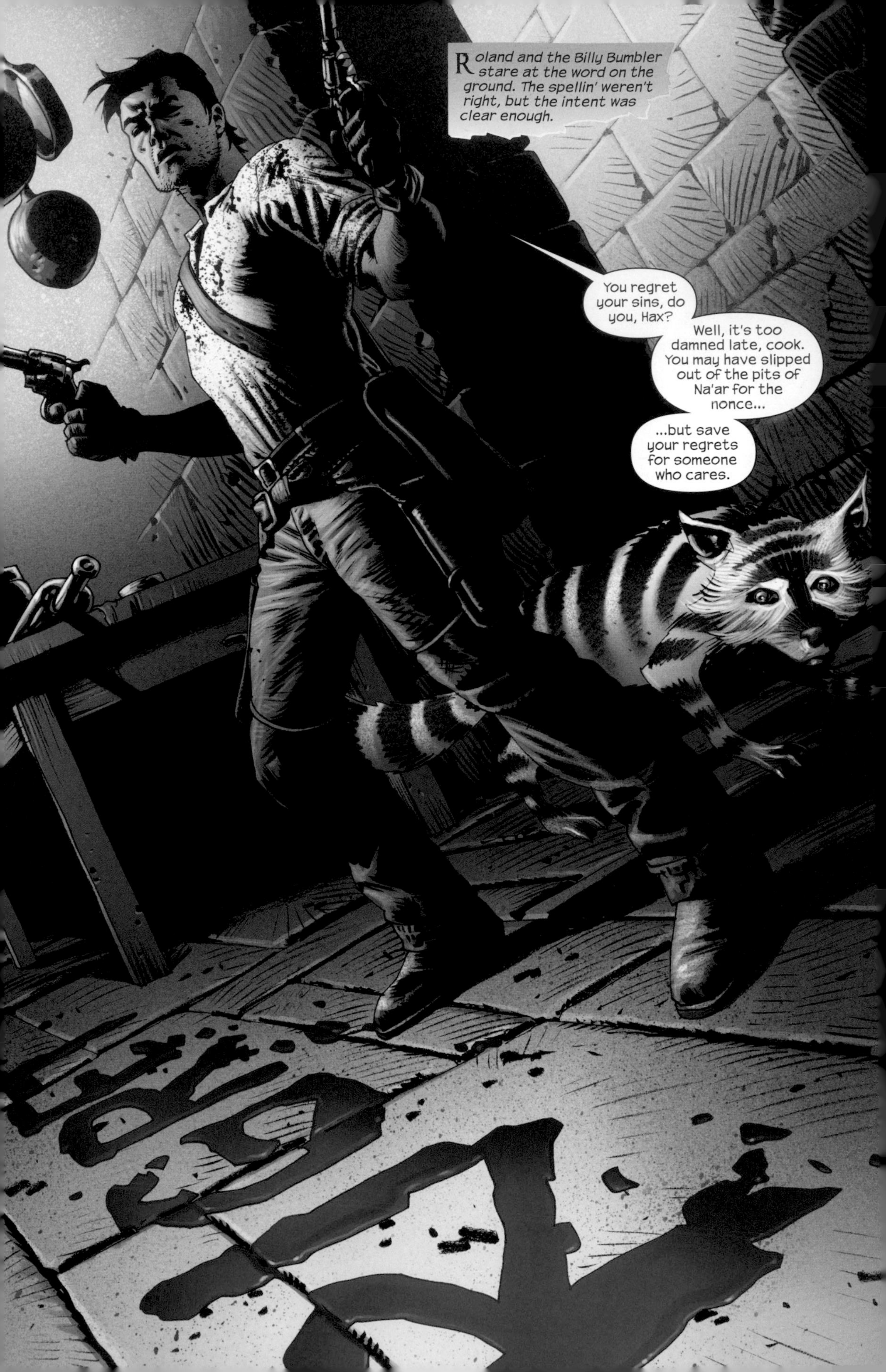
Roland and the Billy Bumbler stare at the word on the ground. The spellin' weren't right, but the intent was clear enough.
You regret your sins, do you, Hax?
Well, it's too damned late, cook. You may have slipped out of the pits of Na'ar for the nonce...
...but save your regrets for someone who cares.

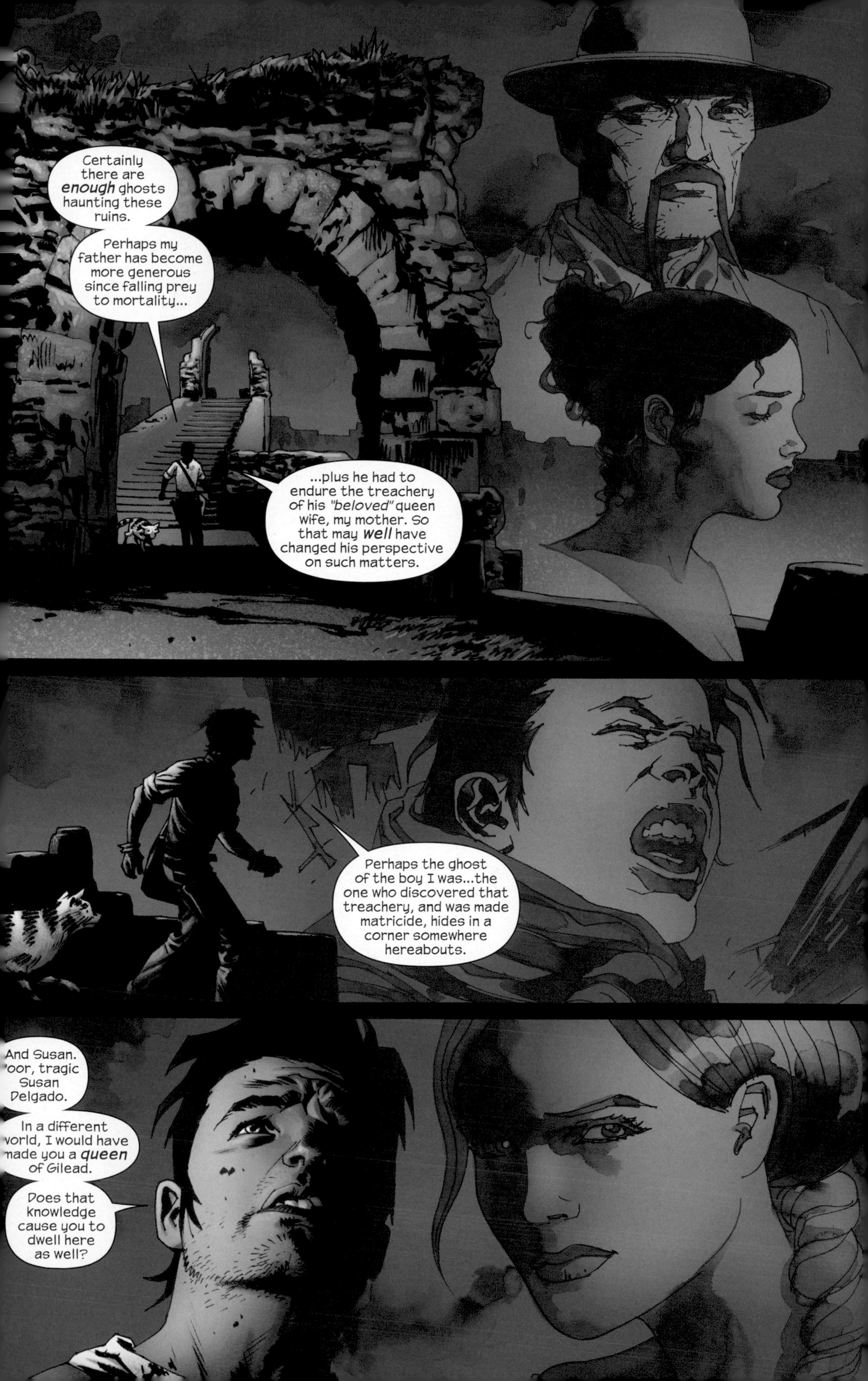
Certainly there are *enough* ghosts haunting these ruins.
Perhaps my father has become more generous since falling prey to mortality...
...plus he had to endure the treachery of his *"beloved"* queen wife, my mother. So that may *well* have changed his perspective on such matters.
Perhaps the ghost of the boy I was...the one who discovered that treachery, and was made matricide, hides in a corner somewhere hereabouts.
And Susan. oor, tragic Susan Delgado.
In a different vorld, I would have nade you a *queen* of Gilead.
Does that knowledge cause you to dwell here as well?

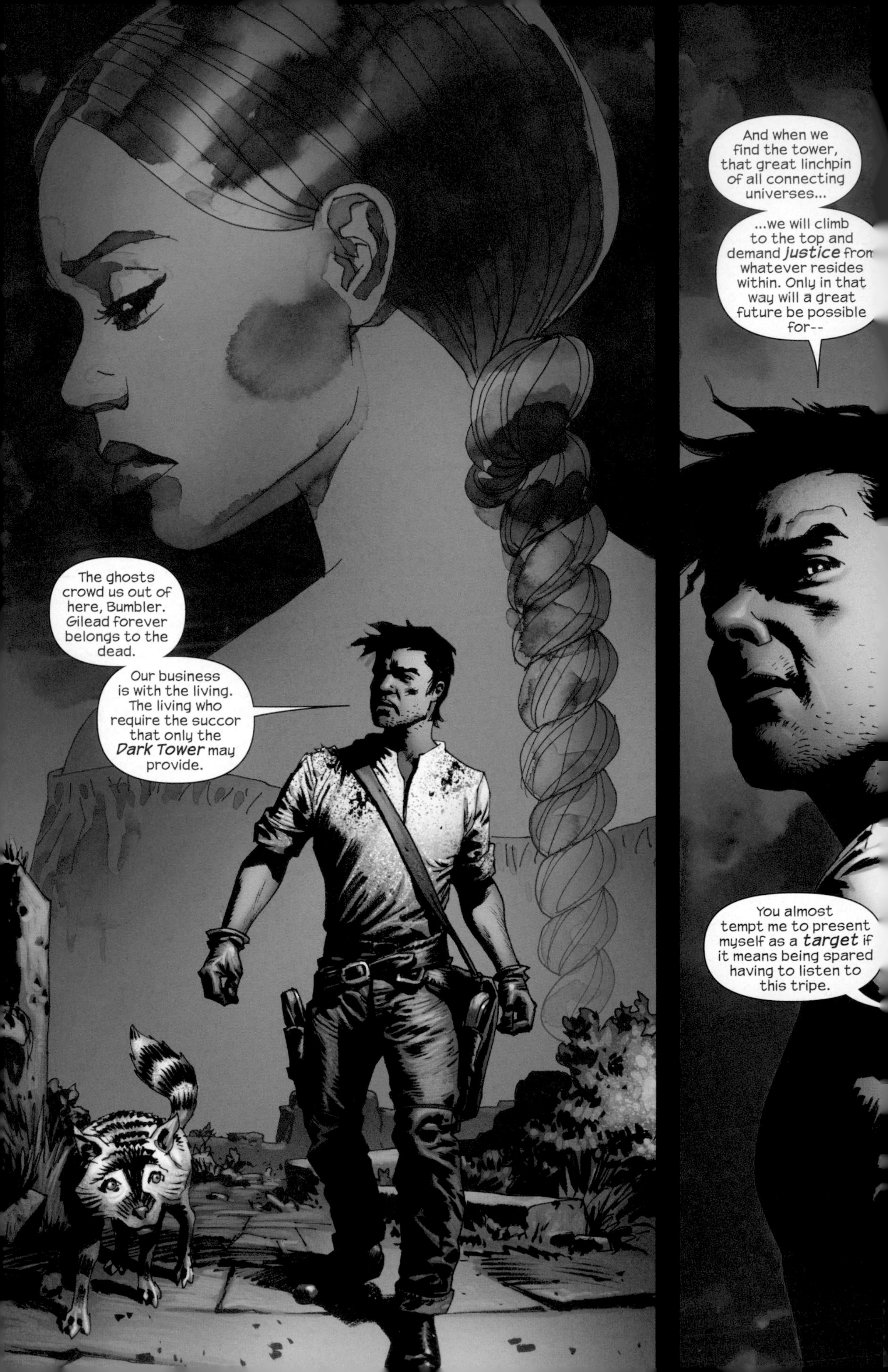

The ghosts crowd us out of here, Bumbler. Gilead forever belongs to the dead.
Our business is with the living. The living who require the succor that only the Dark Tower may provide.
And when we find the tower, that great linchpin of all connecting universes...
...we will climb to the top and demand justice from whatever resides within. Only in that way will a great future be possible for--
You almost tempt me to present myself as a target if it means being spared having to listen to this tripe.

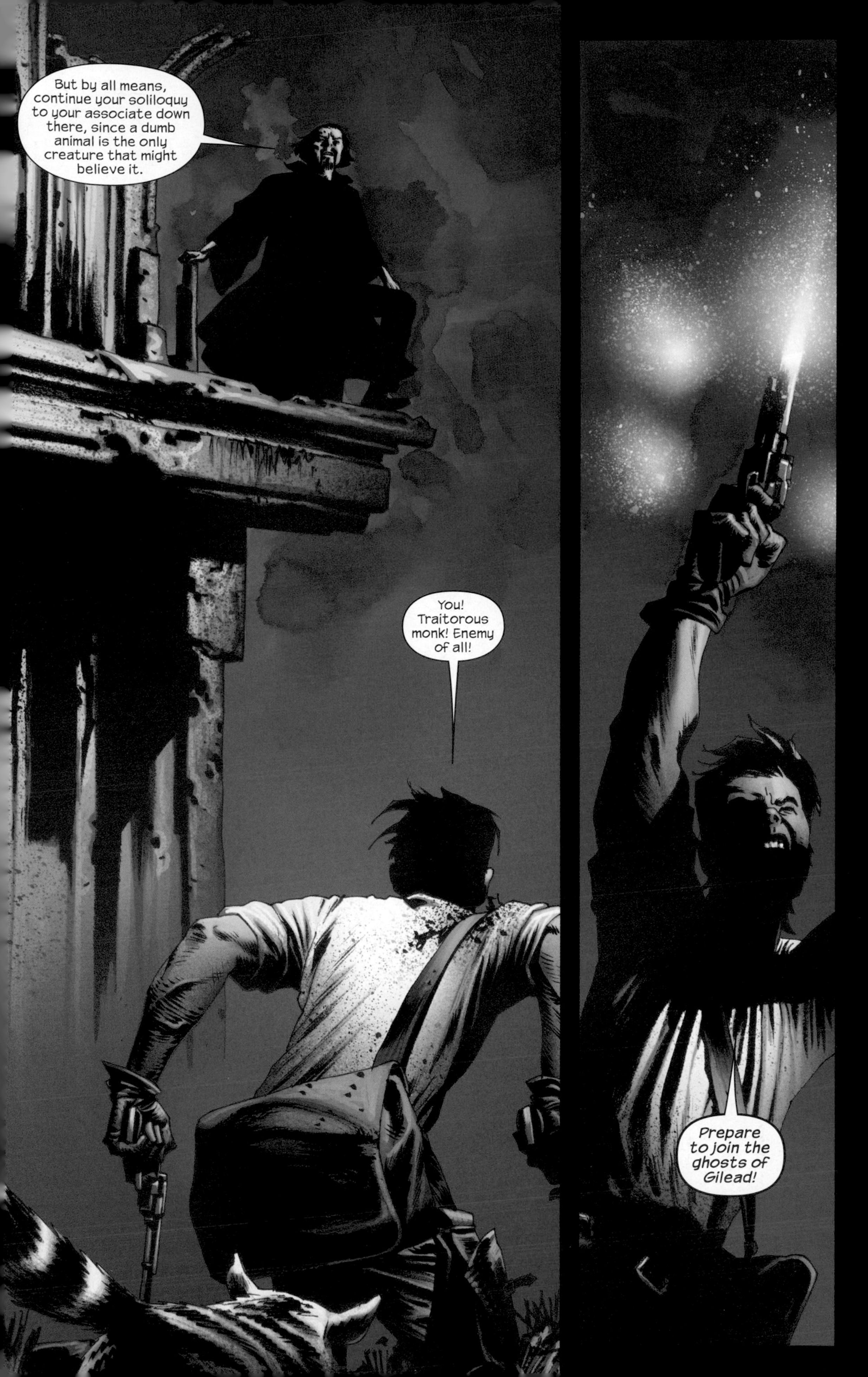
But by all means, continue your soliloquy to your associate down there, since a dumb animal is the only creature that might believe it.
You! Traitorous monk! Enemy of all!
Prepare to join the ghosts of Gilead!

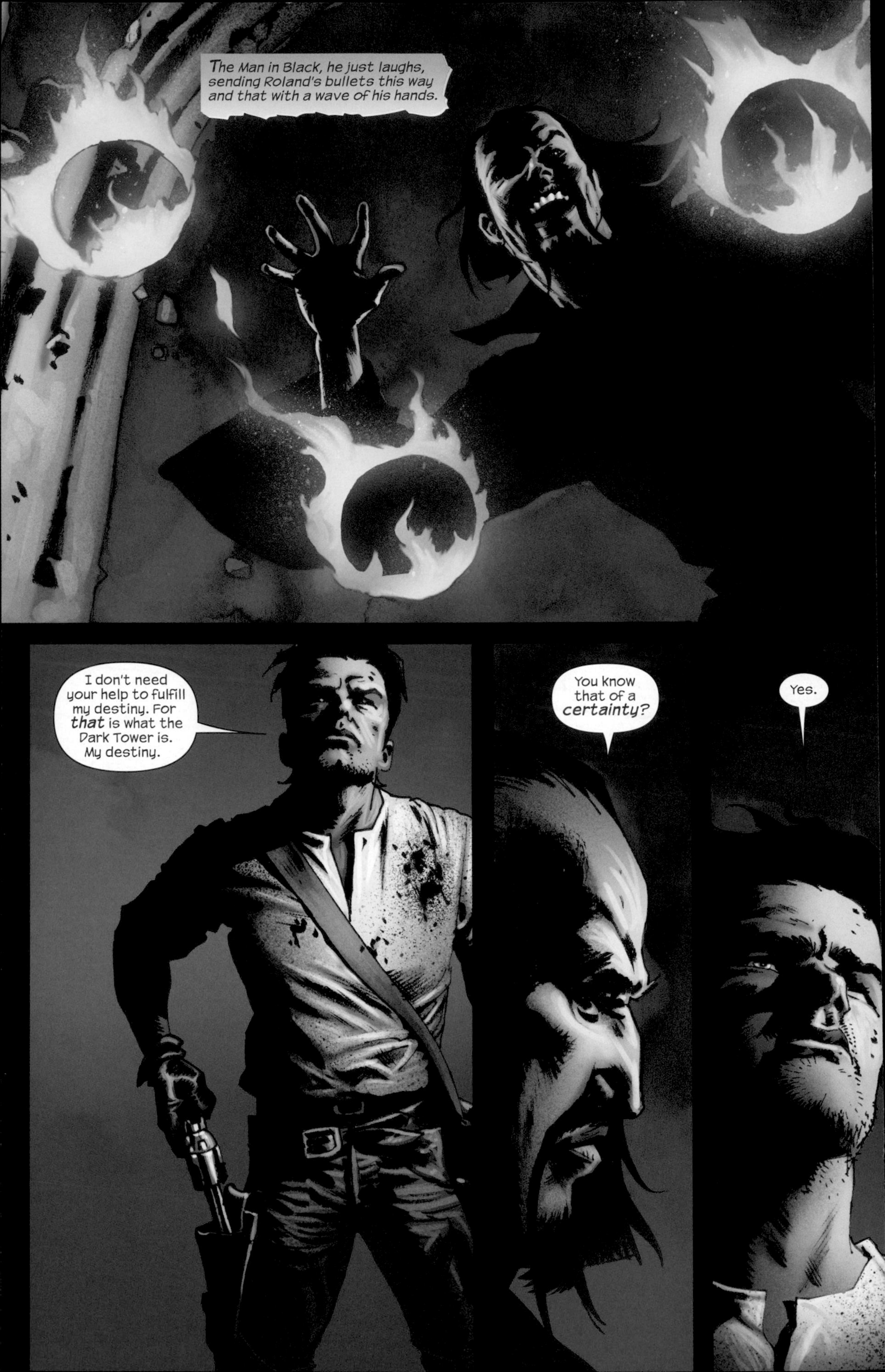
The Man in Black, he just laughs, sending Roland's bullets this way and that with a wave of his hands.
I don't need your help to fulfill my destiny. For *that* is what the Dark Tower is. My destiny.
You know that of a *certainty*?
Yes.

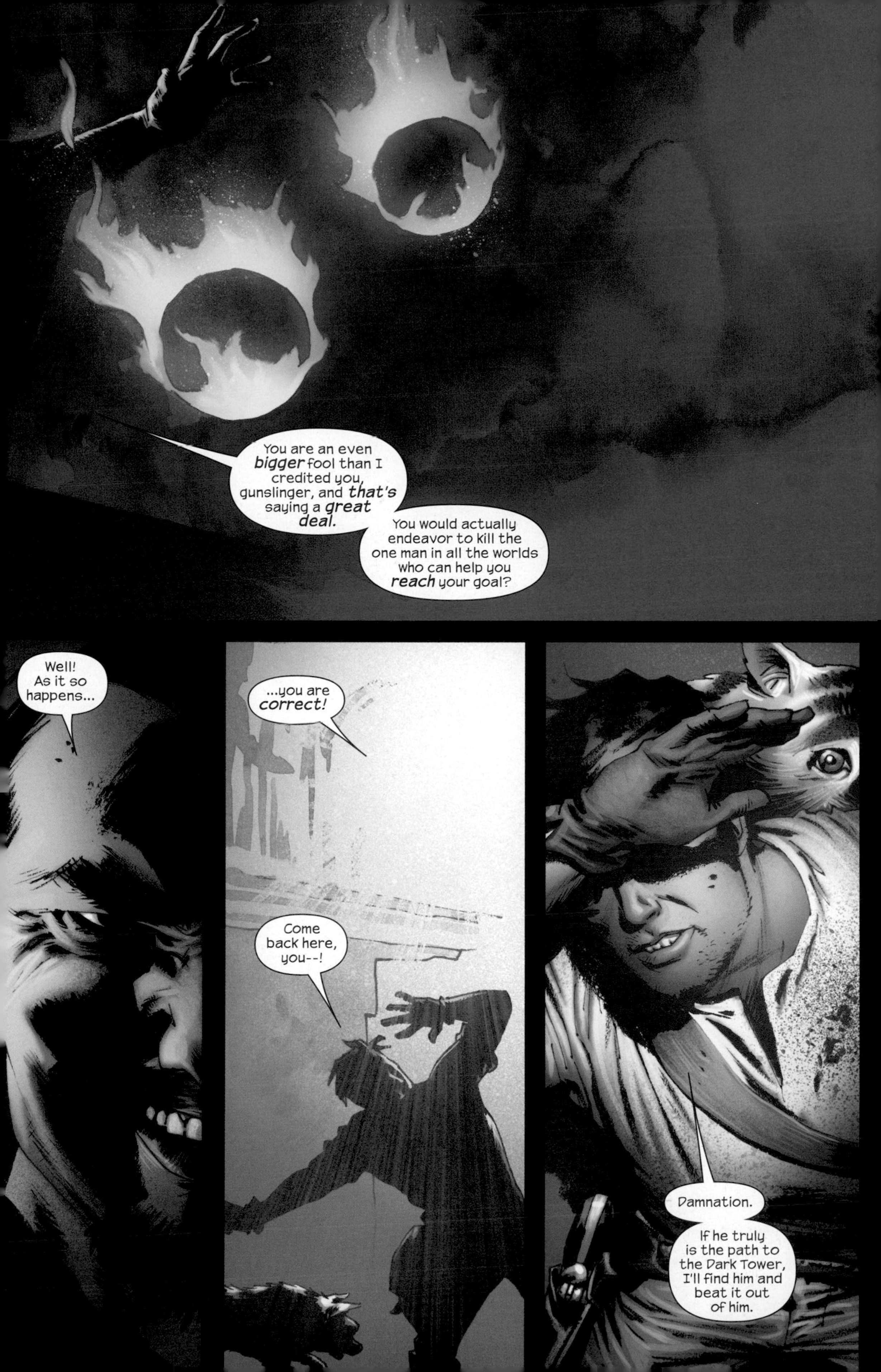
You are an even *bigger* fool than I credited you, gunslinger, and *that's* saying a *great deal.*
You would actually endeavor to kill the one man in all the worlds who can help you *reach* your goal?
Well! As it so happens...
...you are *correct!*
Come back here, you--!
Damnation.
If he truly is the path to the Dark Tower, I'll find him and beat it out of him.

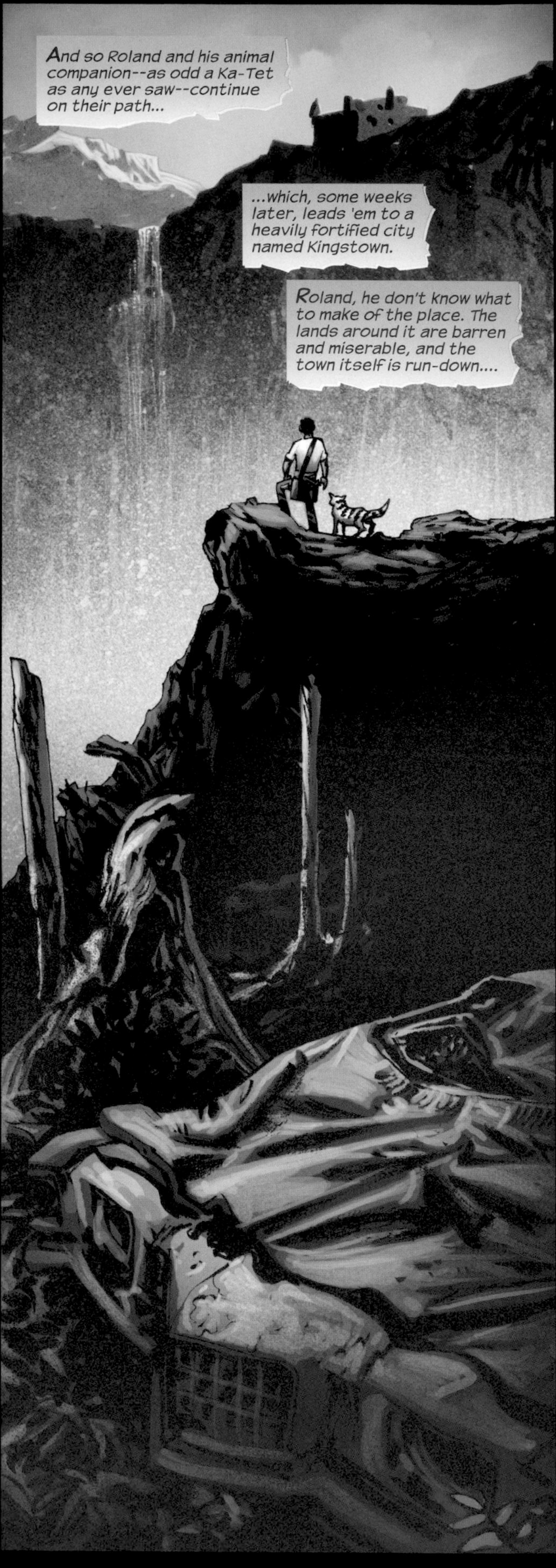
And so Roland and his animal companion--as odd a Ka-Tet as any ever saw--continue on their path...
...which, some weeks later, leads 'em to a heavily fortified city named Kingstown.
Roland, he don't know what to make of the place. The lands around it are barren and miserable, and the town itself is run-down....
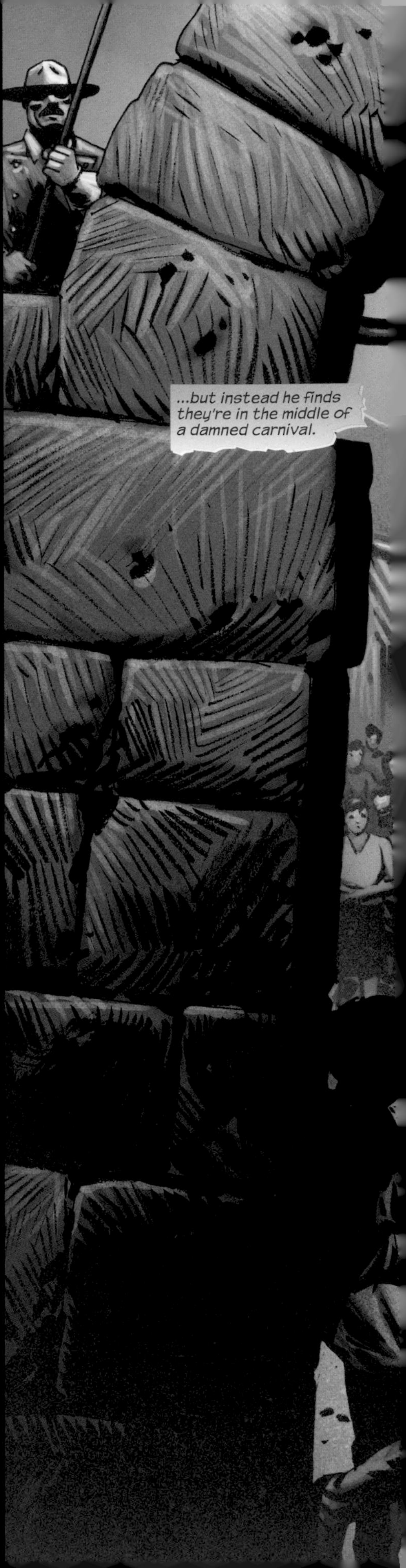
...but instead he finds they're in the middle of a damned carnival.

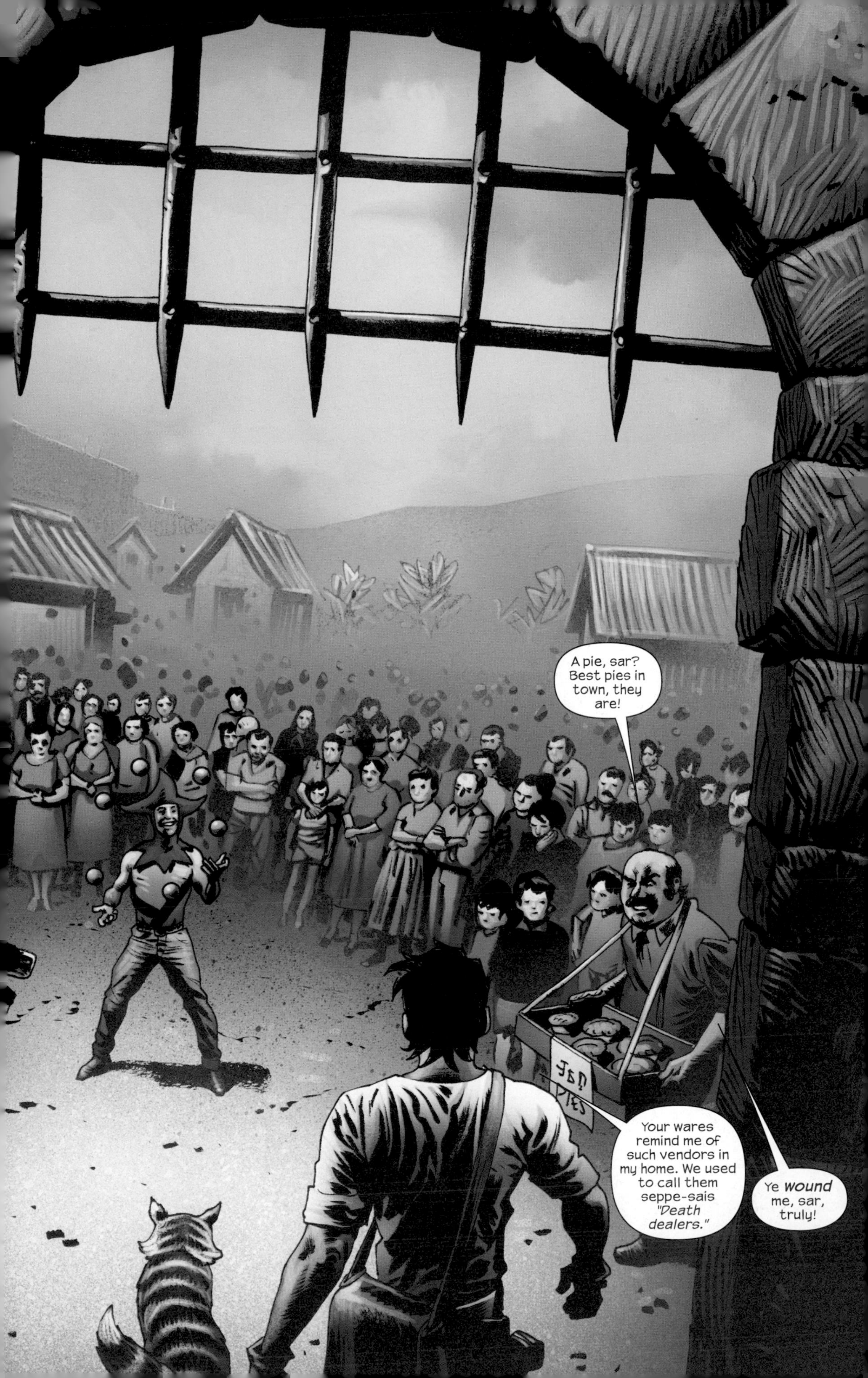
A pie, sar? Best pies in town, they are!
J&D PIES
Your wares remind me of such vendors in my home. We used to call them seppe-sais "Death dealers."
Ye wound me, sar, truly!

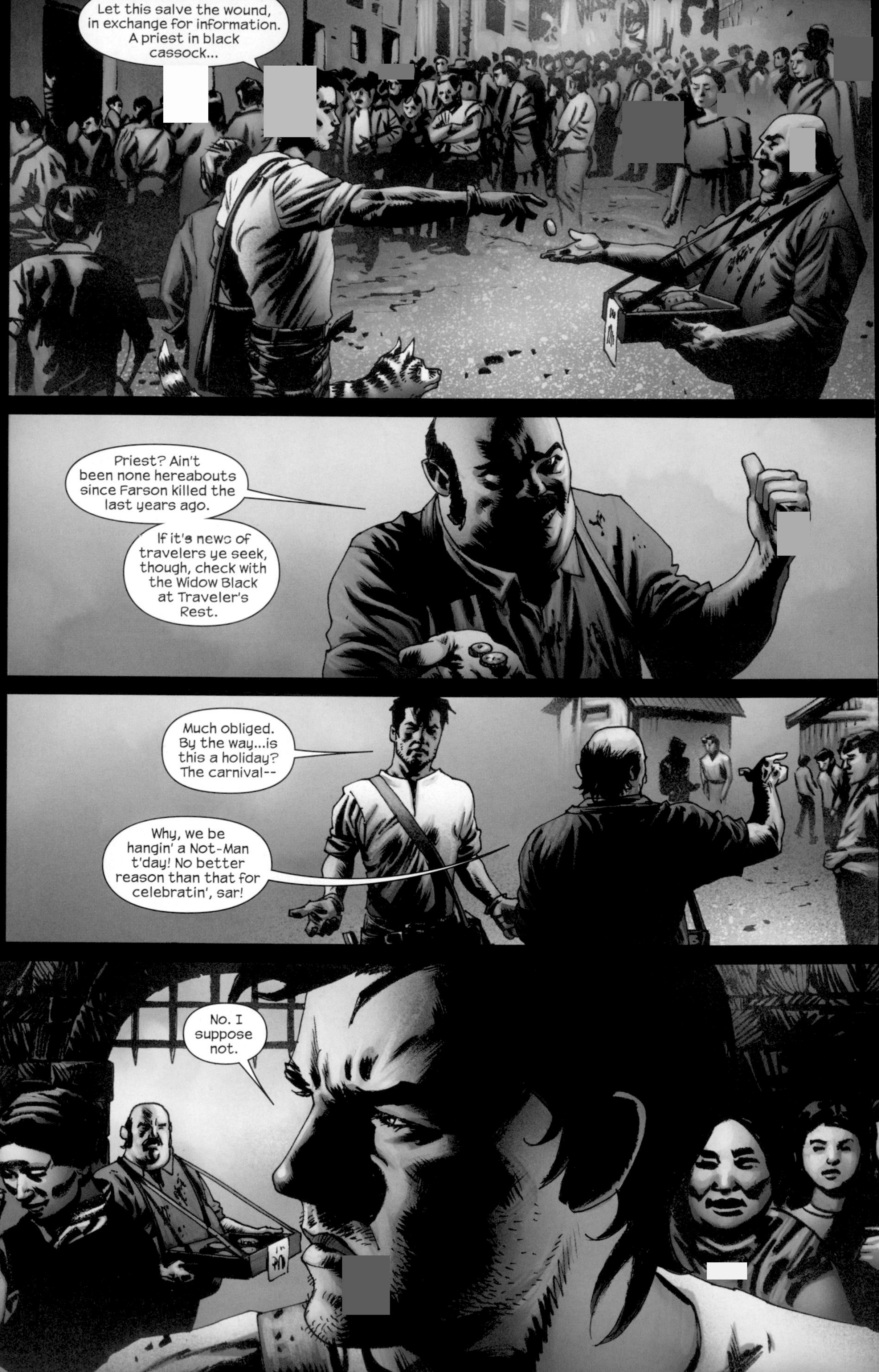
Let this salve the wound, in exchange for information. A priest in black cassock...
Priest? Ain't been none hereabouts since Farson killed the last years ago.
If it's news of travelers ye seek, though, check with the Widow Black at Traveler's Rest.
Much obliged. By the way...is this a holiday? The carnival--
Why, we be hangin' a Not-Man t'day! No better reason than that for celebratin', sar!
No. I suppose not.

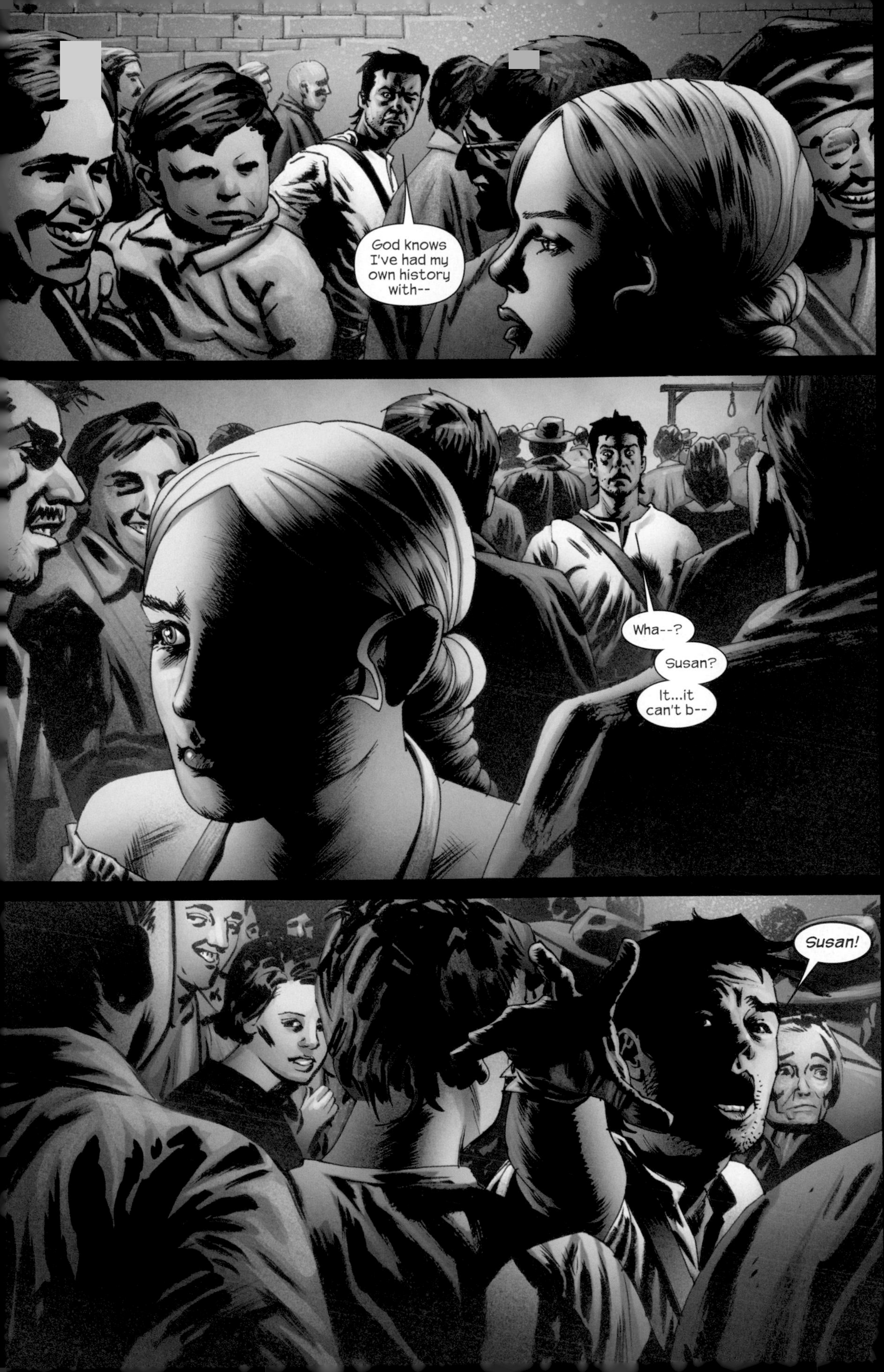
God knows I've had my own history with--
Wha--?
Susan?
It...it can't b--
Susan!

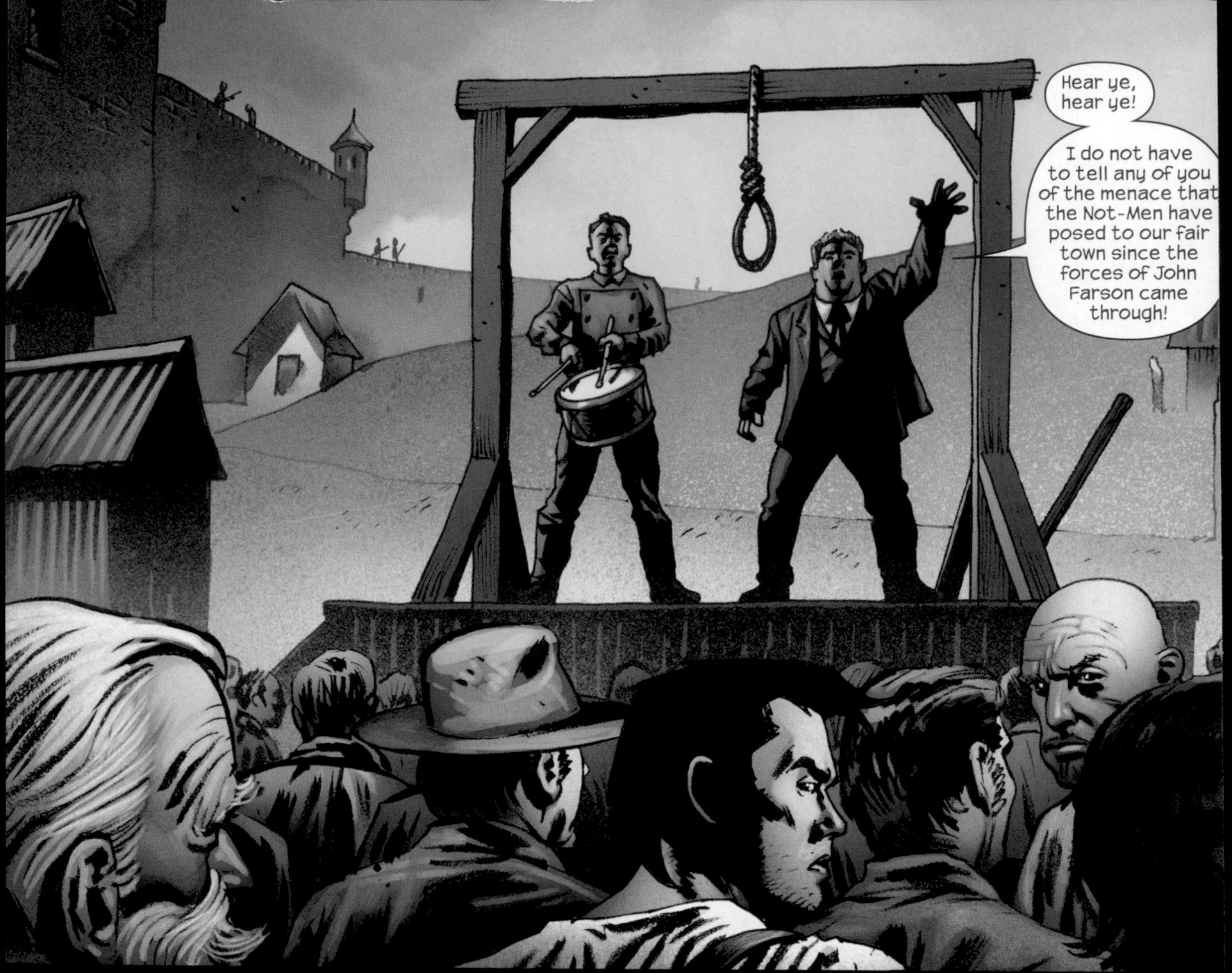
Hear ye, hear ye!
I do not have to tell any of you of the menace that the Not-Men have posed to our fair town since the forces of John Farson came through!

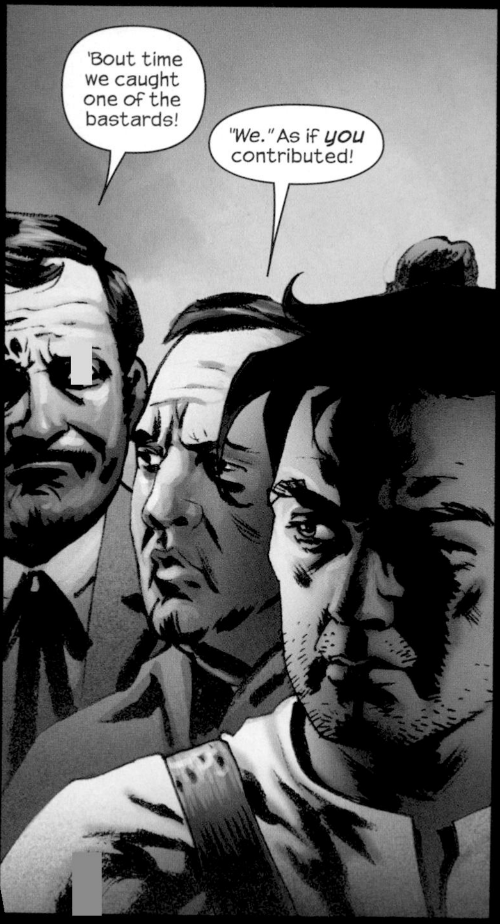
'Bout time we caught one of the bastards!
"We." As if *you* contributed!

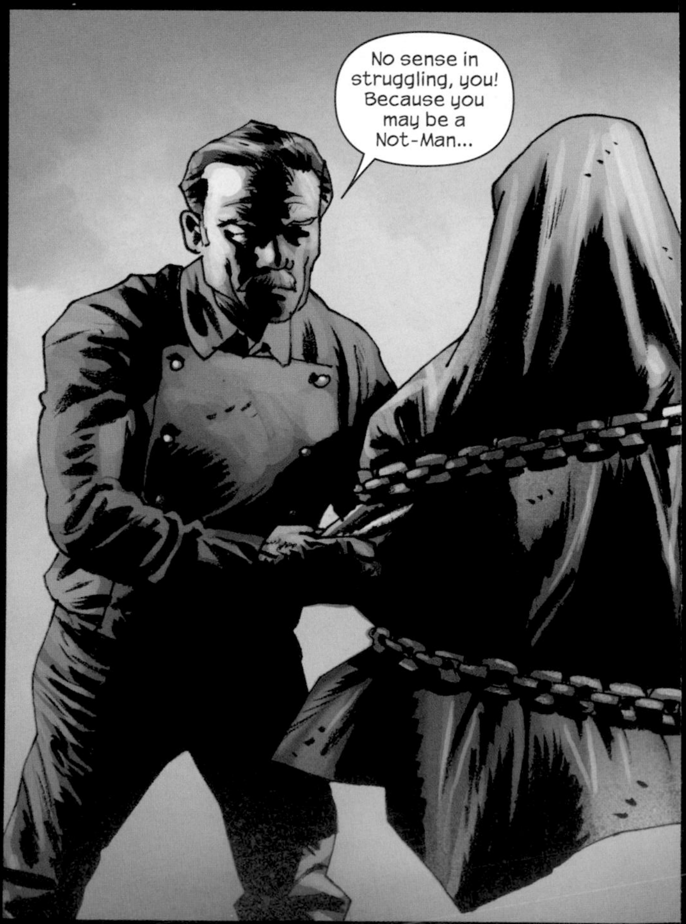
No sense in struggling, you! Because you may be a Not-Man...

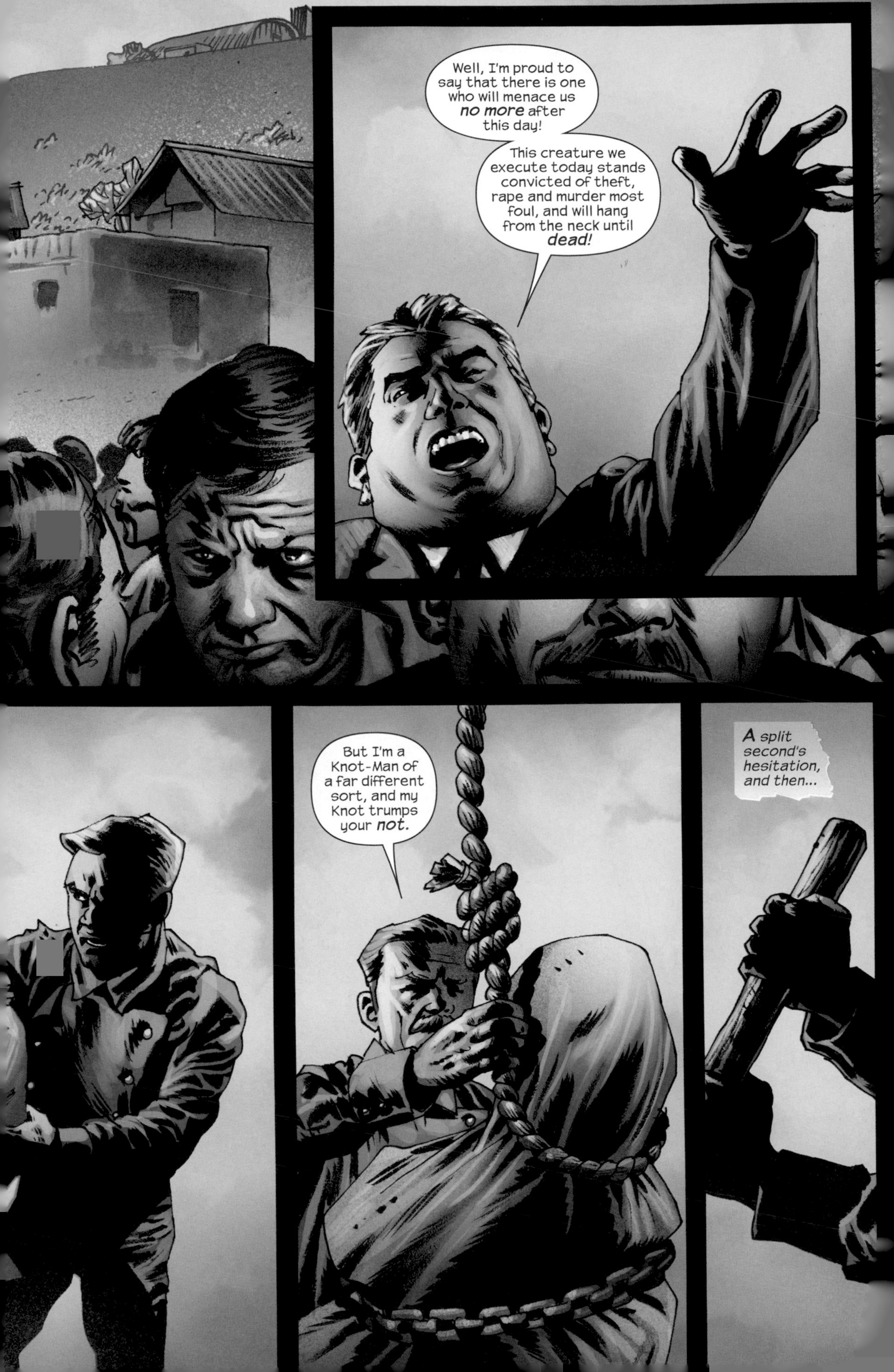
Well, I'm proud to say that there is one who will menace us *no more* after this day!
This creature we execute today stands convicted of theft, rape and murder most foul, and will hang from the neck until *dead!*
But I'm a Knot-Man of a far different sort, and my Knot trumps your *not.*
A split second's hesitation, and then...

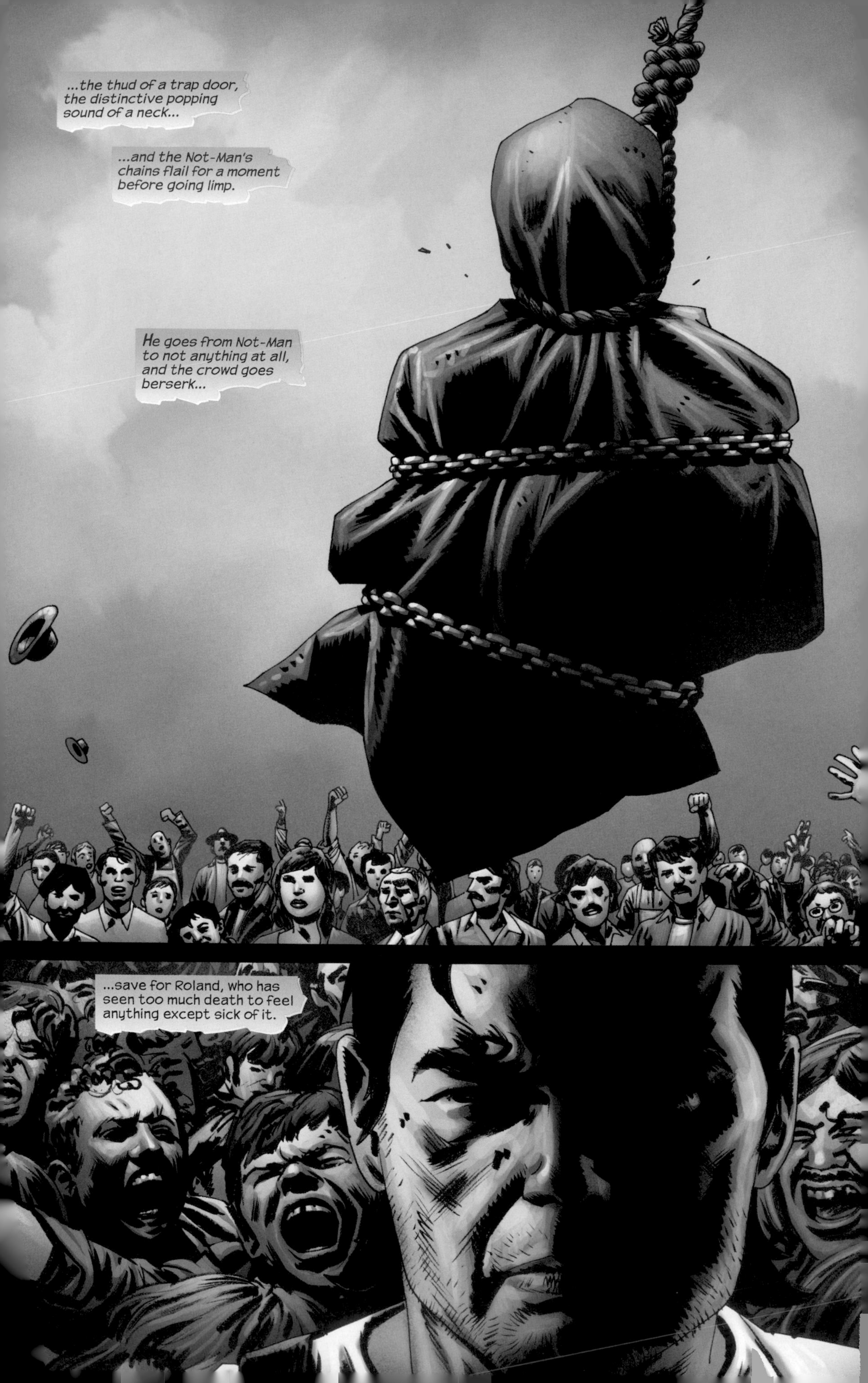
...the thud of a trap door, the distinctive popping sound of a neck...
...and the Not-Man's chains flail for a moment before going limp.
He goes from Not-Man to not anything at all, and the crowd goes berserk...
...save for Roland, who has seen too much death to feel anything except sick of it.

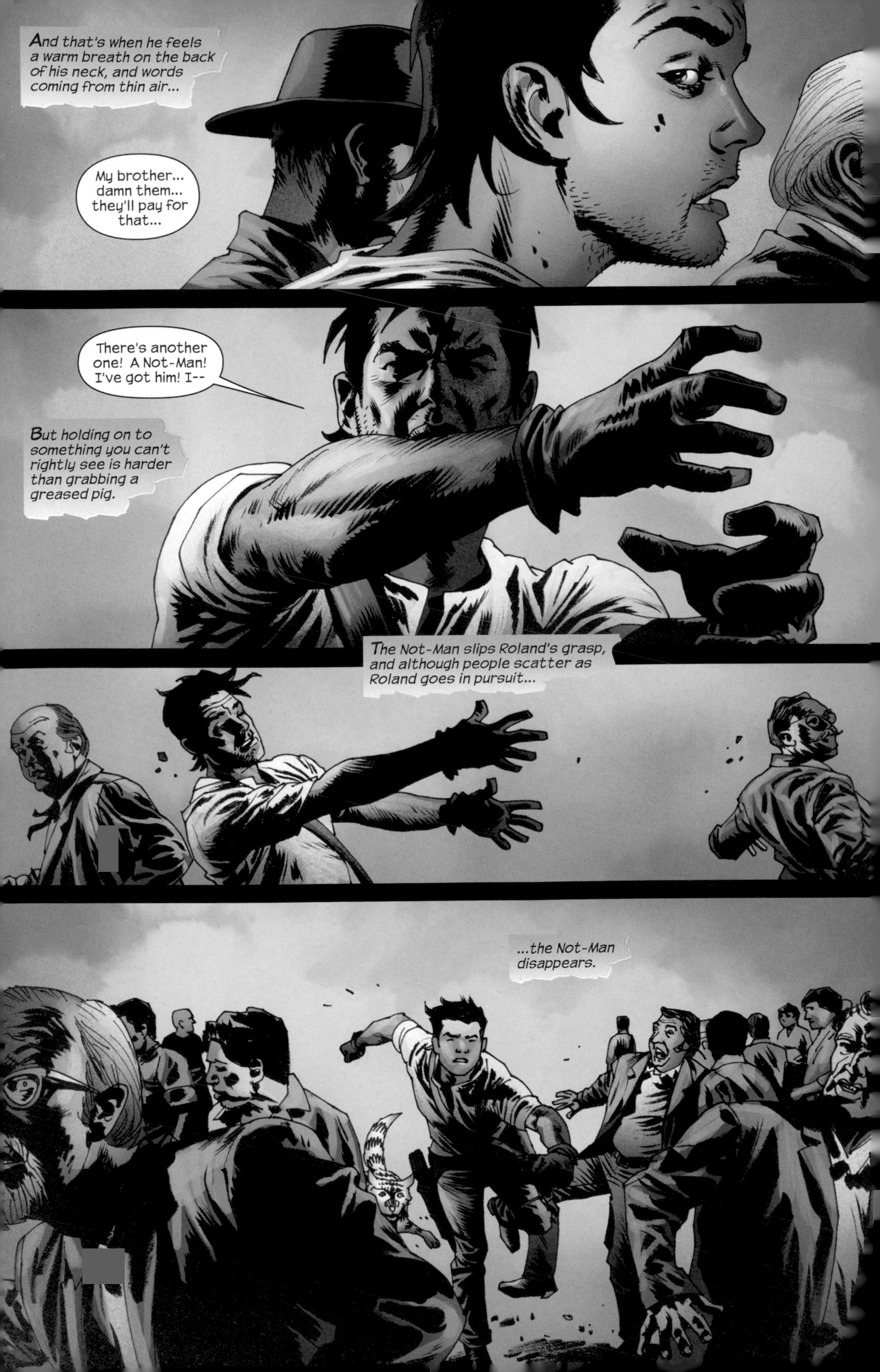
And that's when he feels a warm breath on the back of his neck, and words coming from thin air...
My brother... damn them... they'll pay for that...
There's another one! A Not-Man! I've got him! I--
But holding on to something you can't rightly see is harder than grabbing a greased pig.
The Not-Man slips Roland's grasp, and although people scatter as Roland goes in pursuit...
...the Not-Man disappears.

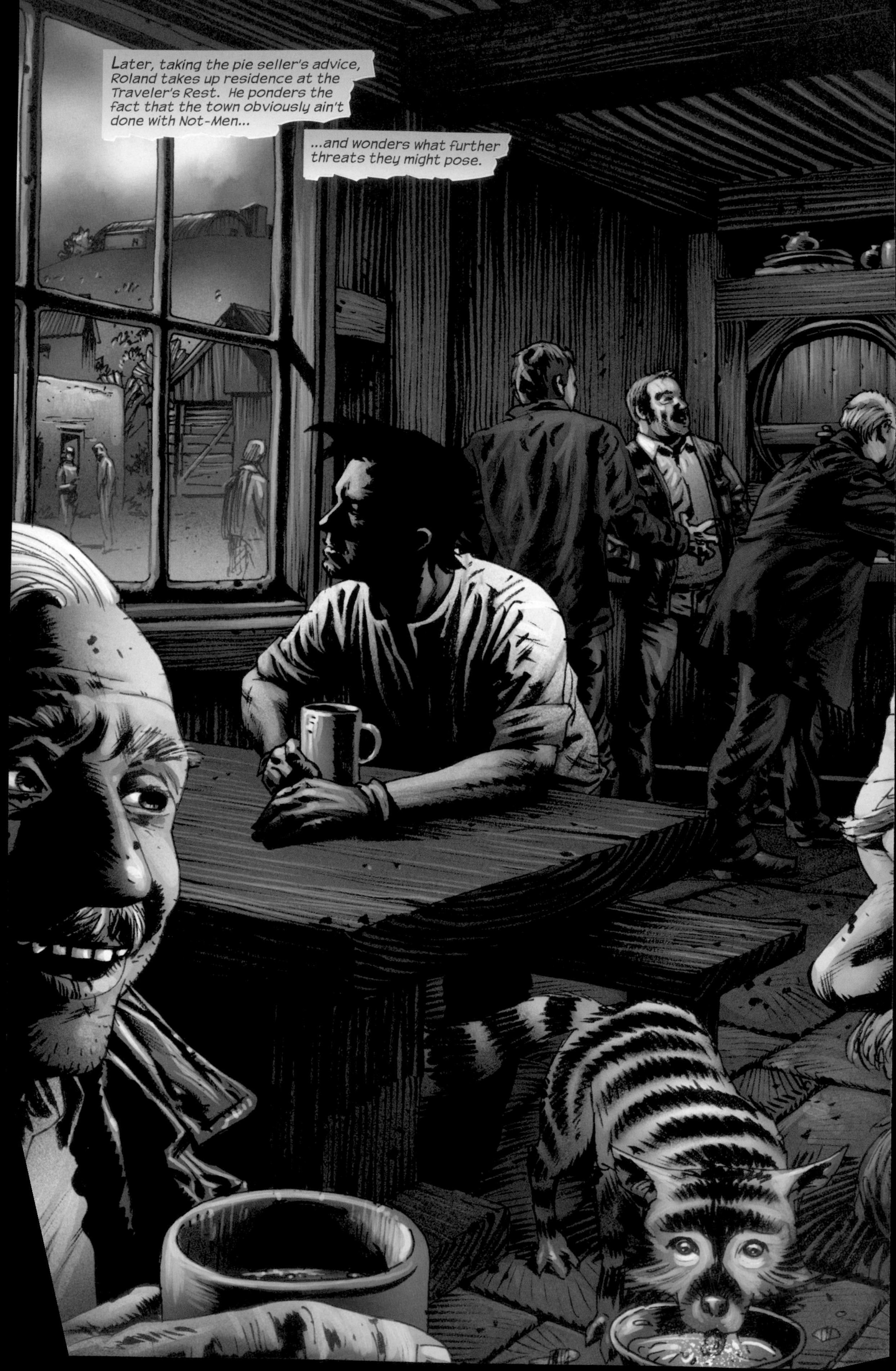
Later, taking the pie seller's advice, Roland takes up residence at the Traveler's Rest. He ponders the fact that the town obviously ain't done with Not-Men...
...and wonders what further threats they might pose.

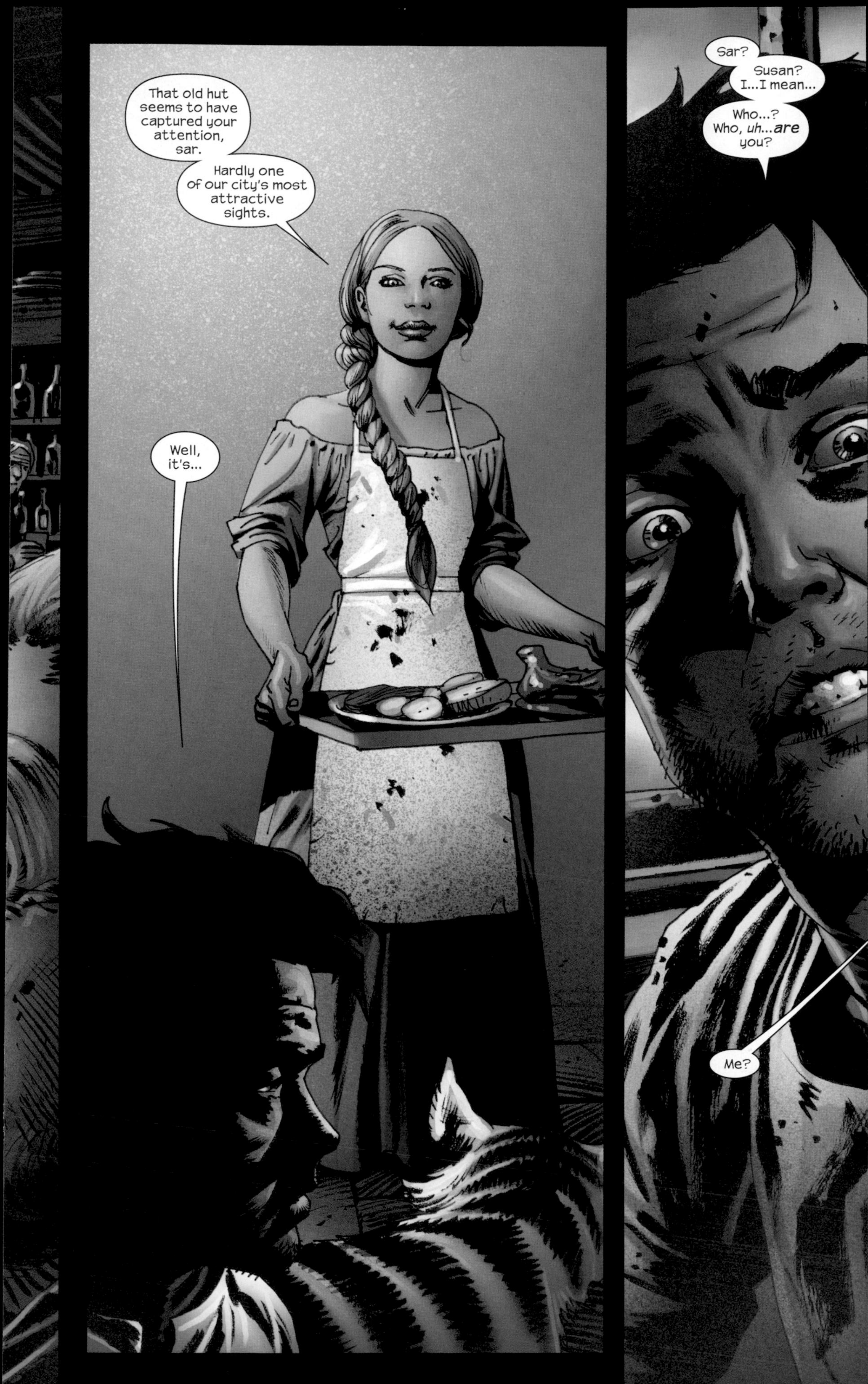
That old hut seems to have captured your attention, sar.
Hardly one of our city's most attractive sights.
Well, it's...
Sar?
Susan? I...I mean...
Who...? Who, *uh*...**are** you?
Me?

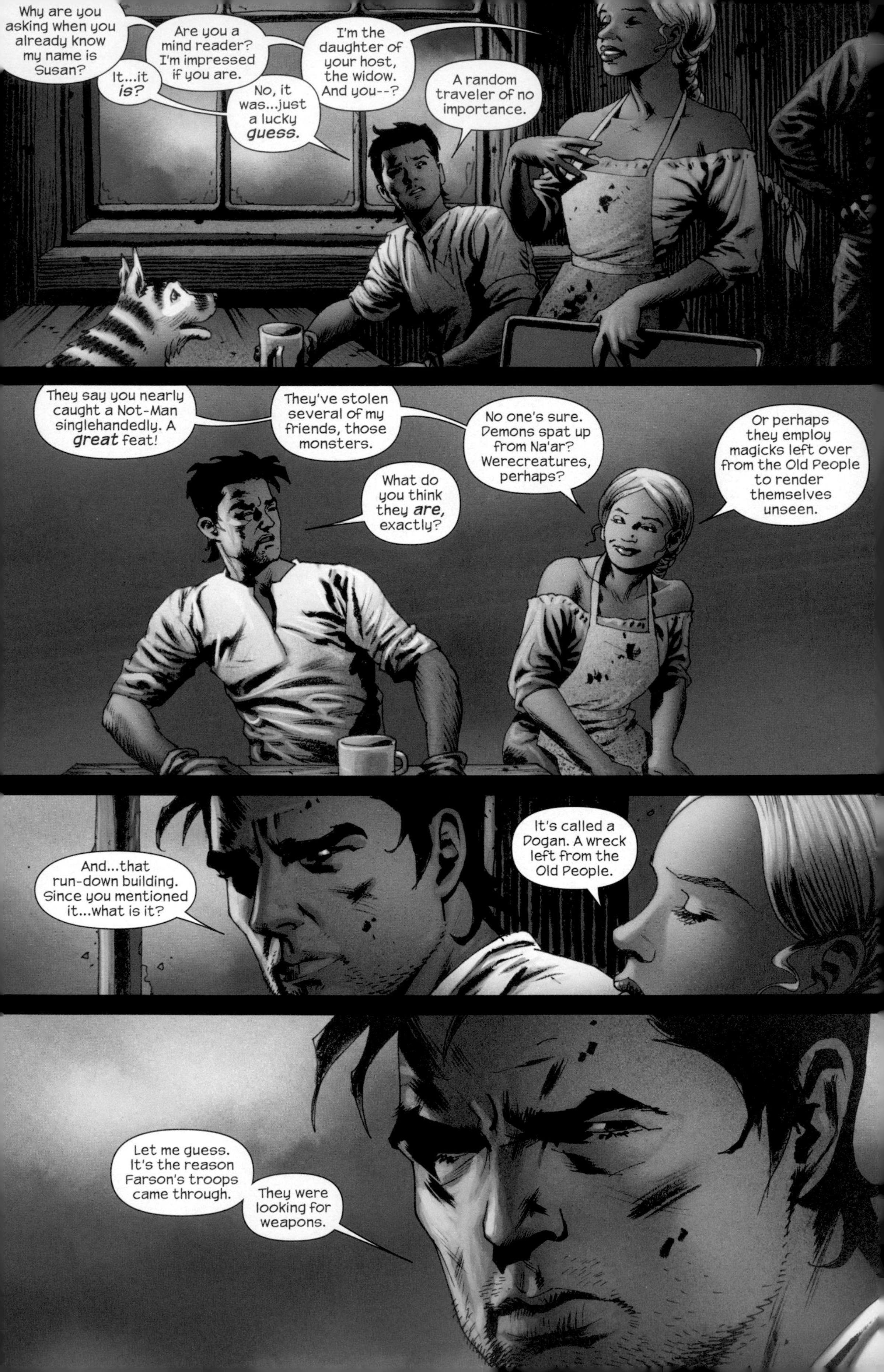

Why are you asking when you already know my name is Susan?
Are you a mind reader? I'm impressed if you are.
It...it *is?*
No, it was...just a lucky *guess.*
I'm the daughter of your host, the widow. And you--?
A random traveler of no importance.
They say you nearly caught a Not-Man singlehandedly. A *great* feat!
They've stolen several of my friends, those monsters.
What do you think they *are,* exactly?
No one's sure. Demons spat up from Na'ar? Werecreatures, perhaps?
Or perhaps they employ magicks left over from the Old People to render themselves unseen.
And...that run-down building. Since you mentioned it...what is it?
It's called a Dogan. A wreck left from the Old People.
Let me guess. It's the reason Farson's troops came through.
They were looking for weapons.

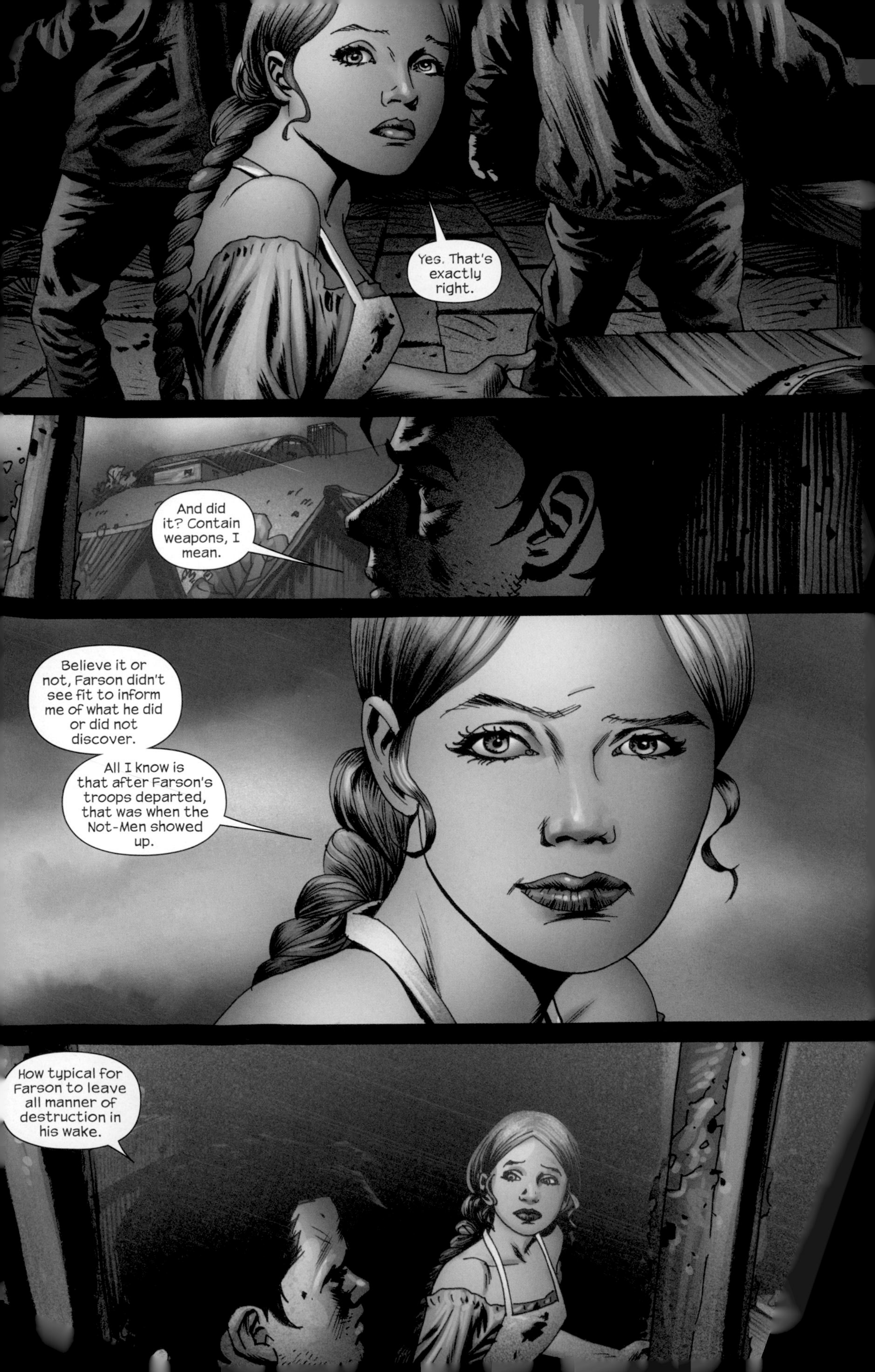
Yes. That's exactly right.
And did it? Contain weapons, I mean.
Believe it or not, Farson didn't see fit to inform me of what he did or did not discover.
All I know is that after Farson's troops departed, that was when the Not-Men showed up.
How typical for Farson to leave all manner of destruction in his wake.

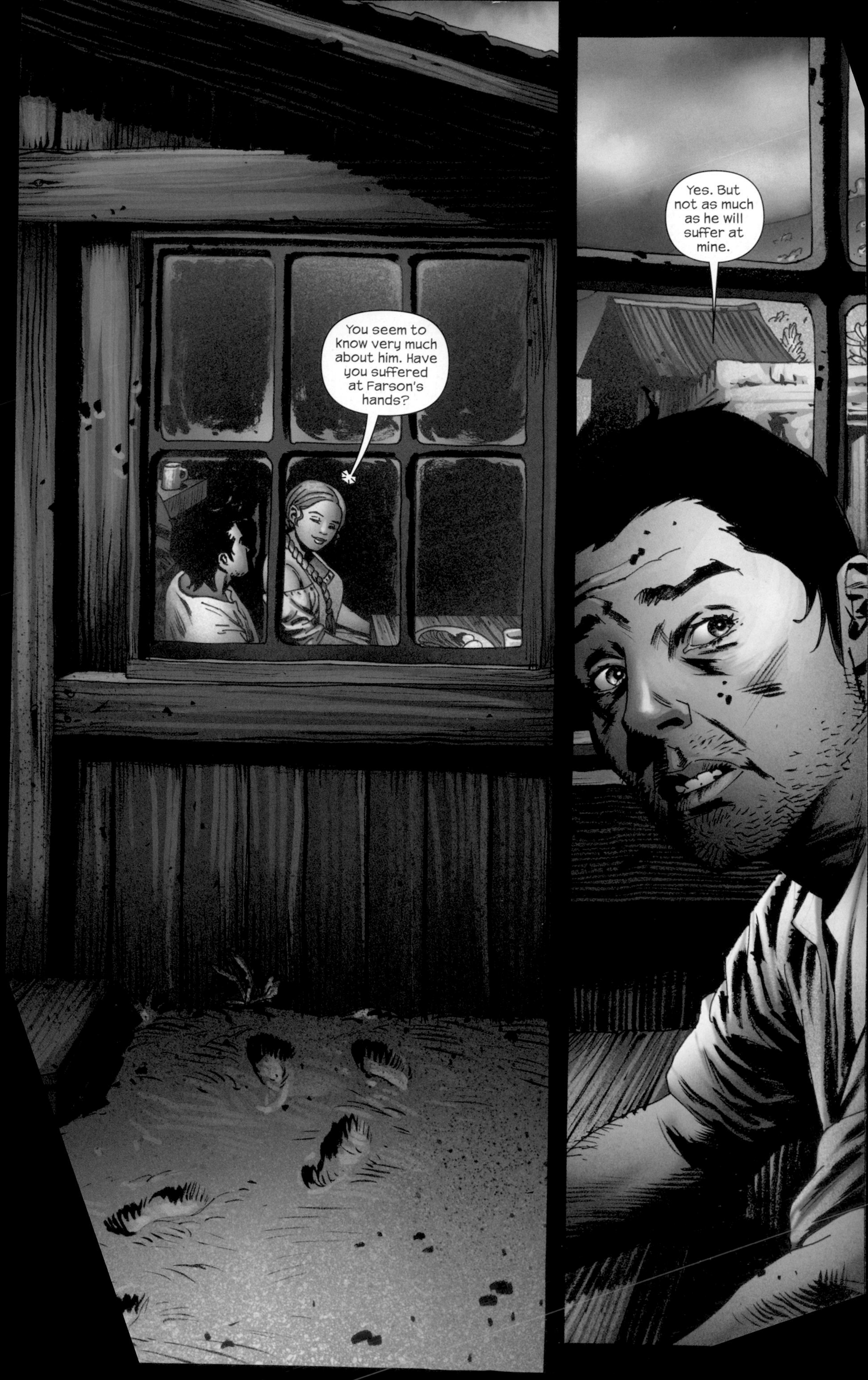
You seem to know very much about him. Have you suffered at Farson's hands?
Yes. But not as much as he will suffer at mine.

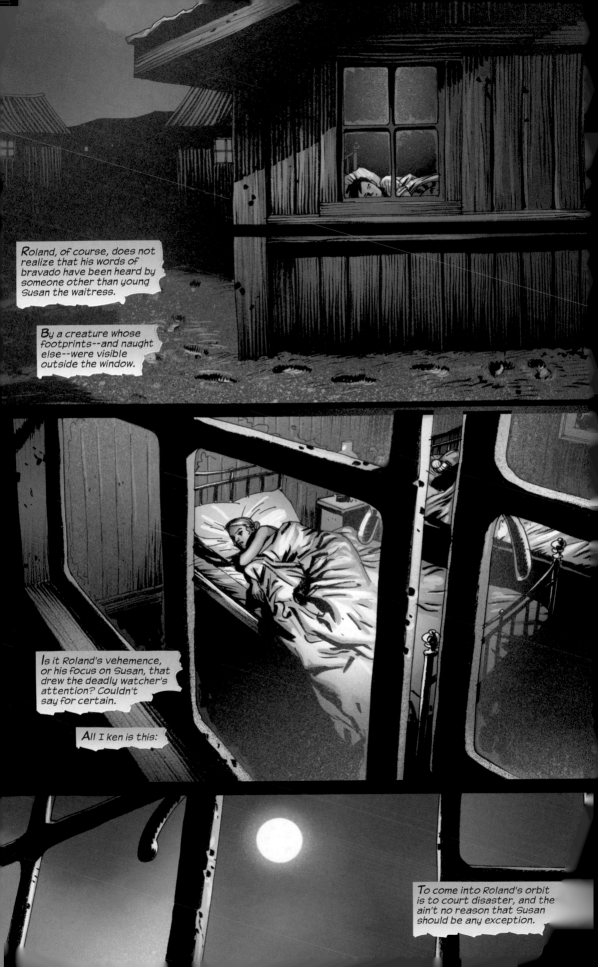

Roland, of course, does not realize that his words of bravado have been heard by someone other than young Susan the waitress.

By a creature whose footprints--and naught else--were visible outside the window.

Is it Roland's vehemence, or his focus on Susan, that drew the deadly watcher's attention? Couldn't say for certain.

All I ken is this:

To come into Roland's orbit is to court disaster, and the ain't no reason that Susan should be any exception.

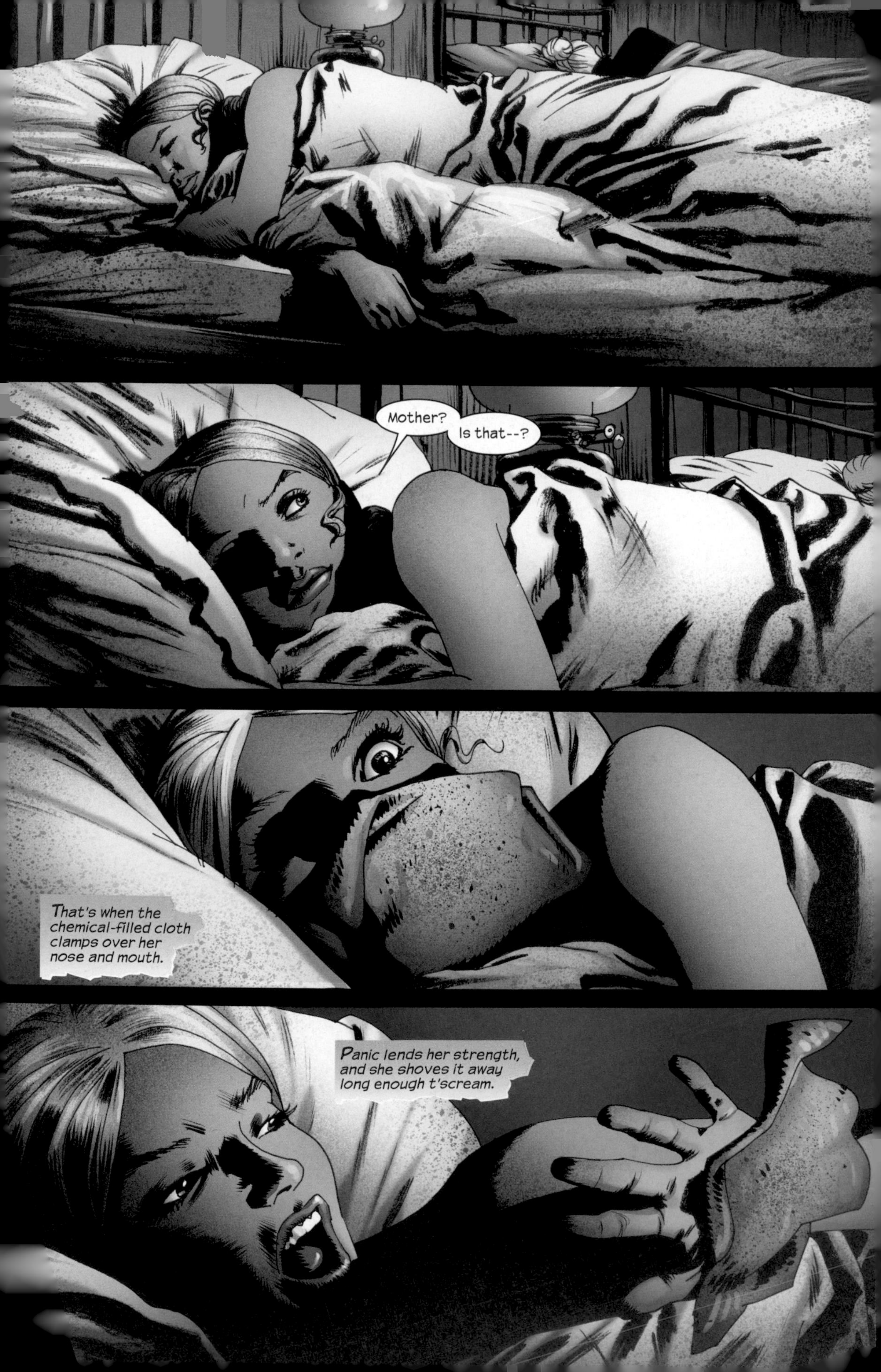

Mother?
Is that--?
That's when the chemical-filled cloth clamps over her nose and mouth.
Panic lends her strength, and she shoves it away long enough t'scream.

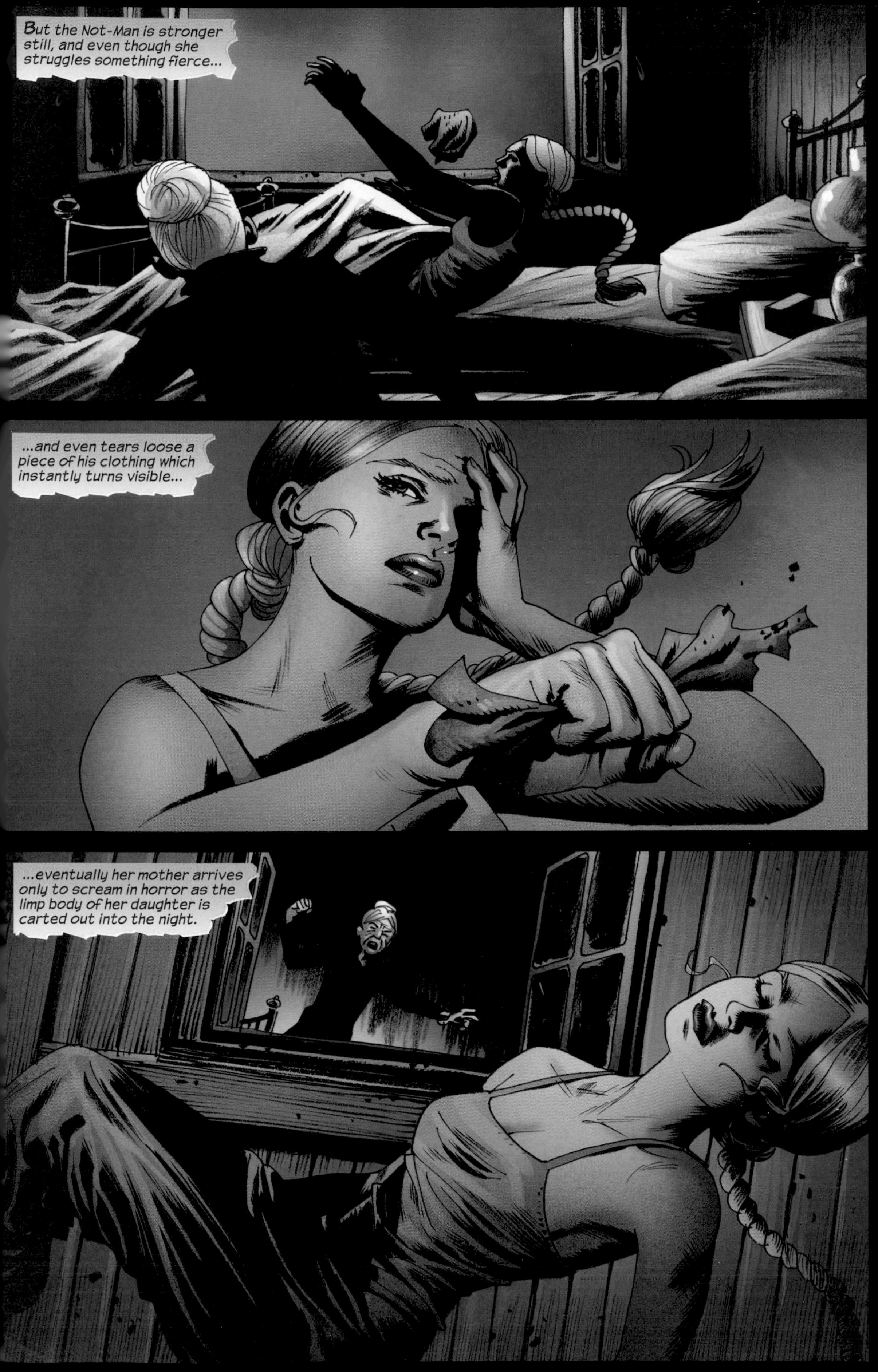

But the Not-Man is stronger still, and even though she struggles something fierce...
...and even tears loose a piece of his clothing which instantly turns visible...
...eventually her mother arrives only to scream in horror as the limp body of her daughter is carted out into the night.

STEPHEN KING

THE DARK TOWER
~ THE GUNSLINGER ~

THE JOURNEY BEGINS
CHAPTER FIVE

Truth to tell, the Widow Black is a dyspeptic creature with scarcely a kind word for anyone.

But even she don't deserve to have her daughter yanked away by invisible monsters called Not-Men.

Straight as a bullet, the Billy Bumbler leads him to the Dogan on the Hill.

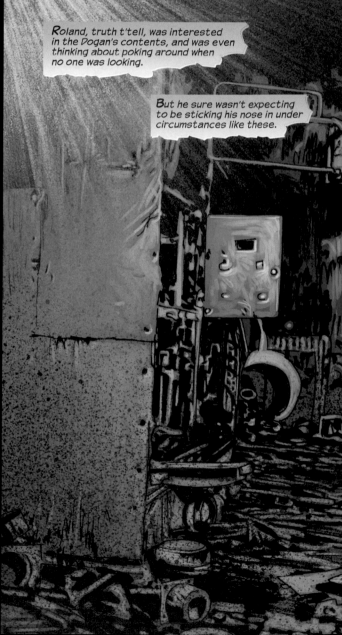

Roland, truth t'tell, was interested in the Dogan's contents, and was even thinking about poking around when no one was looking.

But he sure wasn't expecting to be sticking his nose in under circumstances like these.

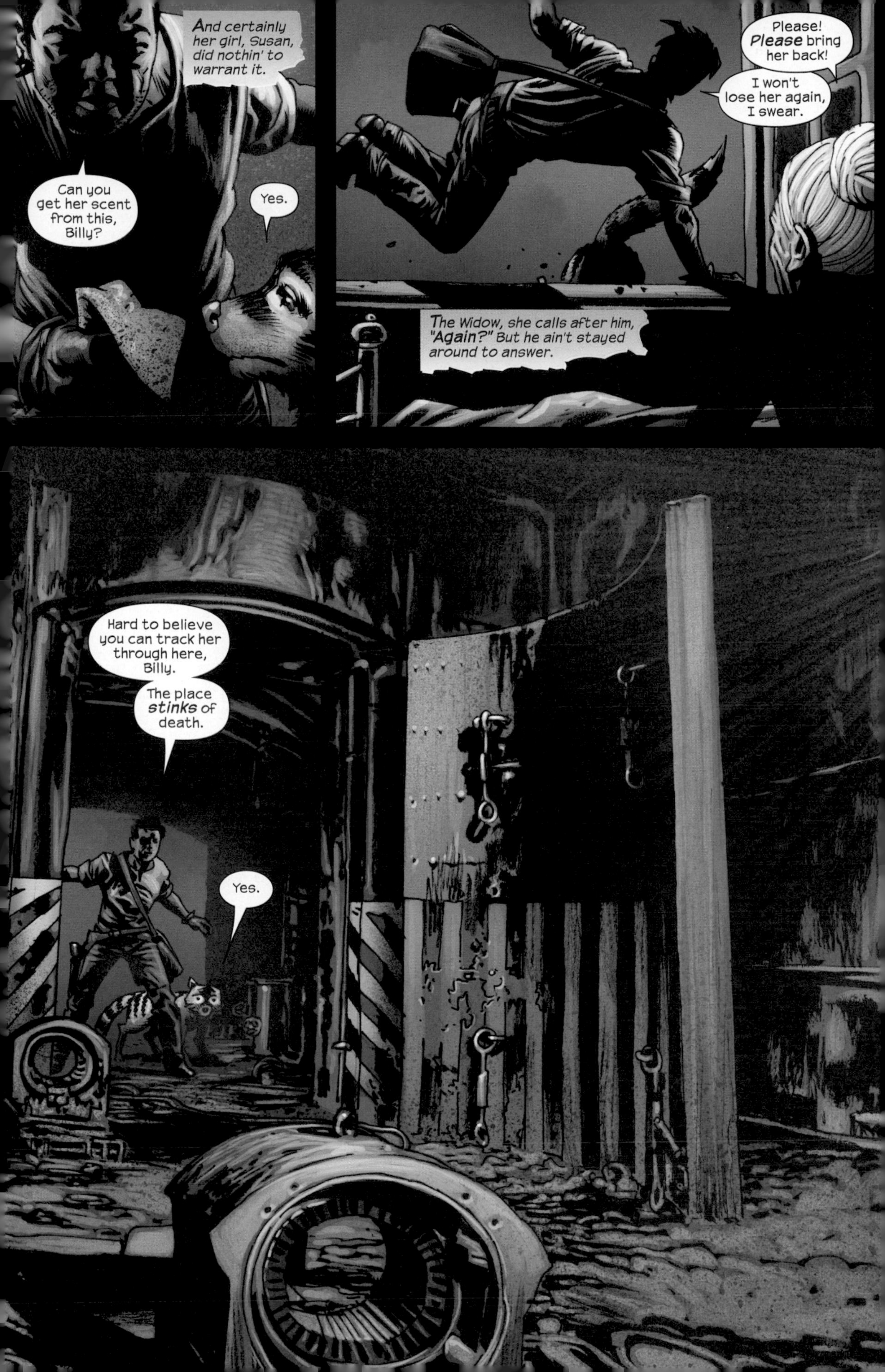
And certainly her girl, Susan, did nothin' to warrant it.
Can you get her scent from this, Billy?
Yes.
Please! *Please* bring her back!
I won't lose her again, I swear.
The Widow, she calls after him, "Again?" But he ain't stayed around to answer.
Hard to believe you can track her through here, Billy.
The place *stinks* of death.
Yes.

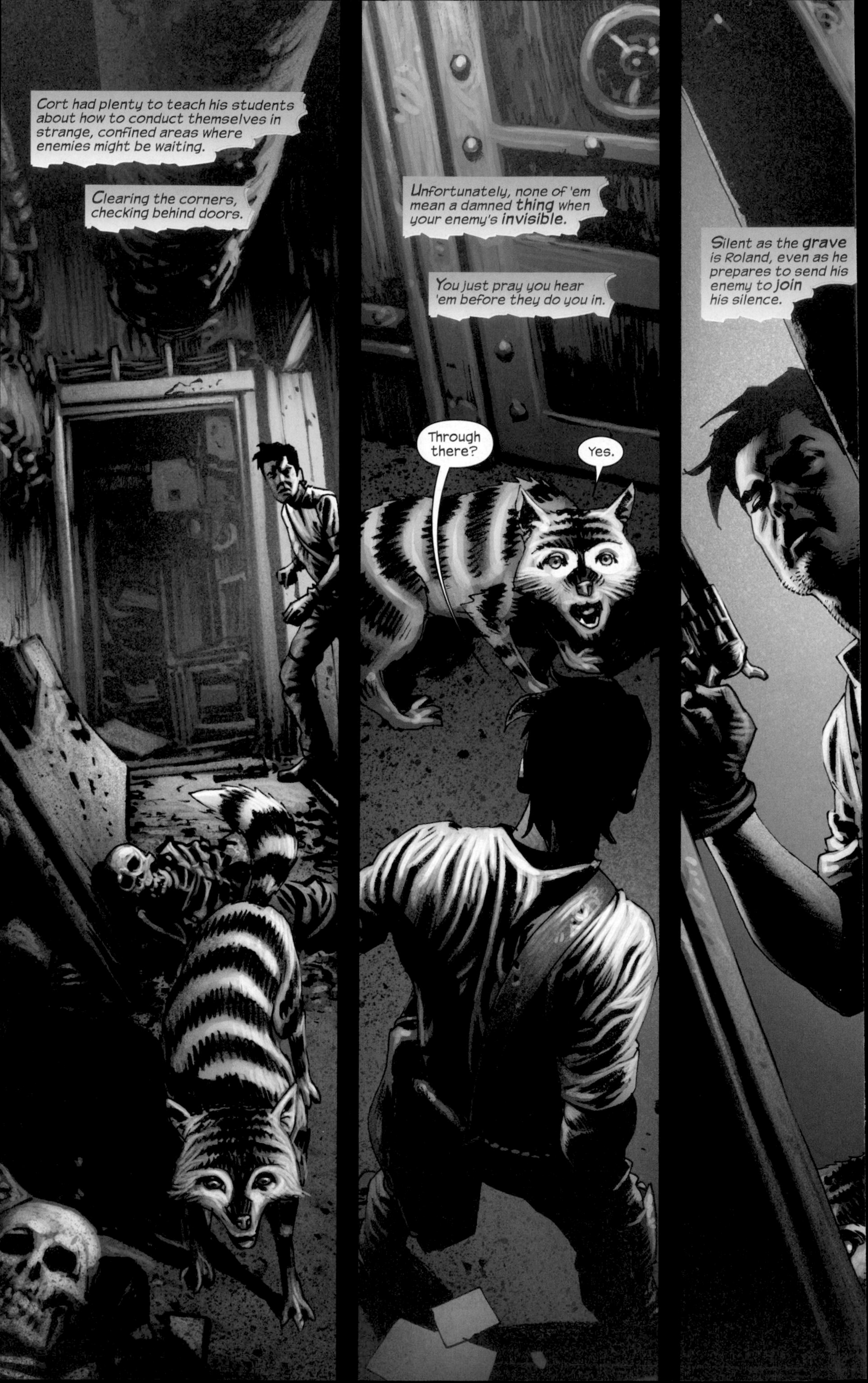
Cort had plenty to teach his students about how to conduct themselves in strange, confined areas where enemies might be waiting.
Clearing the corners, checking behind doors.
Unfortunately, none of 'em mean a damned thing when your enemy's invisible.
You just pray you hear 'em before they do you in.
Through there?
Yes.
Silent as the grave is Roland, even as he prepares to send his enemy to join his silence.

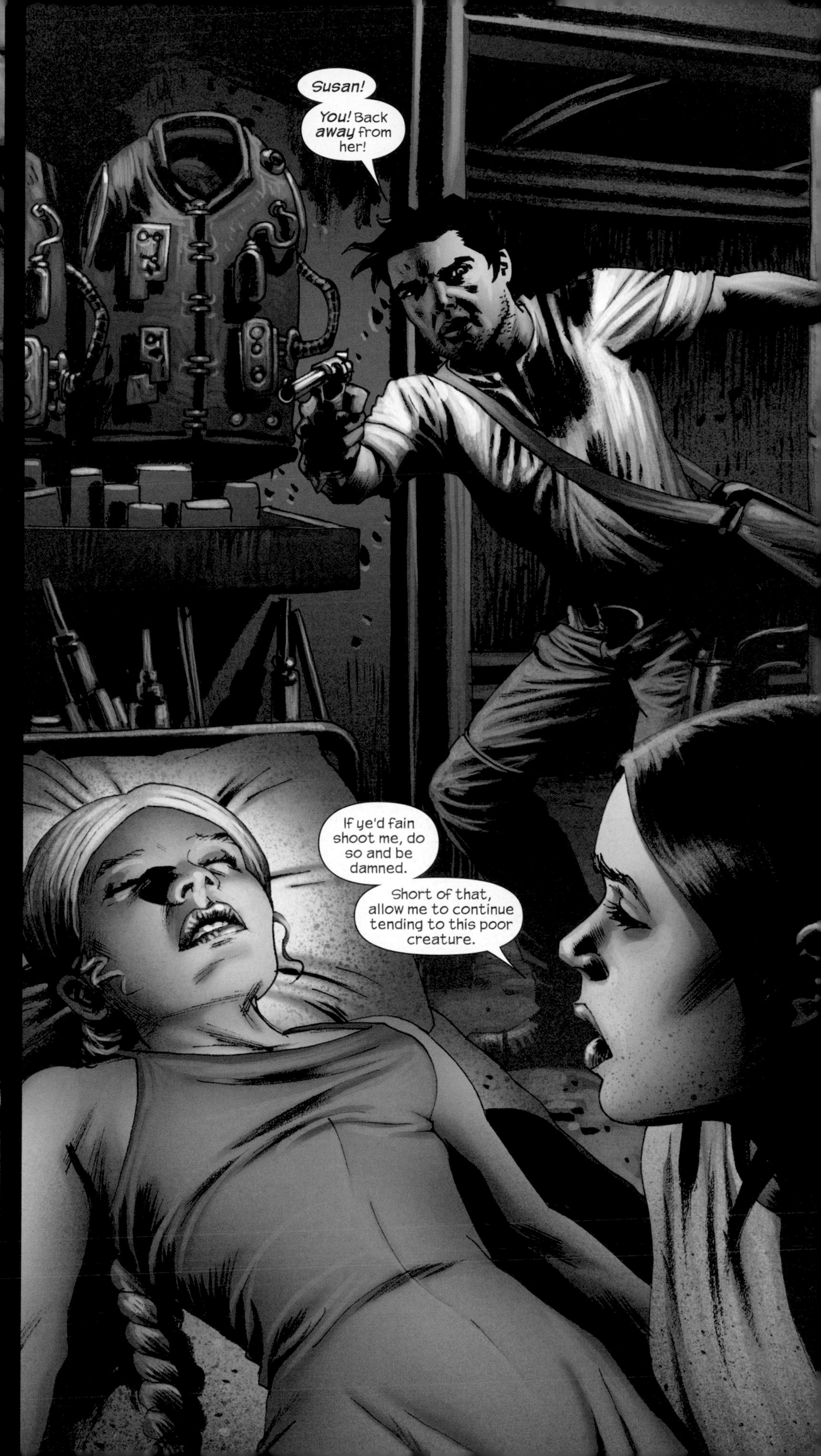
Susan!
You! Back away from her!
If ye'd fain shoot me, do so and be damned.
Short of that, allow me to continue tending to this poor creature.

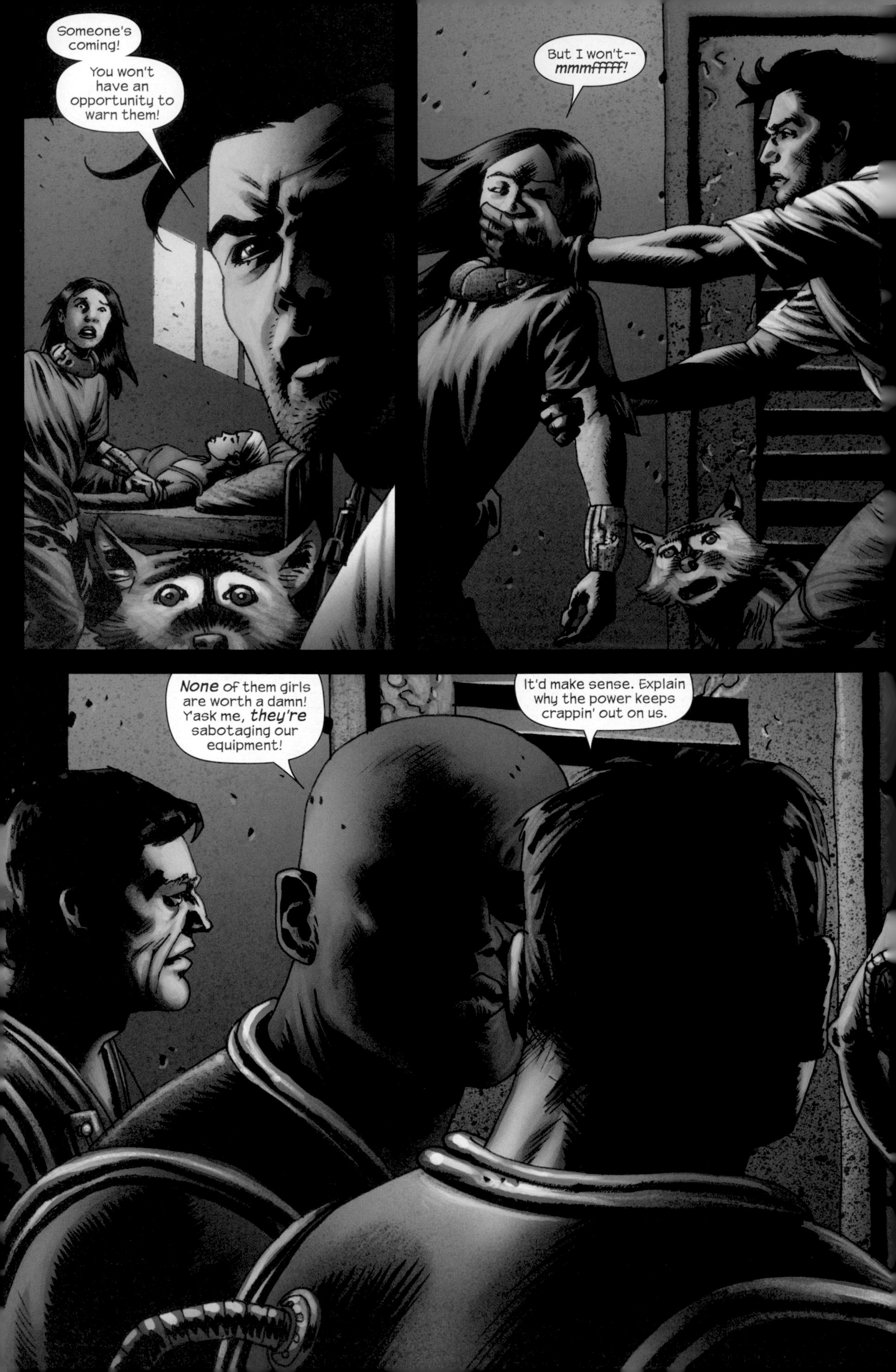
Someone's coming!
You won't have an opportunity to warn them!
But I won't-- *mmmfffff!*
None of them girls are worth a damn! Y'ask me, *they're* sabotaging our equipment!
It'd make sense. Explain why the power keeps crappin' out on us.

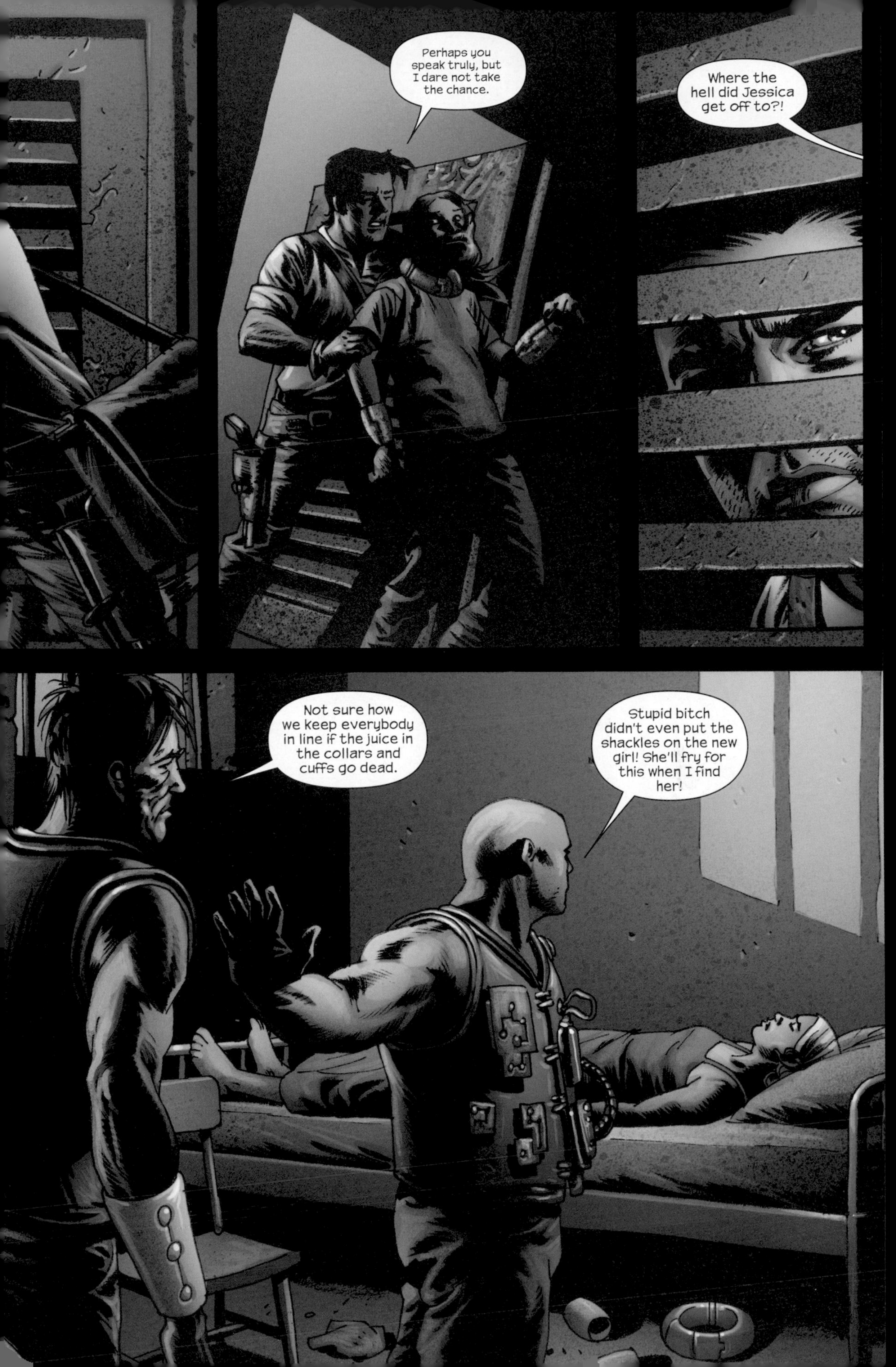
Perhaps you speak truly, but I dare not take the chance.
Where the hell did Jessica get off to?!
Not sure how we keep everybody in line if the juice in the collars and cuffs go dead.
Stupid bitch didn't even put the shackles on the new girl! She'll fry for this when I find her!

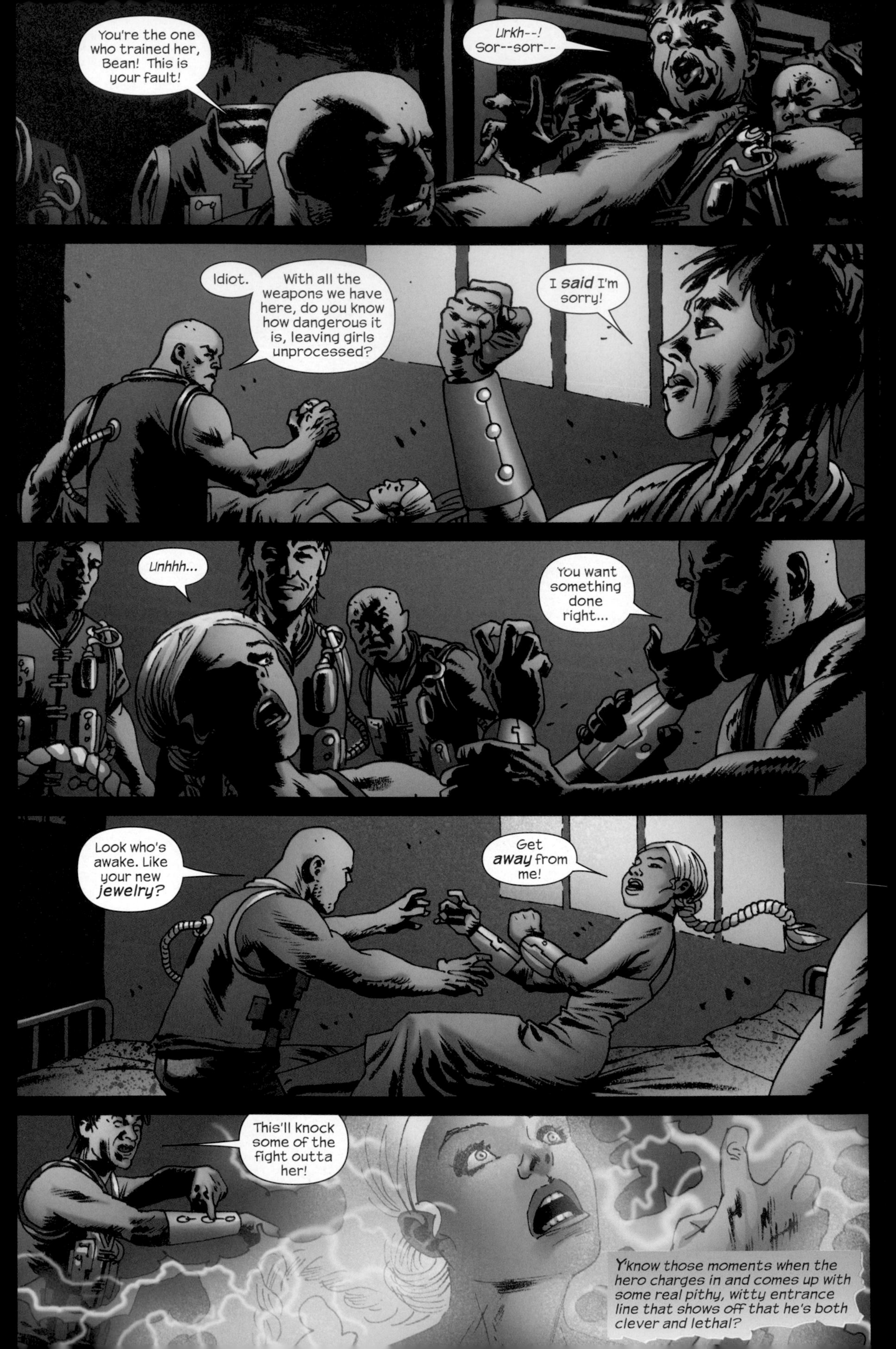

You're the one who trained her, Bean! This is your fault!
Urkh--! Sor--sorr--
Idiot.
With all the weapons we have here, do you know how dangerous it is, leaving girls unprocessed?
I *said* I'm sorry!
Unhhh...
You want something done right...
Look who's awake. Like your new *jewelry*?
Get *away* from me!
This'll knock some of the fight outta her!
Y'know those moments when the hero charges in and comes up with some real pithy, witty entrance line that shows off that he's both clever and lethal?

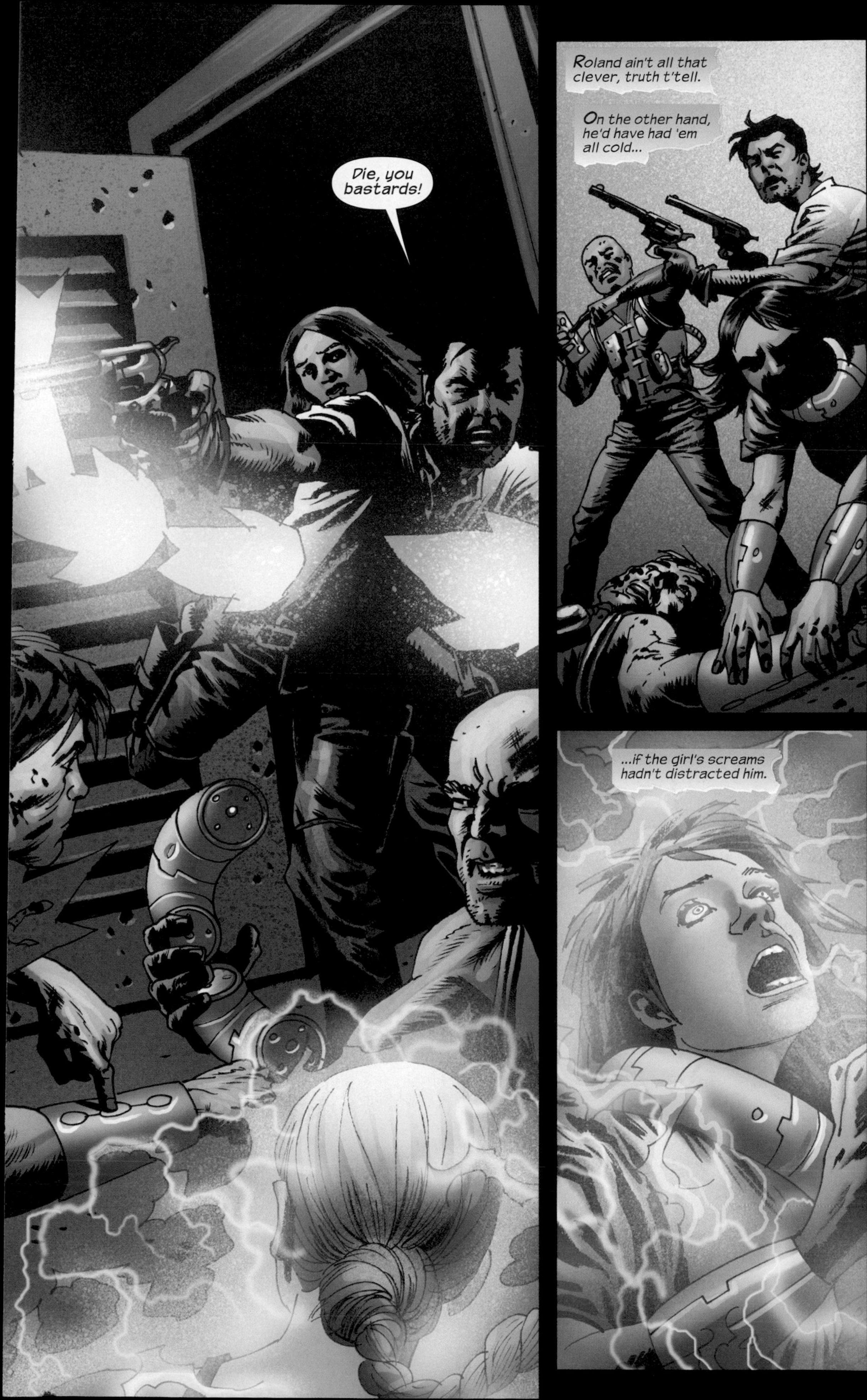
Die, you bastards!
Roland ain't all that clever, truth t'tell.
On the other hand, he'd have had 'em all cold...
...if the girl's screams hadn't distracted him.

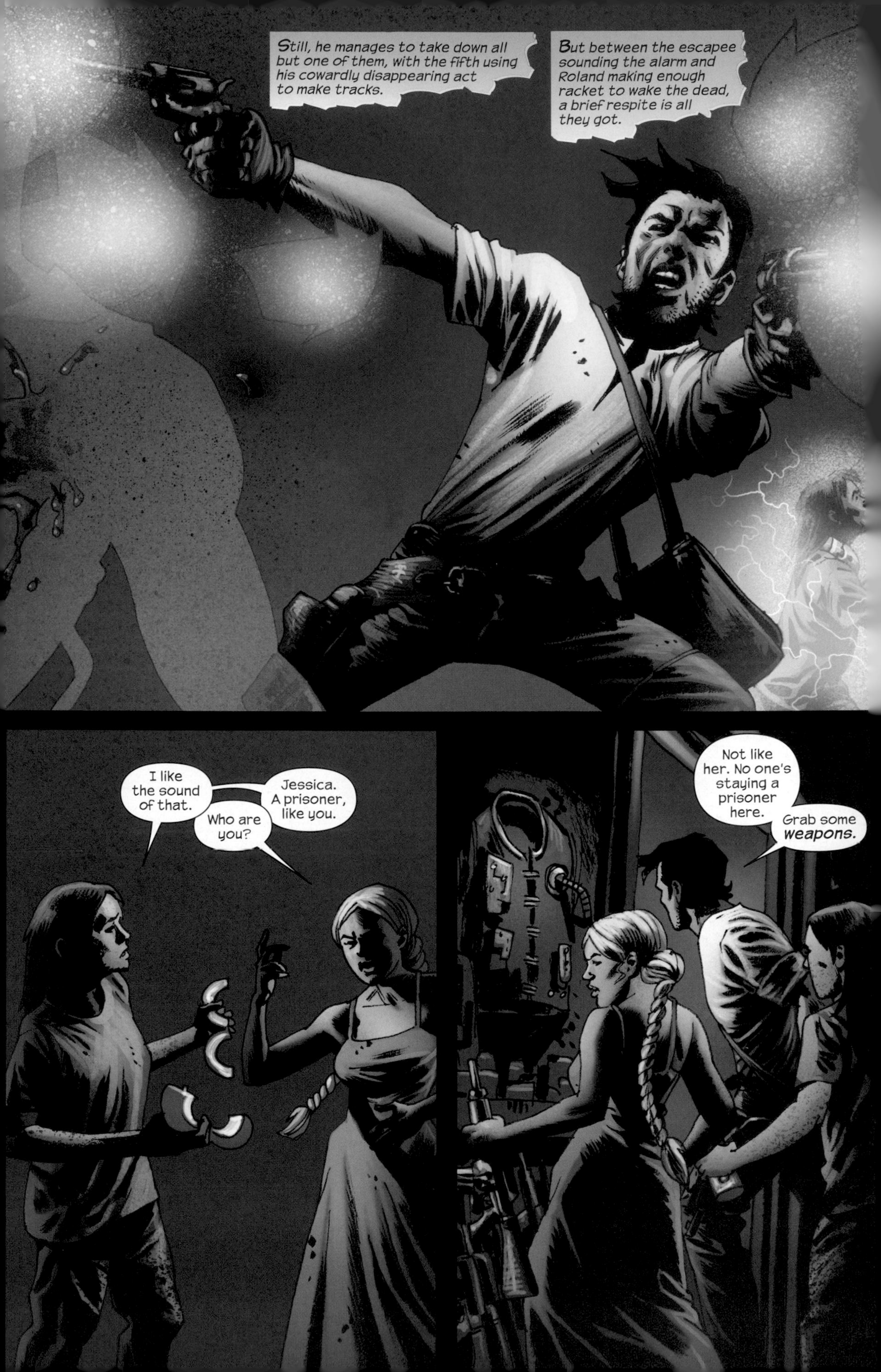
Still, he manages to take down all but one of them, with the fifth using his cowardly disappearing act to make tracks.
But between the escapee sounding the alarm and Roland making enough racket to wake the dead, a brief respite is all they got.
I like the sound of that.
Who are you?
Jessica. A prisoner, like you.
Not like her. No one's staying a prisoner here.
Grab some *weapons.*

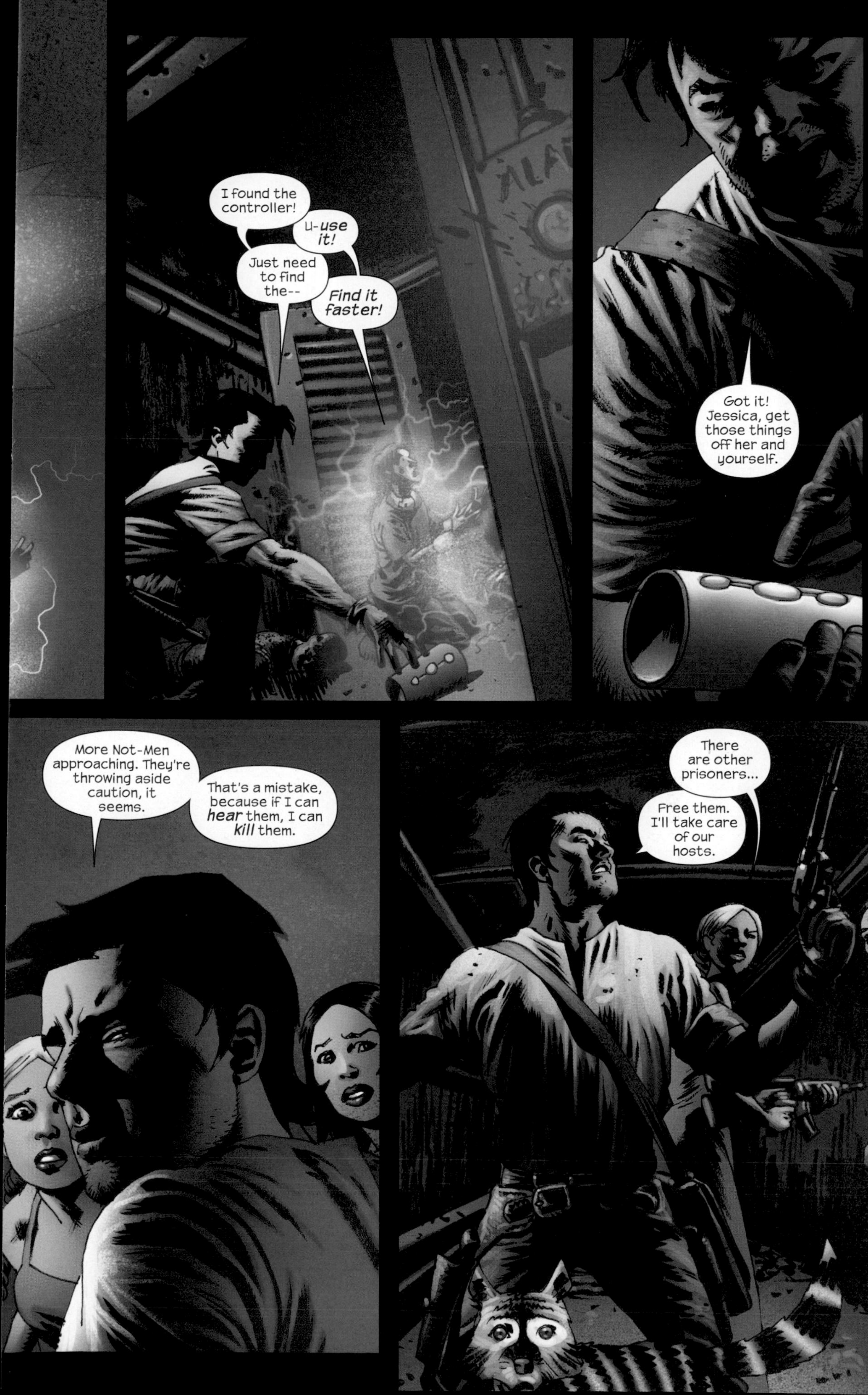

I found the controller!
U-use it!
Just need to find the--
Find it faster!
Got it! Jessica, get those things off her and yourself.
More Not-Men approaching. They're throwing aside caution, it seems.
That's a mistake, because if I can *hear* them, I can *kill* them.
There are other prisoners...
Free them. I'll take care of our hosts.

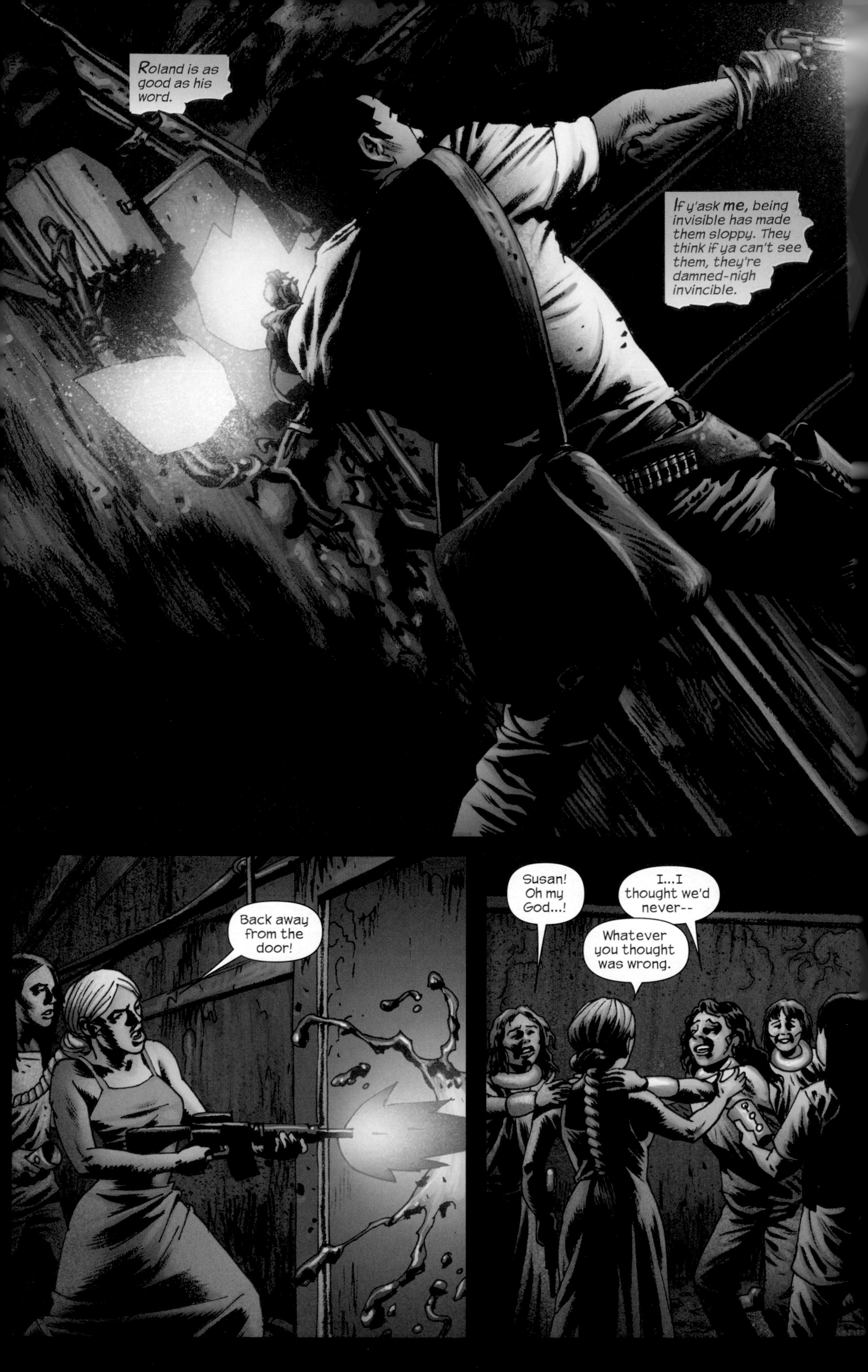
Roland is as good as his word.
If y'ask me, being invisible has made them sloppy. They think if ya can't see them, they're damned-nigh invincible.
Back away from the door!
Susan! Oh my God...!
I...I thought we'd never--
Whatever you thought was wrong.

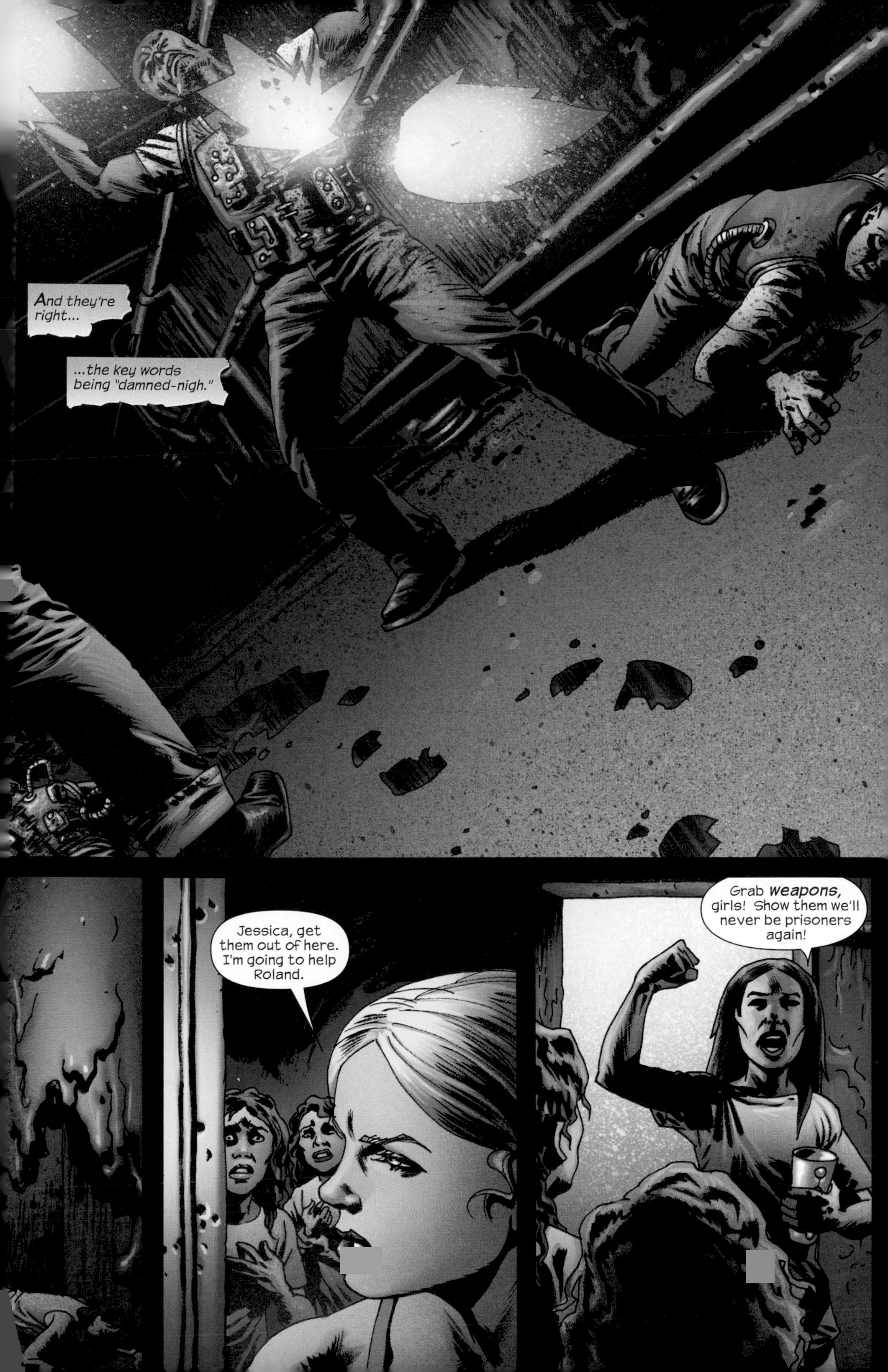
And they're right...
...the key words being "damned-nigh."
Jessica, get them out of here. I'm going to help Roland.
Grab *weapons,* girls! Show them we'll never be prisoners again!

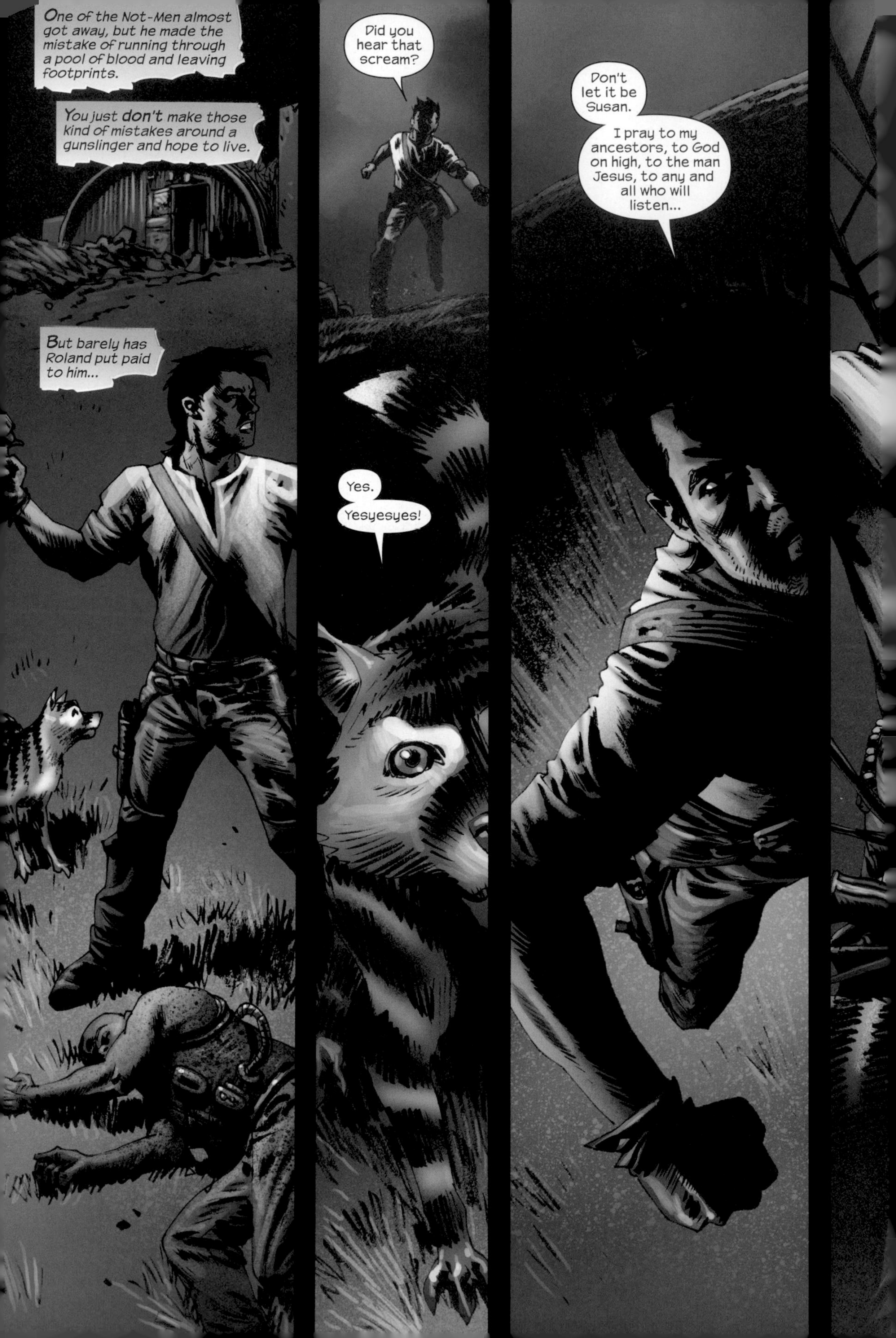
One of the Not-Men almost got away, but he made the mistake of running through a pool of blood and leaving footprints.
You just don't make those kind of mistakes around a gunslinger and hope to live.
But barely has Roland put paid to him...
Did you hear that scream?
Yes.
Yesyesyes!
Don't let it be Susan.
I pray to my ancestors, to God on high, to the man Jesus, to any and all who will listen...

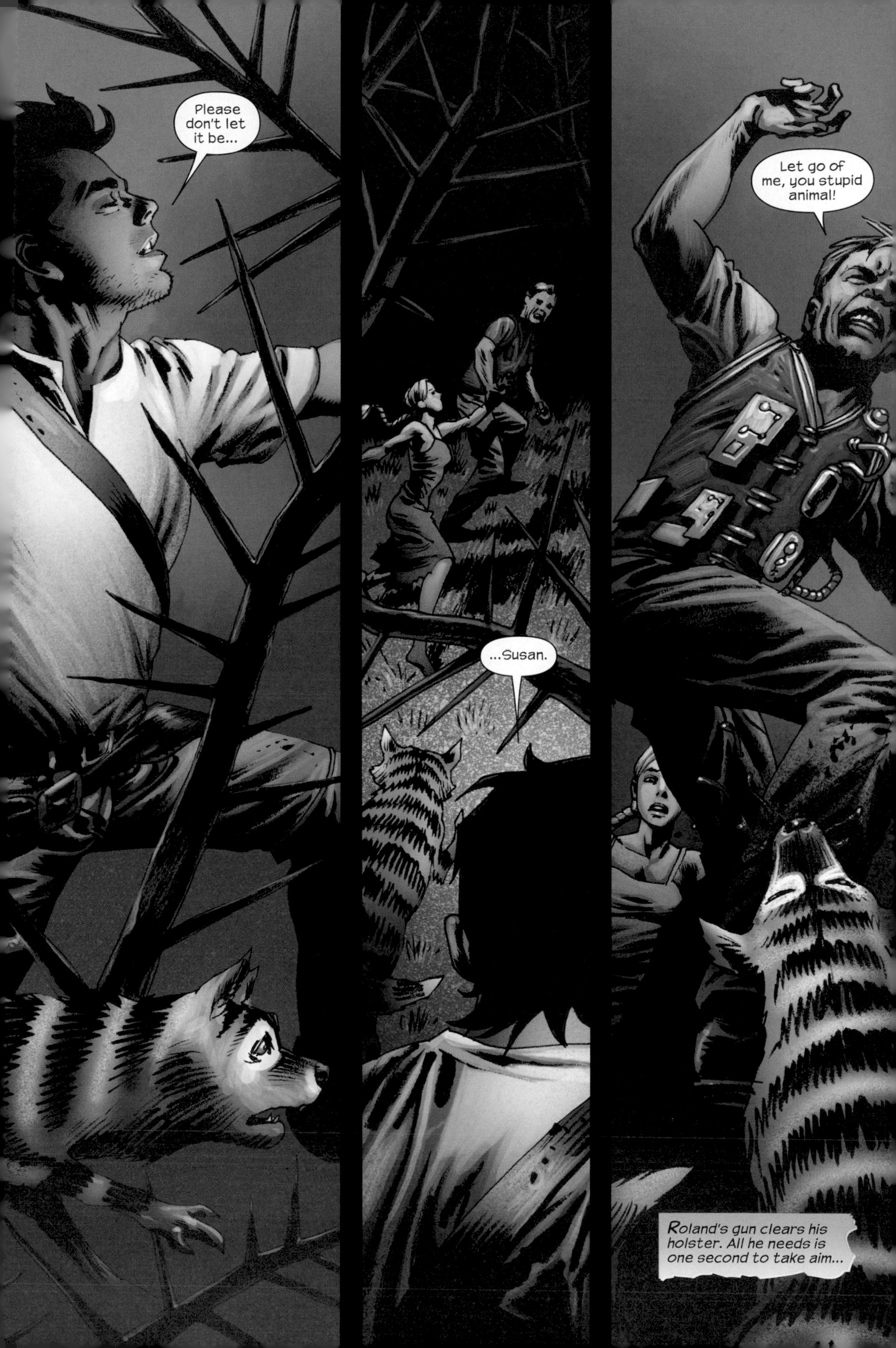
Please don't let it be...
...Susan.
Let go of me, you stupid animal!
Roland's gun clears his holster. All he needs is one second to take aim...

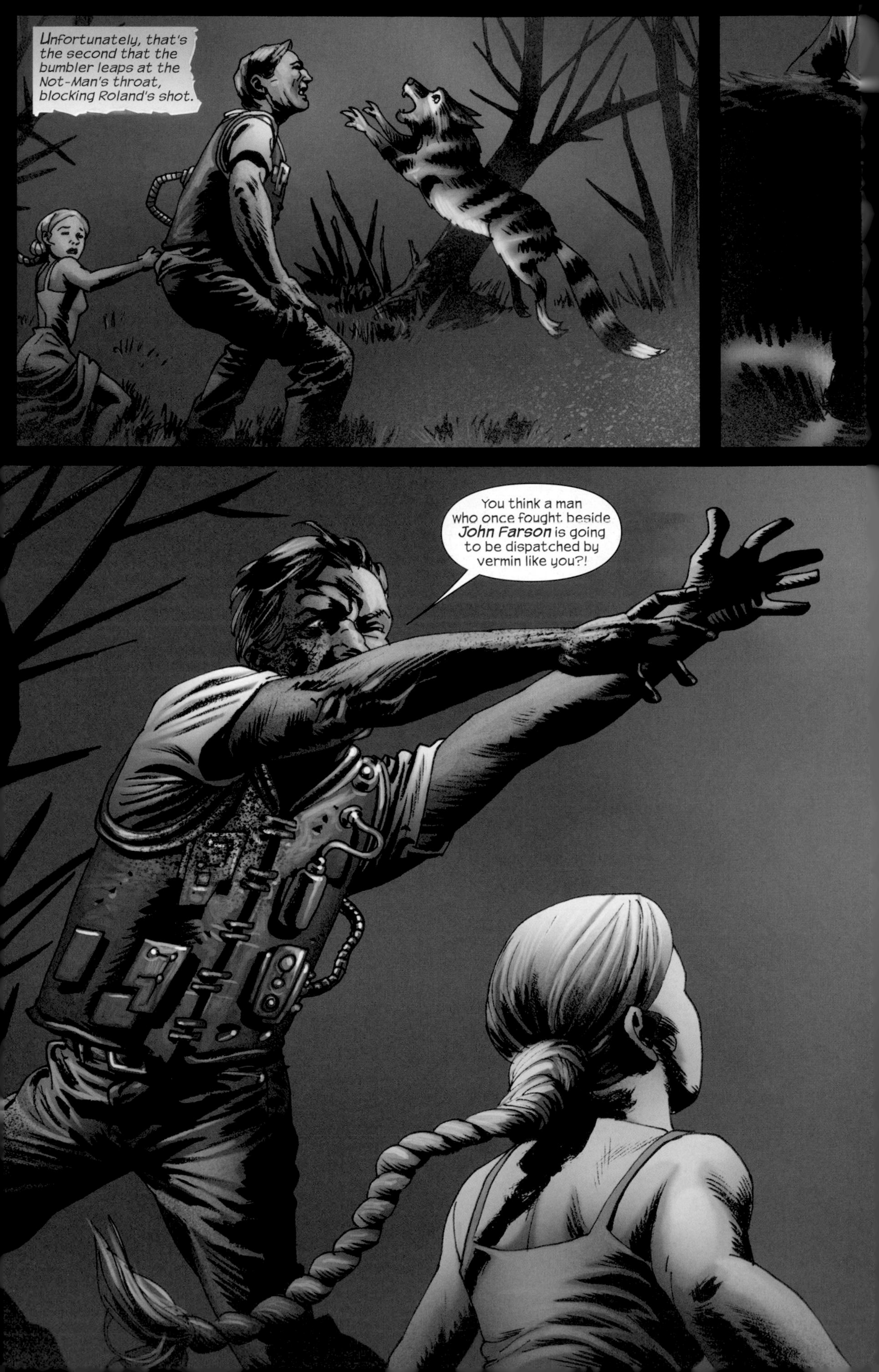
Unfortunately, that's the second that the bumbler leaps at the Not-Man's throat, blocking Roland's shot.
You think a man who once fought beside John Farson is going to be dispatched by vermin like you?!

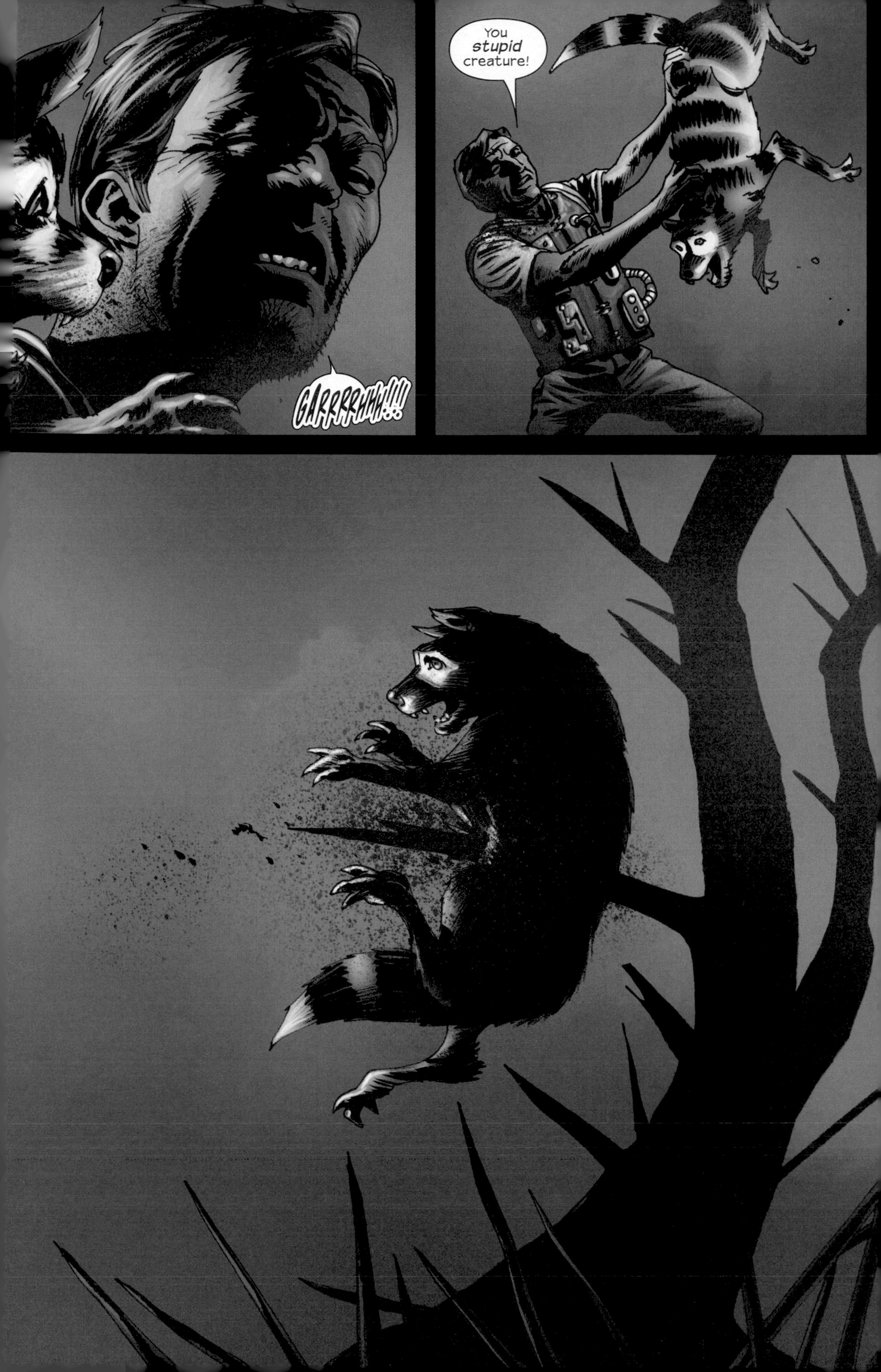
GARRRRHHH!!!
You stupid creature!

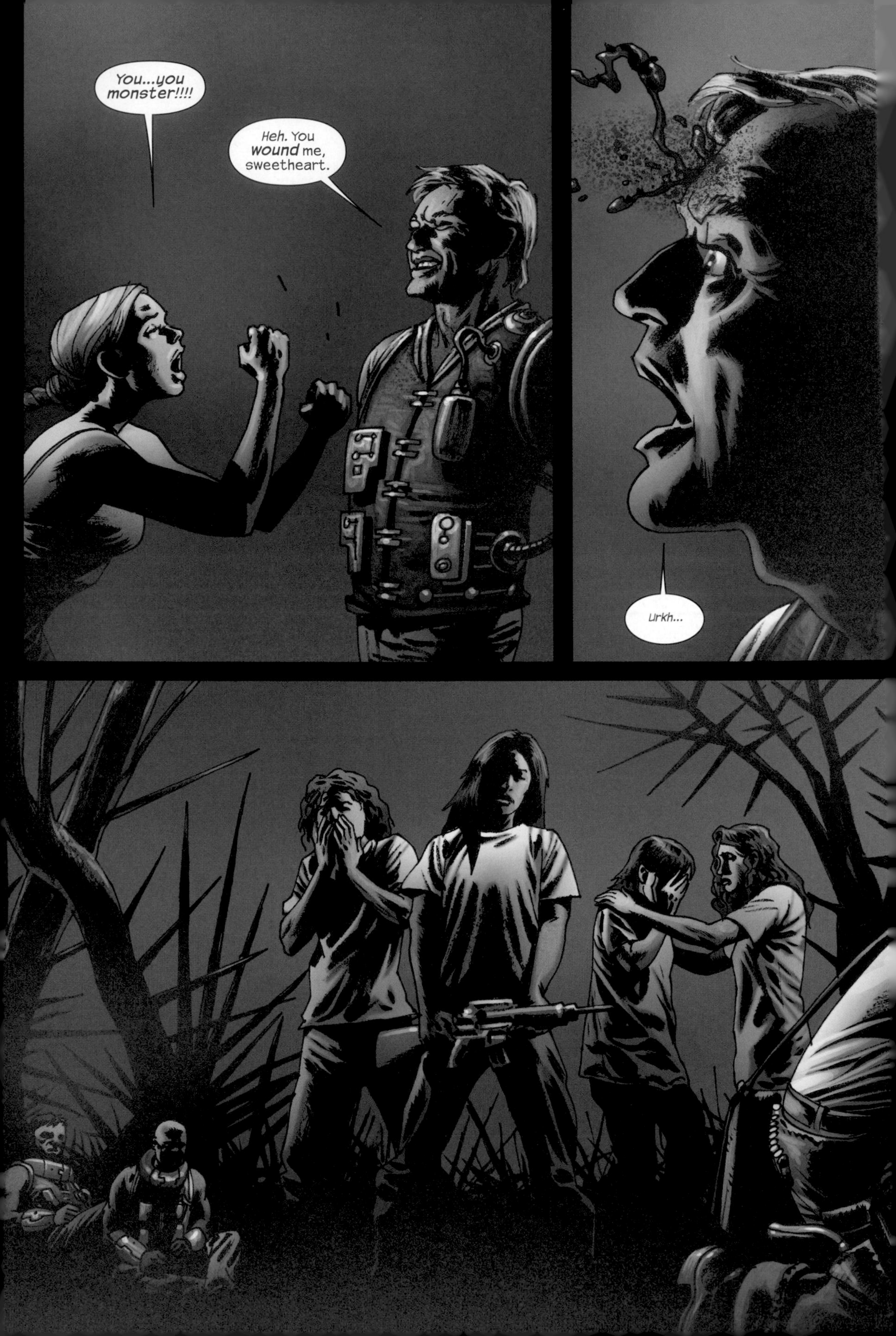
You...you monster!!!!
Heh. You wound me, sweetheart.
Urkh...

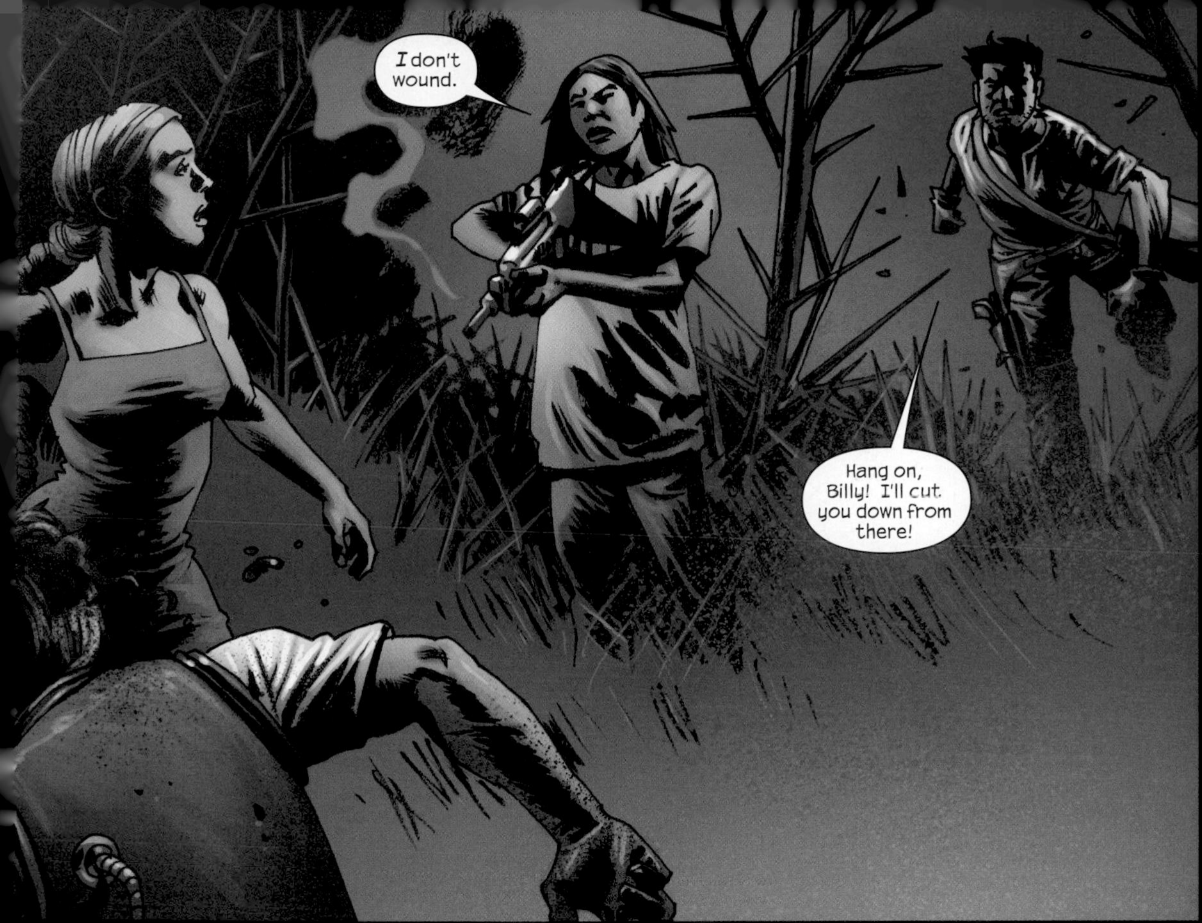
I don't wound.
Hang on, Billy! I'll cut you down from there!

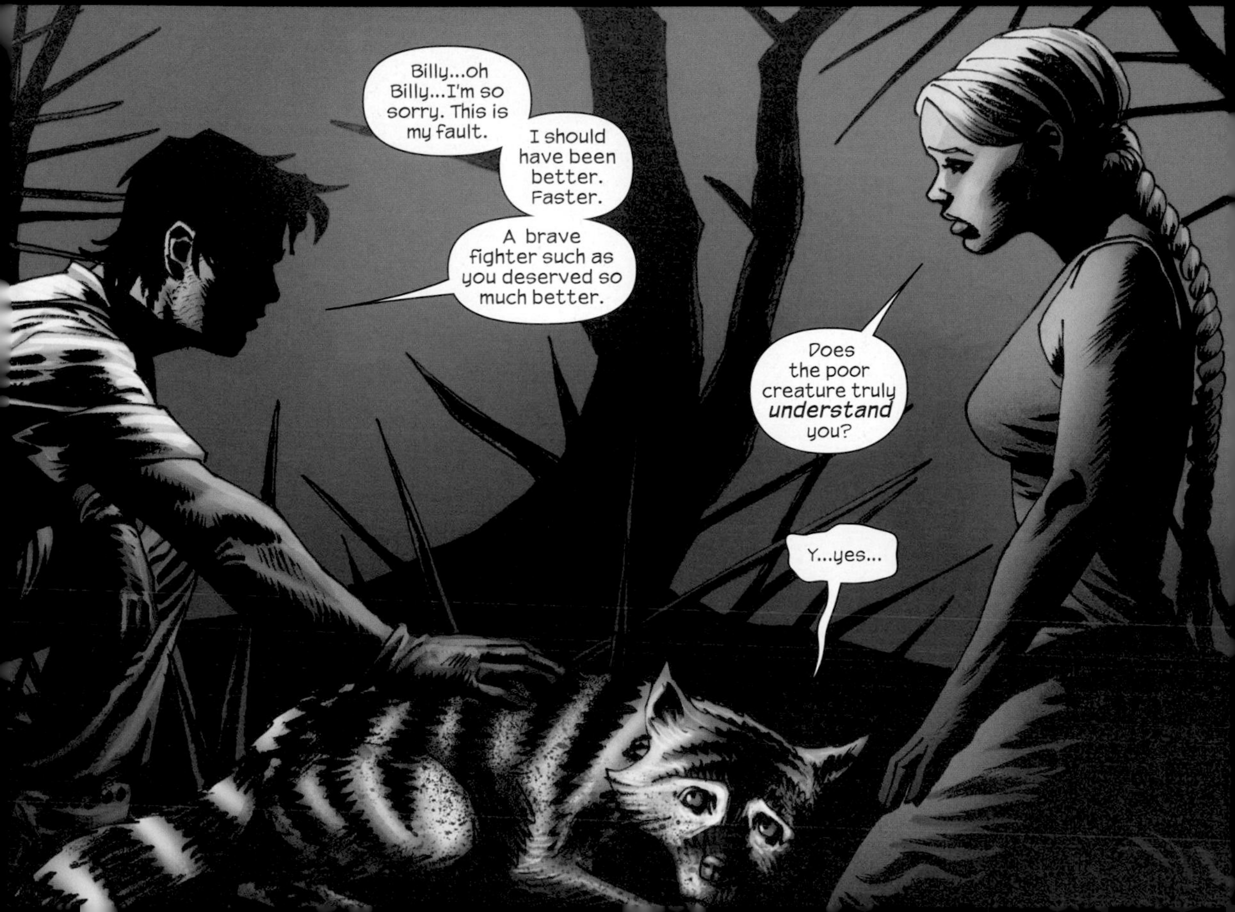
Billy...oh Billy...I'm so sorry. This is my fault.
I should have been better. Faster.
A brave fighter such as you deserved so much better.
Does the poor creature truly *understand* you?
Y...yes...

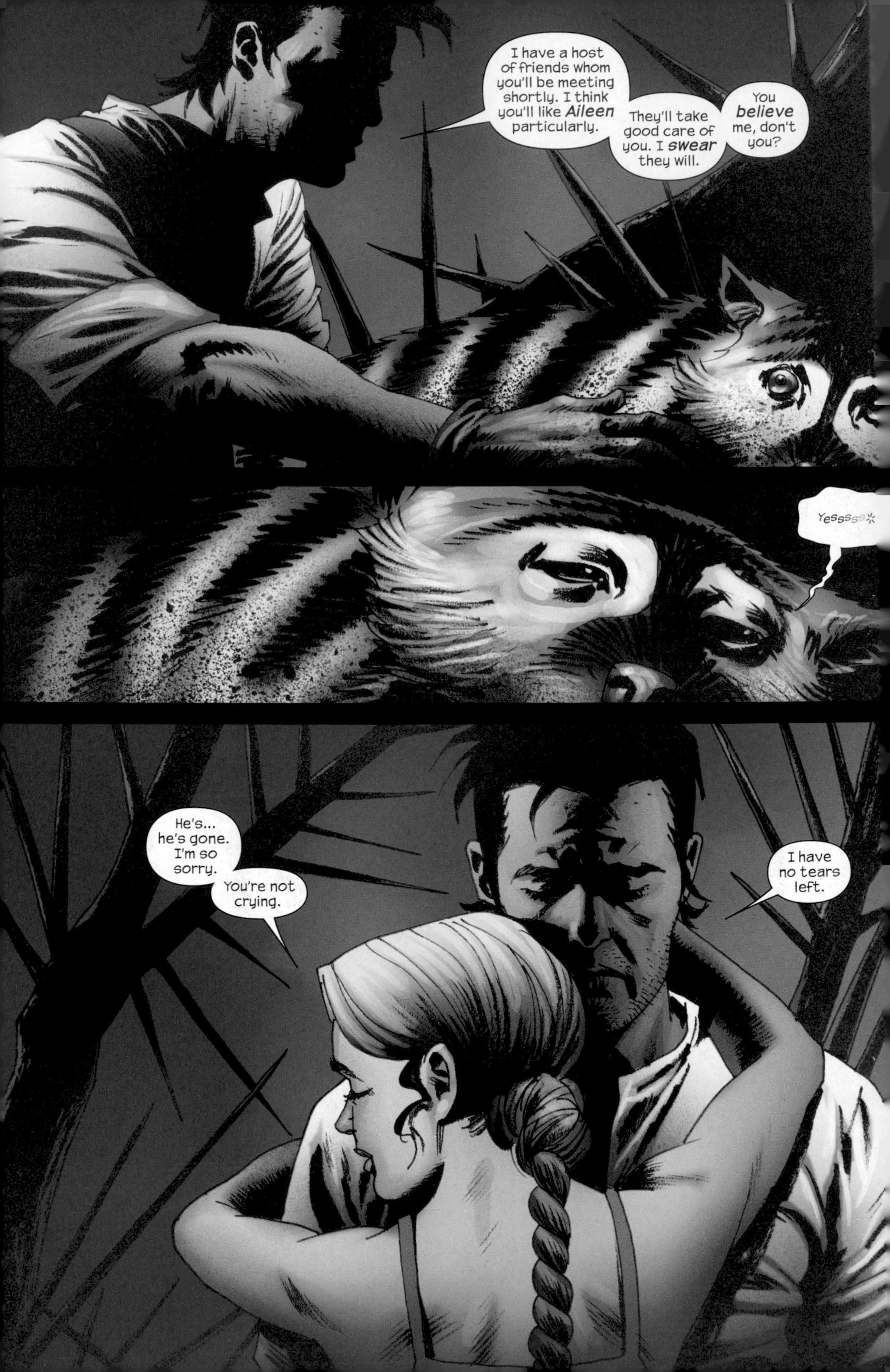

I have a host of friends whom you'll be meeting shortly. I think you'll like *Aileen* particularly.
They'll take good care of you. I *swear* they will.
You *believe* me, don't you?
Yessss
He's... he's gone. I'm so sorry.
You're not crying.
I have no tears left.

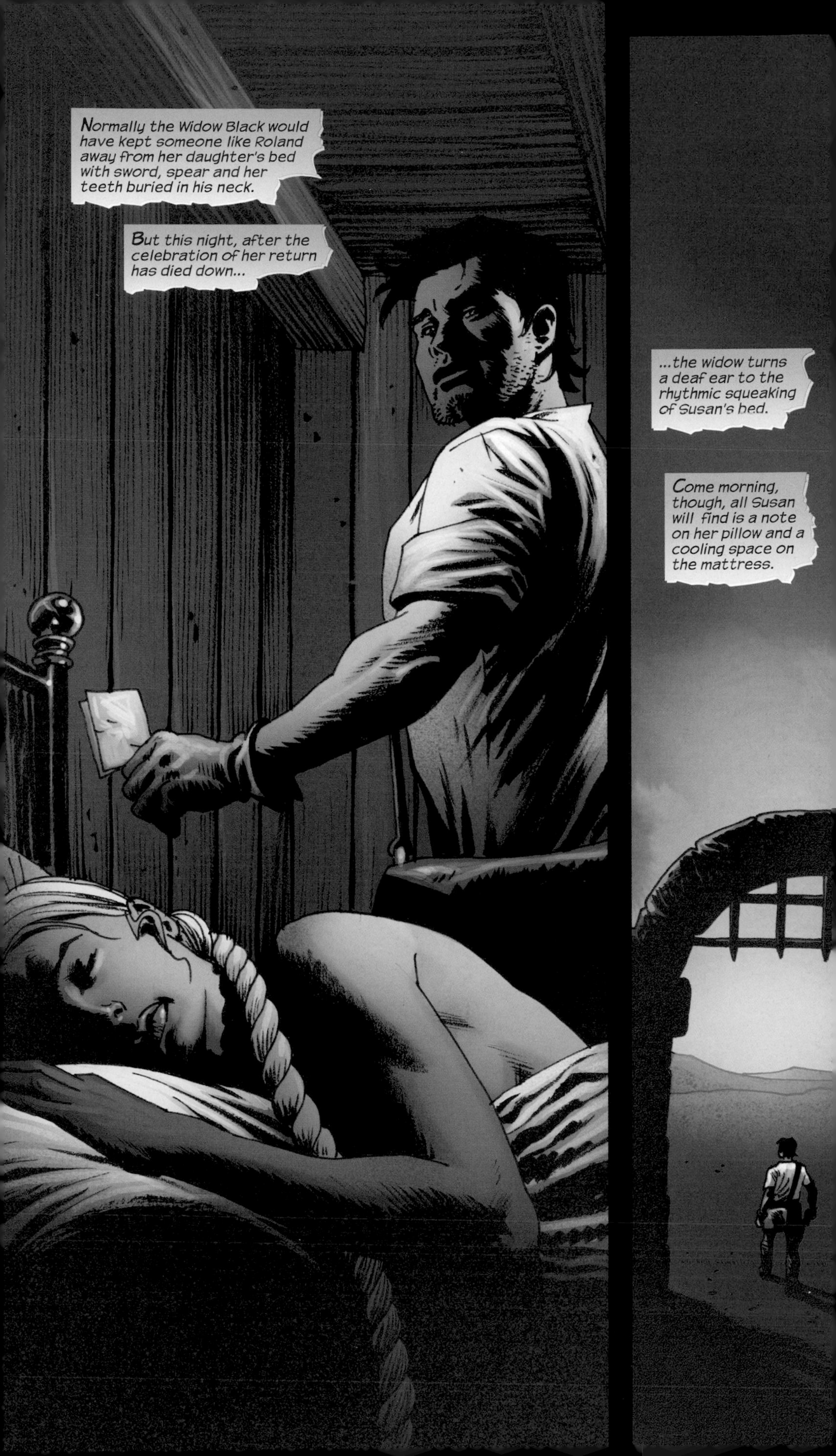
Normally the Widow Black would have kept someone like Roland away from her daughter's bed with sword, spear and her teeth buried in his neck.
But this night, after the celebration of her return has died down...
...the widow turns a deaf ear to the rhythmic squeaking of Susan's bed.
Come morning, though, all Susan will find is a note on her pillow and a cooling space on the mattress.

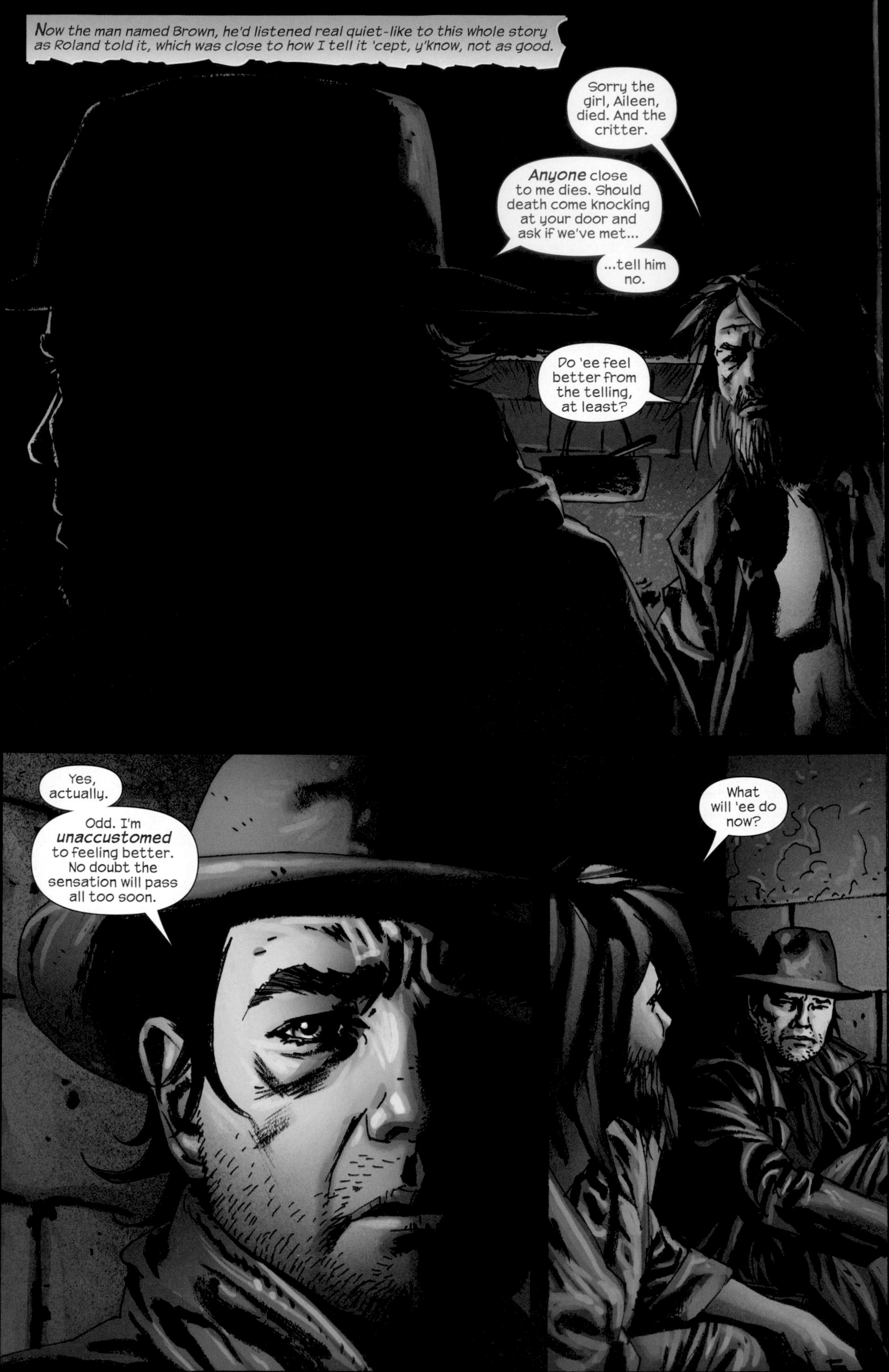
Now the man named Brown, he'd listened real quiet-like to this whole story as Roland told it, which was close to how I tell it 'cept, y'know, not as good.
Sorry the girl, Aileen, died. And the critter.
Anyone close to me dies. Should death come knocking at your door and ask if we've met...
...tell him no.
Do 'ee feel better from the telling, at least?
Yes, actually.
Odd. I'm ***unaccustomed*** to feeling better. No doubt the sensation will pass all too soon.
What will 'ee do now?

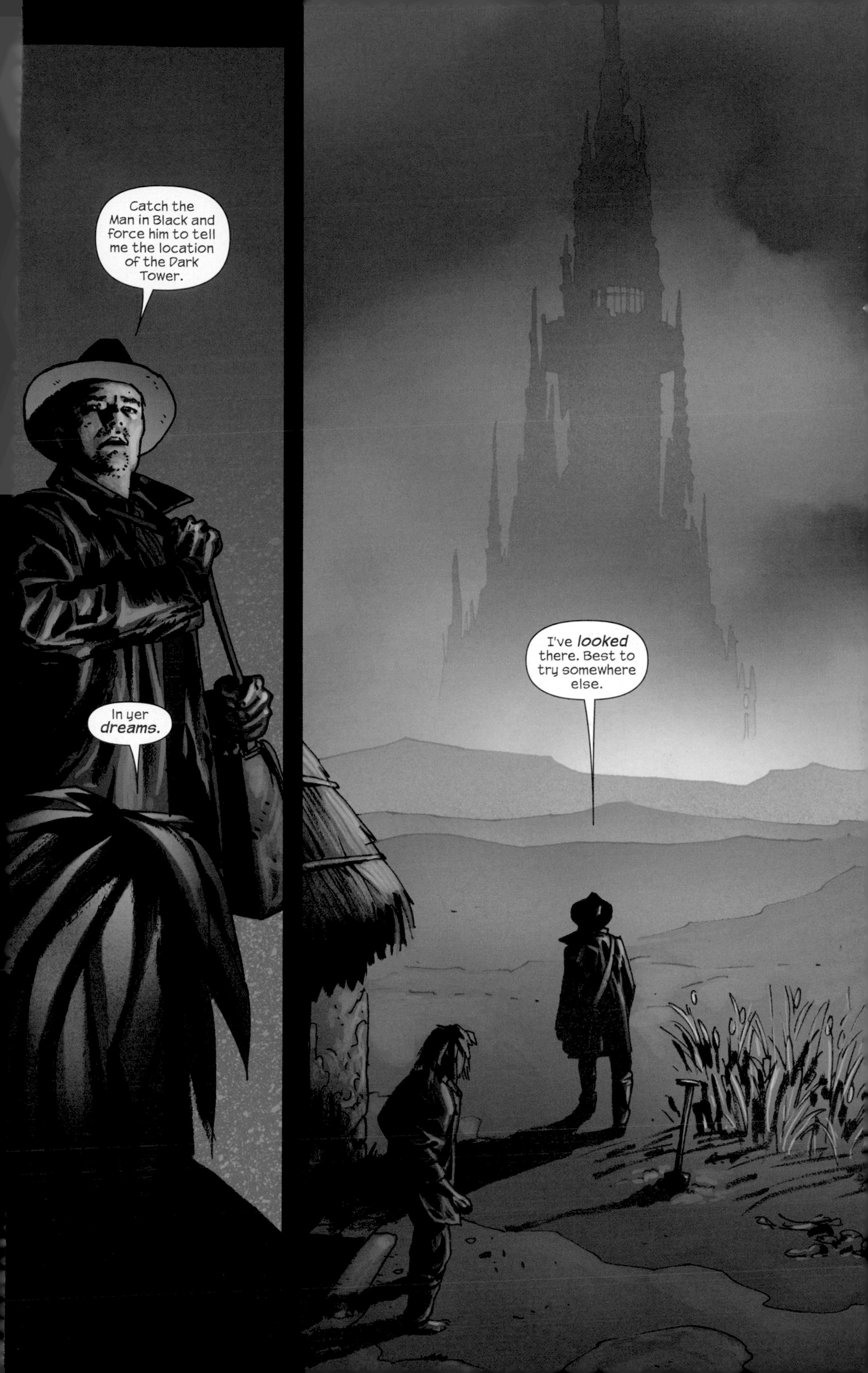
Catch the Man in Black and force him to tell me the location of the Dark Tower.
In yer *dreams.*
I've *looked* there. Best to try somewhere else.

The story continues in Dark Tower: The Gunslinger – The Little Sisters of Eluria

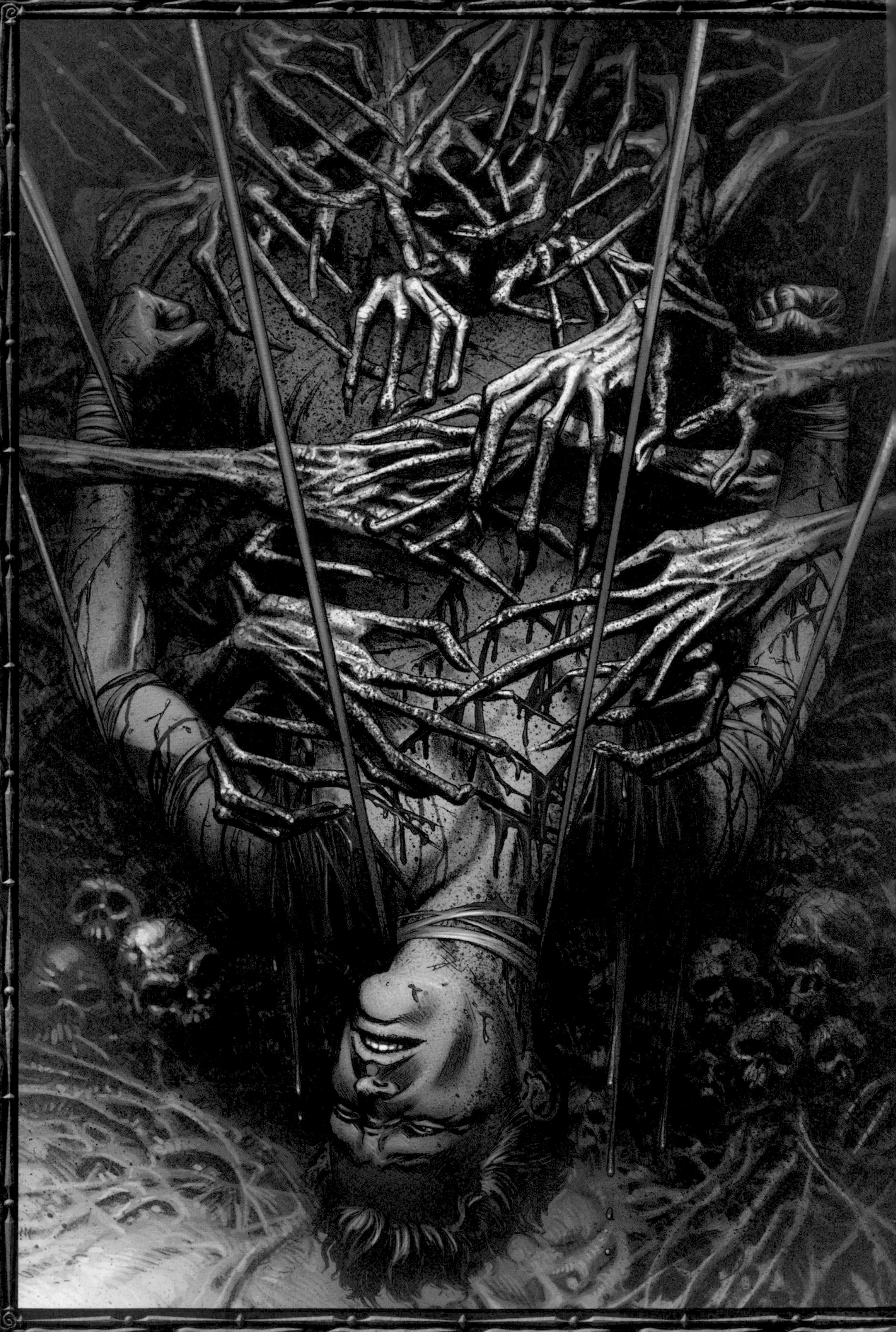

THE DARK TOWER READING CHRONOLOGY

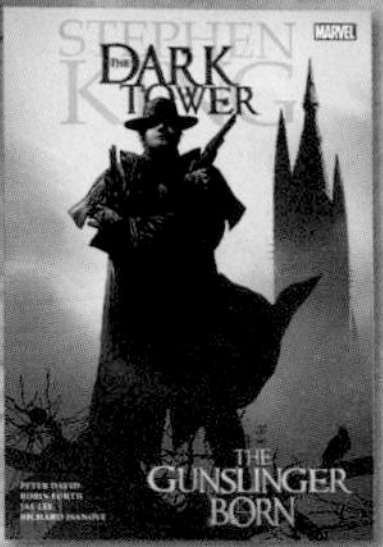
MARVEL
STEPHEN KING
DARK TOWER
THE GUNSLINGER BORN

THE DARK TOWER
THE GUNSLINGER BORN

BOOK 1

ISBN: 978 0 7851 2144 2

A man's quest begins with a boy's test. The world of Roland Deschain — the world of the Dark Tower — has been a thirty-year obsession for Stephen King. And now, King carries his masterwork of fantasy to Marvel, bringing stunning new textures to his epic story! *The Gunslinger Born* seamlessly integrates the wonder of Mid-World and the story of its hard-bitten cast of characters into the finest Marvel Comics storytelling tradition.

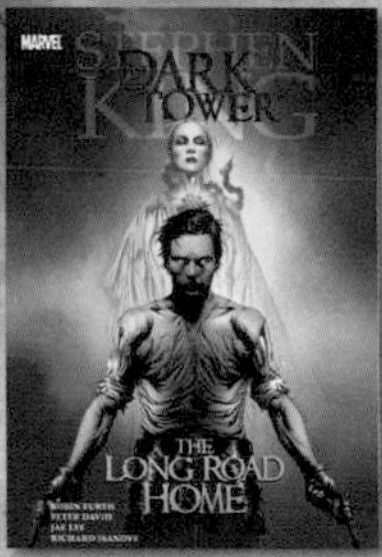
MARVEL
STEPHEN KING
DARK TOWER
THE LONG ROAD HOME

THE DARK TOWER
THE LONG ROAD HOME

BOOK 2

ISBN: 978 0 7851 2709 3

The gunslinger is born into a harsh world of mystery and violence. Susan Delgado is dead. Clay Reynolds and the vestiges of the Big Coffin Hunters are in pursuit. The ka-tet fragments as evil abounds. It will be a long road home. With Roland seemingly lost inside the haunted world of Maerlyn's Grapefruit, and the dark forces therein tugging at his soul, it will take all the courage of his ka-tet to get him out of Hambry and back home. But as the Dogan stirs, portending an evil of which Roland and his ka-tet have no ken, it may very well be that the gunslinger born walks a long road home to death.

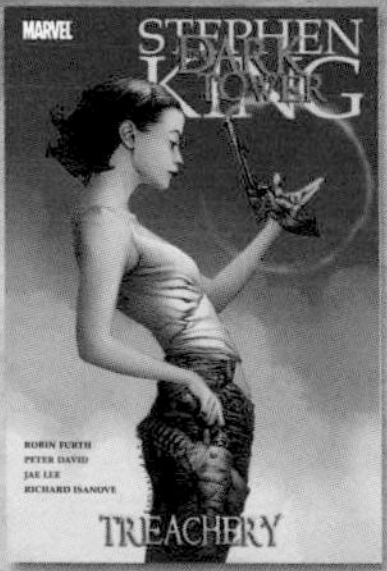
MARVEL
STEPHEN KING
DARK TOWER
TREACHERY

THE DARK TOWER
TREACHERY

BOOK 3

ISBN: 978 0 7851 3574 6

From the creative team that brought Roland's early adventures to life in *Dark Tower: The Gunslinger Born* and *Dark Tower: The Long Road Home* comes the third chapter of this dark saga of friendship, betrayal and a cosmic quest as conceived by master storyteller Stephen King.

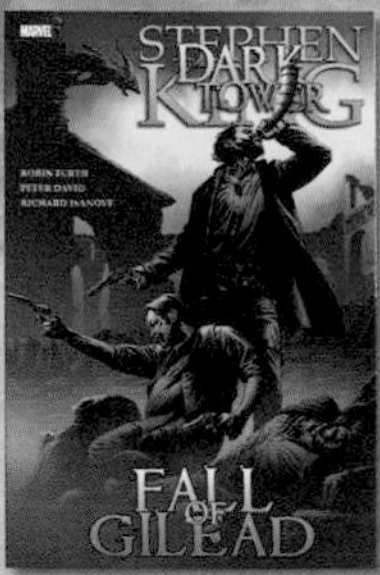
MARVEL
STEPHEN KING
DARK TOWER
FALL OF GILEAD

THE DARK TOWER
FALL OF GILEAD

BOOK 4

ISBN: 978 0 7851 2951 6

How could you have done it, Roland? How could you have killed your own mother? That's what everyone in Gilead's asking — even your grieving father. But you know the answer: Marten Broadcloak and one of them evil grapefruits. That's how. And while you rot in jail, the plot your matricide was only one small part of is wrapping its bloody and black tendrils around Gilead. Your town — the home of the Gunslingers — is the prize possession of the great enemy of the land, John Farson. And he means to have it. Gilead will fall, it will. And it will fall to the death of a thousand cuts. It started with your mother, yes, but it won't end there.

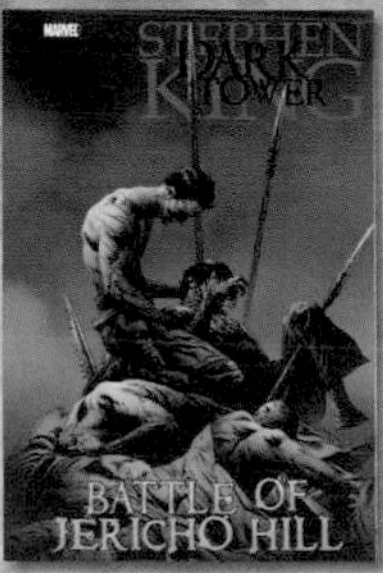
MARVEL
STEPHEN KING
DARK TOWER
BATTLE OF JERICHO HILL

THE DARK TOWER
BATTLE OF JERICHO HILL

BOOK 5

ISBN: 978 0 7851 2953 0

A brand-new story featuring Roland Deschain and his beleaguered ka-tet as they go on the run following the complete destruction of their beloved city of Gilead! And when such as Gilead falls, the pillars of reality itself — the six beams holding all of existence together — begins to crumble. The satanic plan of the Crimson King to return all of existence to the primal state of chaos is nigh.

Dark Tower: The Journey Begins #1 **Cover by Sean Phillips & Richard Isanove**

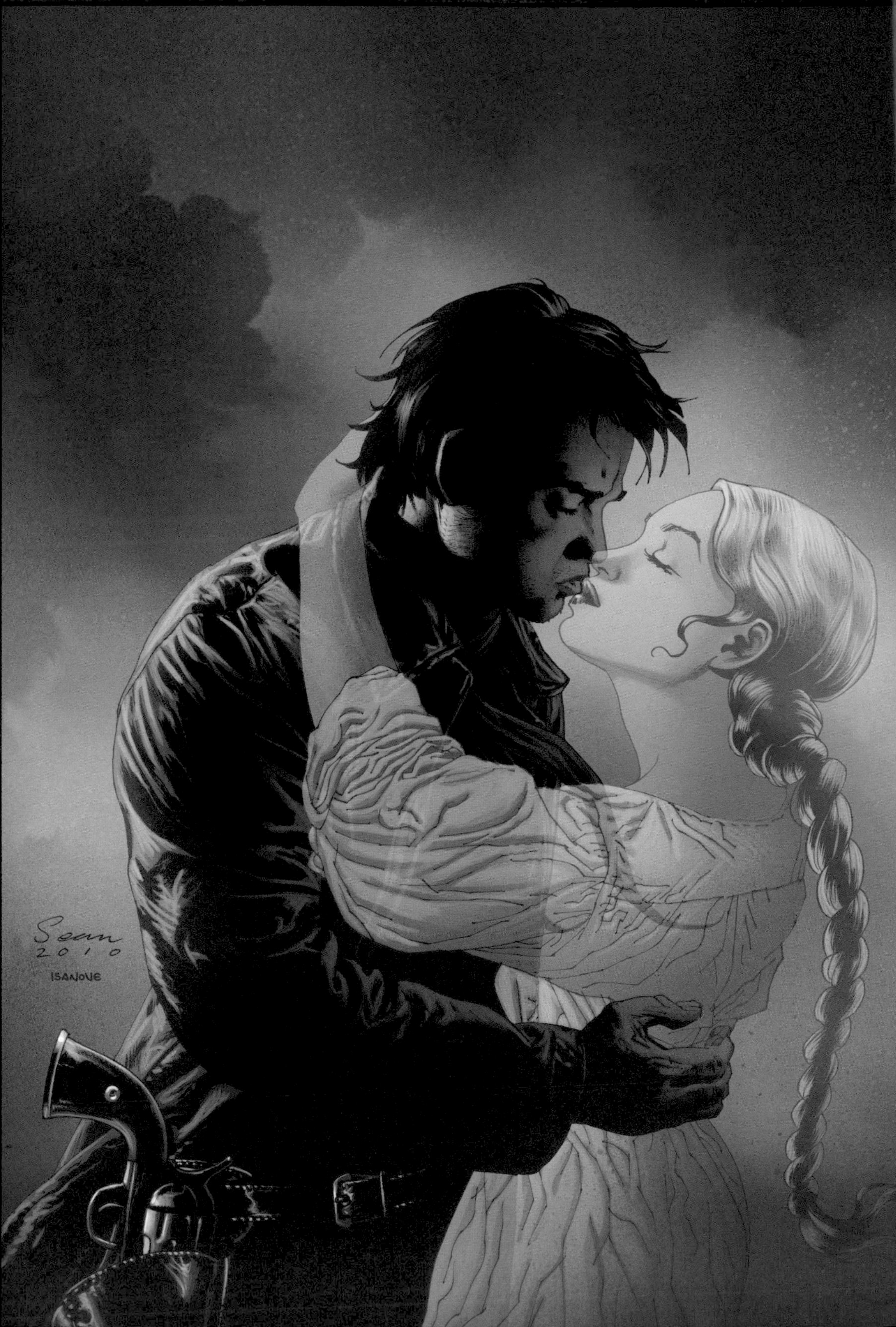
Sean
2010
ISANOVE

Dark Tower: The Journey Begins #1 **Variant Cover by Jae Lee & June Chung**

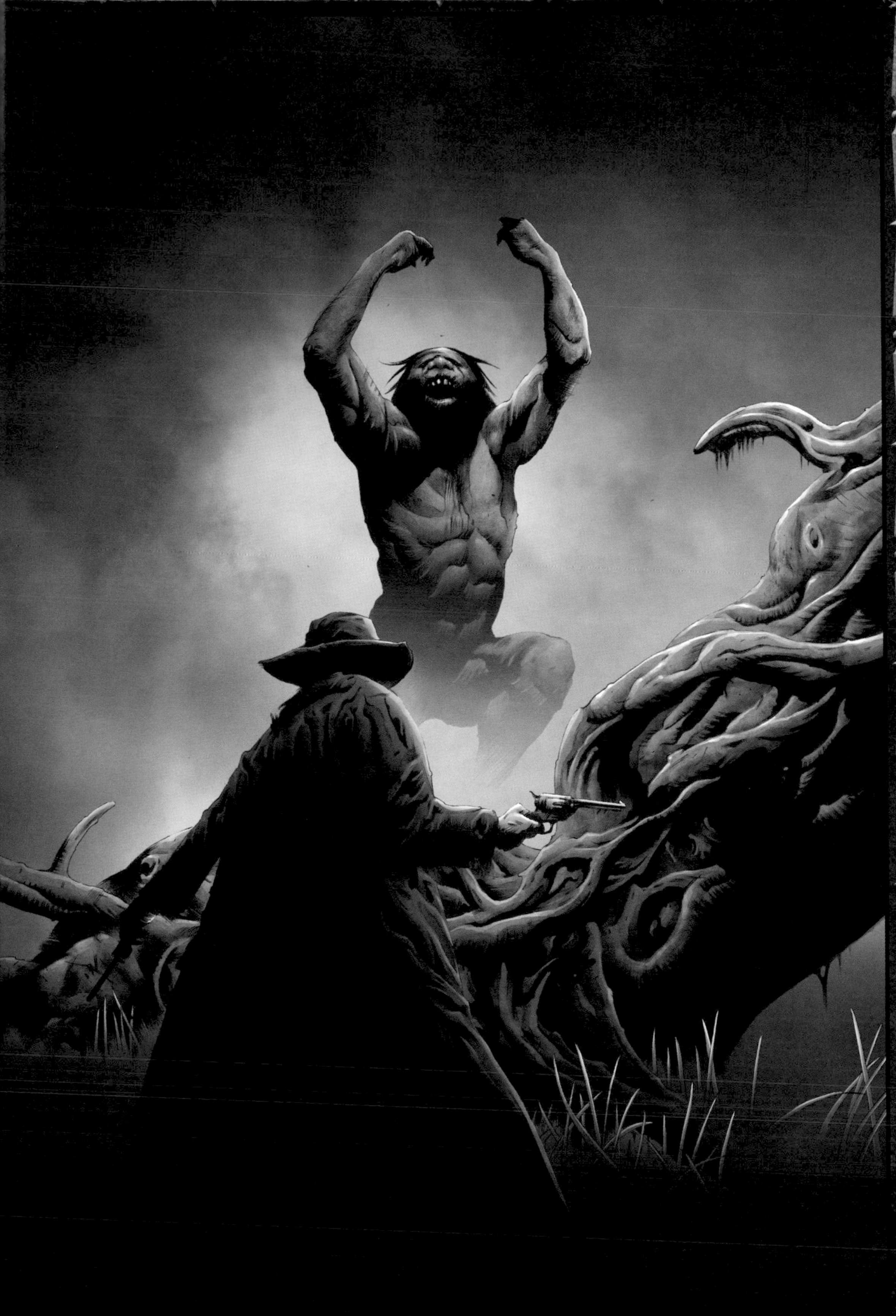

Dark Tower: The Journey Begins #2 **Cover by Sean Phillips & Richard Isanove**

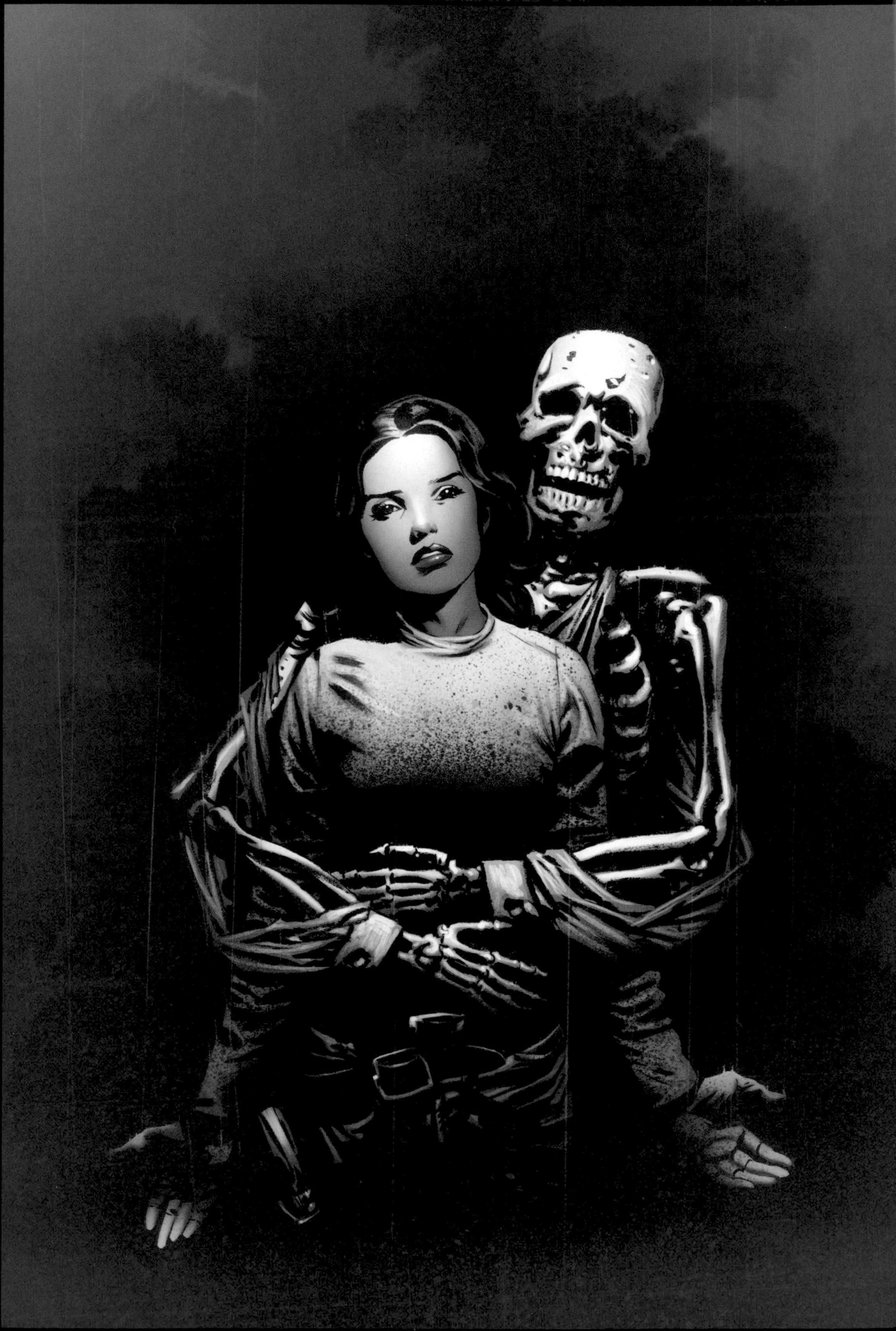

Dark Tower: The Journey Begins #5 **Cover by Sean Phillips & Richard Isanove**

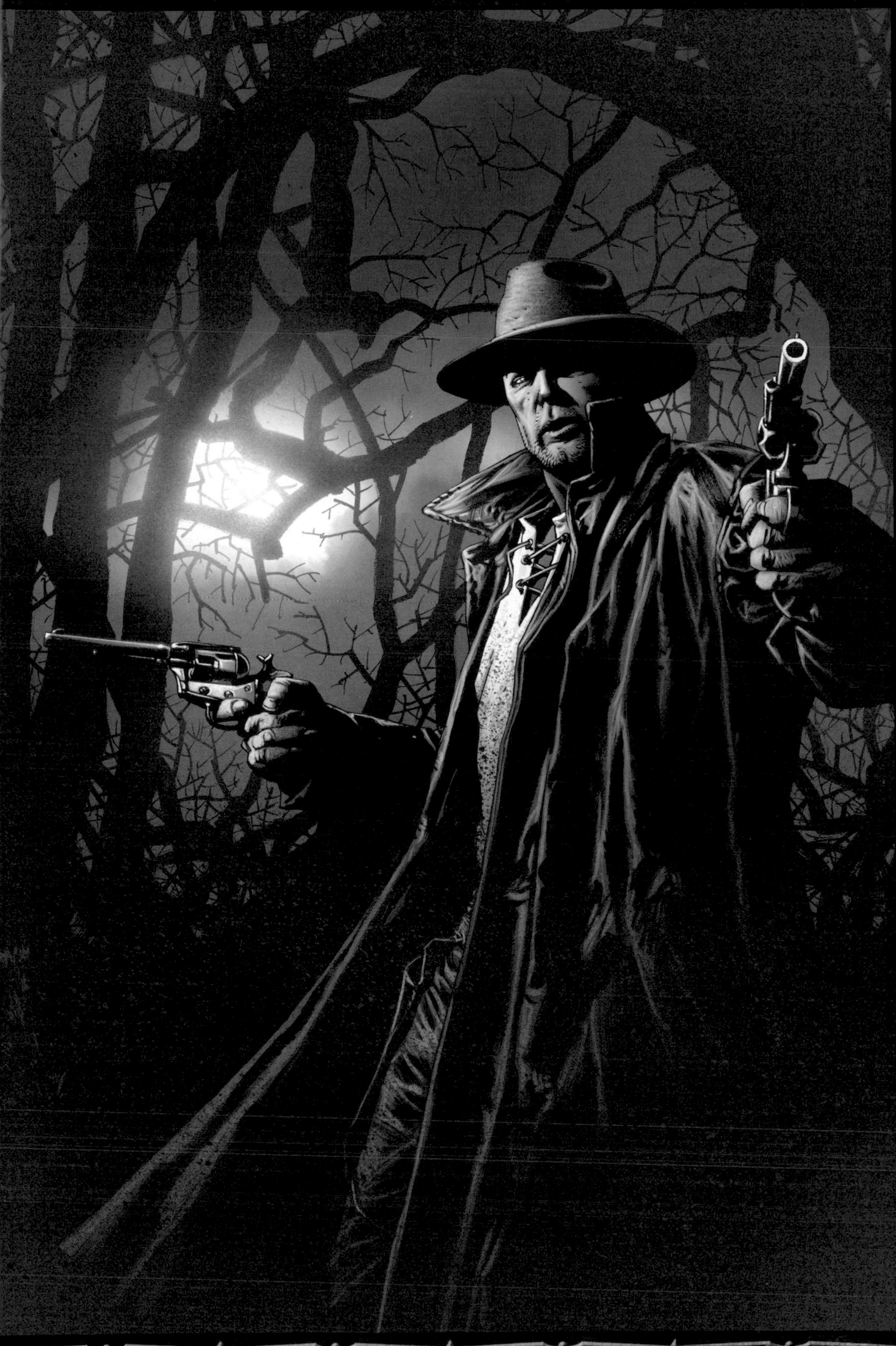

SKETCH

ART EVOLUTION
ISSUE 4, PAGE 2

INKS

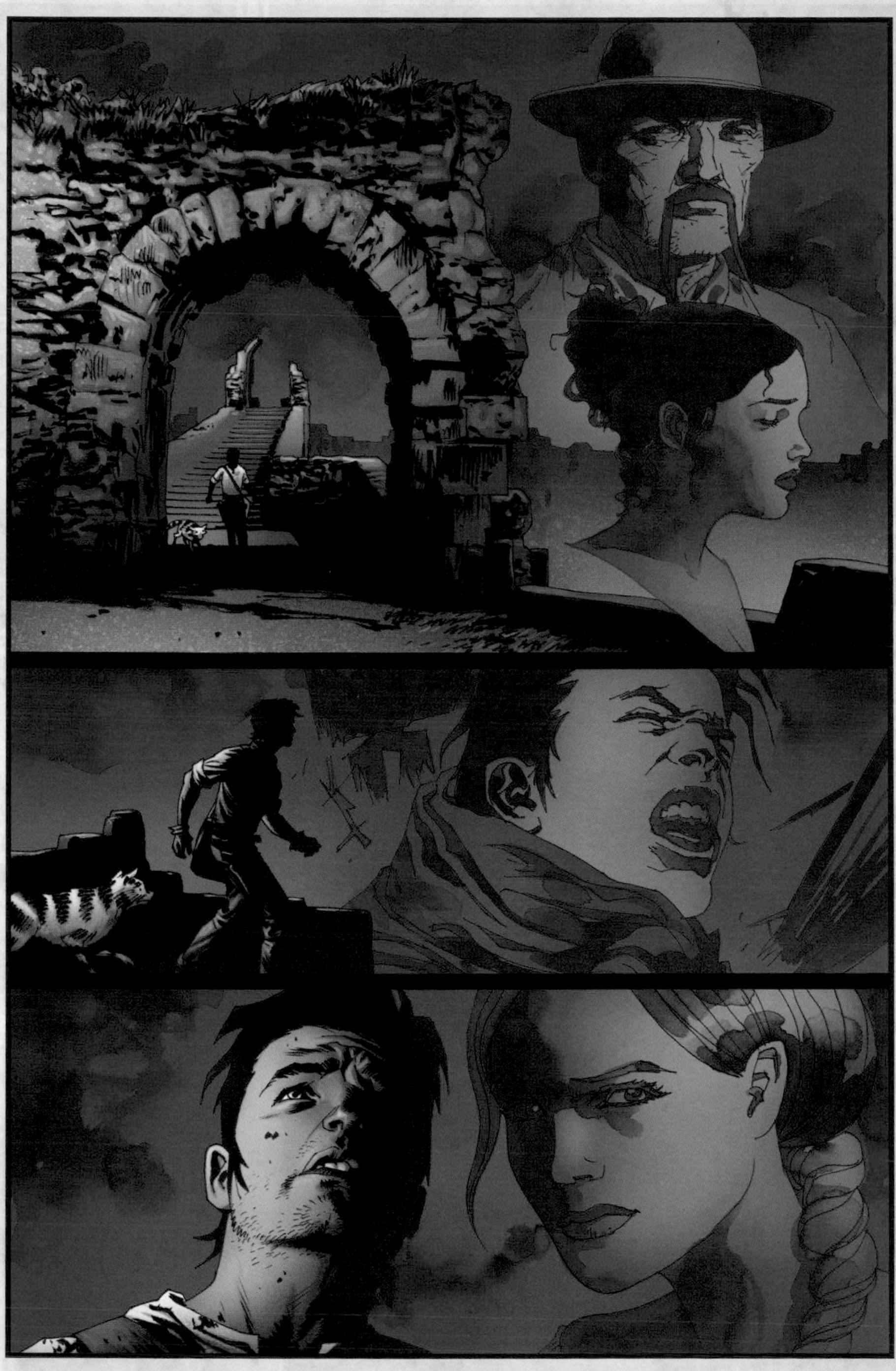

COLORS

SKETCH

ART EVOLUTION
ISSUE 4, PAGE 3

INKS

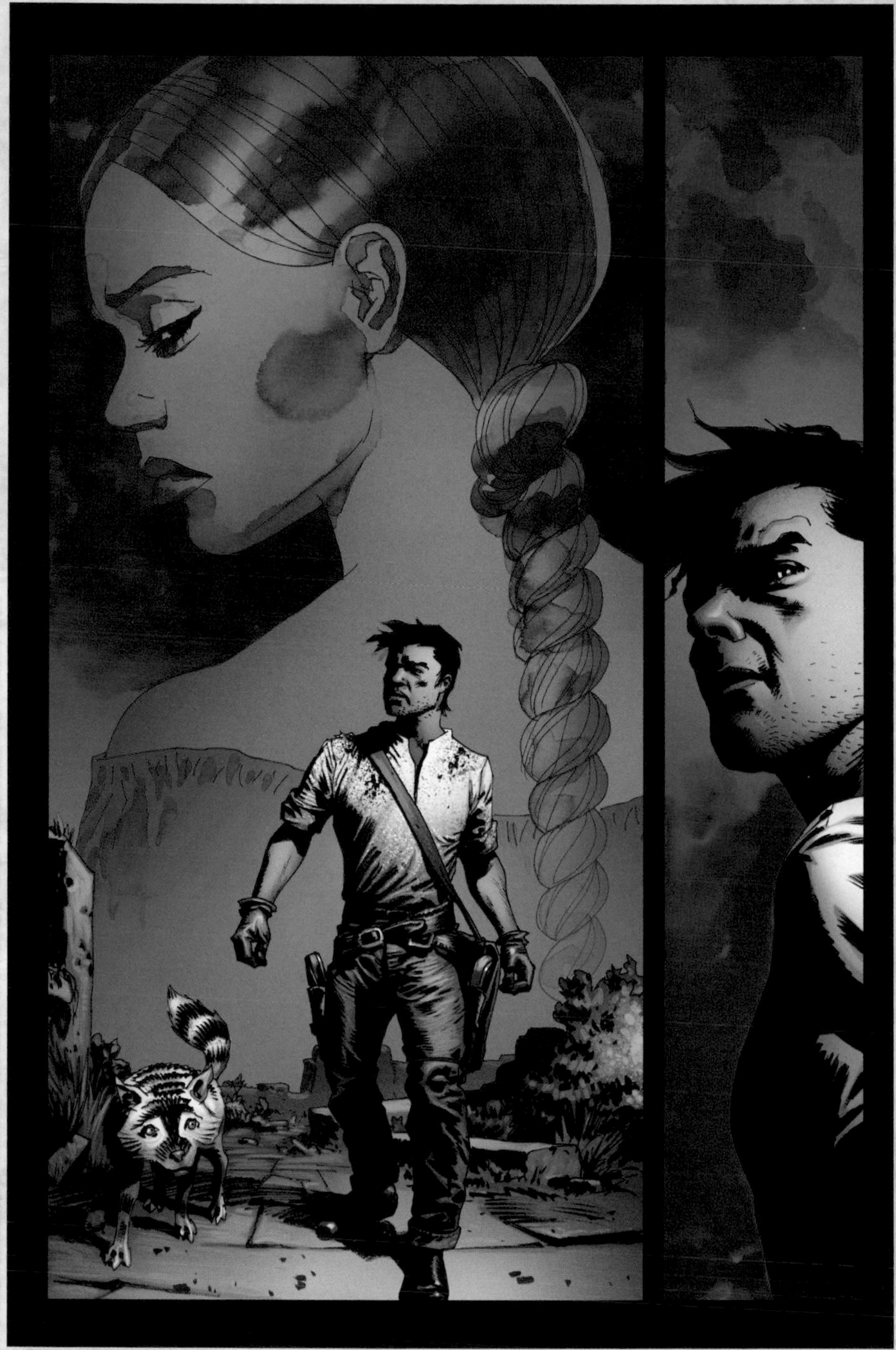

COLORS

ISSUE 4, PAGE 4 INKS

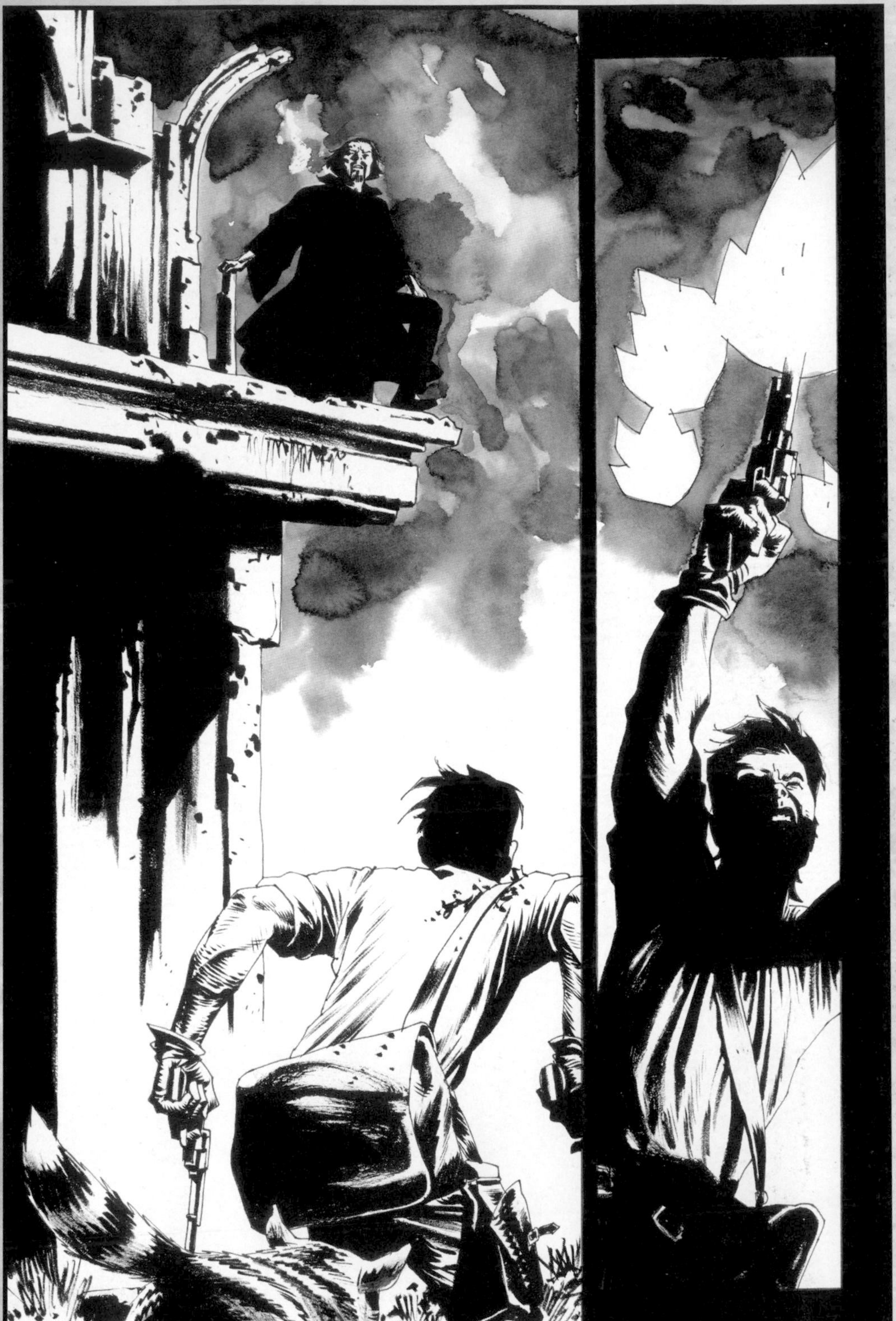